CHRISTMAS FAYRE

Festive Menus, Traditional Customs Gifts and Decorations

Sara Paston-Williams

DAVID & CHARLES
Newton Abbot   London

British Library Cataloguing in Publication Data

Paston-Williams, Sara
  Christmas fayre.
  1. Food. Christmas dishes. Recipes
  I. Title
  641.5′66

ISBN 0-7153-9348-0

Typeset by Typesetters (Birmingham) Ltd,
and printed in West Germany
by Mohndruck GmbH
for David & Charles Publishers plc
Brunel House   Newton Abbot   Devon

Contents

Introduction

Now thrice welcome, Christmas,
Which brings us good cheer,
Minced pies and plum porridge,
Good ale and strong beer.

Anonymous, 17th century

Winter was a season of festivals established by pagan people of both north and south, thousands of years before Christ was born, whether it was the Roman 'Saturnalia' and 'Kalends', or the Teutonic and Celtic 'Jiuleis' and 'Giuli' from which the Scandinavian 'Jul' and our 'Yule' may have come. Herds of animals had to be killed off before winter set in, so their carcasses were roasted and great feasts were held and for a short while, cold, darkness and hunger were forgotten in the celebrations.

The church prudently decided to take over the pagan ceremonies to celebrate the Birth, or Mass, of Christ. As a result, our modern Christmas is a curious blend of Christian and blatant pagan symbolism, with the giving of presents, the decorating of our houses, the burning of the Yule log in the hearth and the feasting mixed with the cribs, candles and church services.

Food and feasting have always been an important part of the Christmas tradition and Christmas feasts have ranged from the sublime to the ridiculous according to custom, availability and wealth. Gilded peacocks, boars' heads with apples in their mouths and elaborate sweetmeats were set before medieval kings, while smoked elephant and fried locusts have graced the table of at least one African adventurer, and the early settlers in Australia bravely tried to reproduce the English plum pudding under the boiling summer sun after tucking into braised kangaroo.

Christmas food also has a sacramental quality. As well as the ceremonial breaking of bread and sipping of wine, there are pagan rituals connected with ensuring the next year's harvest. In most countries animals are given special food and evil spirits have to be appeased with various dishes. The great consumption of meat at Christmas reflects ancient sacrificial rites, while the shape and ingredients of a wide variety of cakes, breads, biscuits and puddings are symbolic to both Christians and heathens alike.

Whatever the menu, Christmas is marked by a determination to prepare and eat something special, a spirit of overwhelming hospitality and a remarkable resolve to cling to national and family customs. I hope this book helps you to do all those things and to enjoy your future Christmasses even more.

Iced Christmas Wreath (page 19)

The Christmas Cake

Most European countries have a traditional cake, pastry, gingerbread or loaf made especially at Christmas time. France has the 'Bûche de Noël' (page 20), a chocolate log, and an elaborately iced 'Christ Bread' containing a coin. 'Christopsomo' also containing a coin is traditional in Greece while Italy has a number of traditional cakes; 'Panetone' (page 22), a dome-shaped fruit cake from Milan, being the most popular. Belgium specialises in a Yule log topped with a fondant baby while the German Christmas markets stock a vast range of decorated spiced cakes and gingerbreads, the best known being 'Lebkuchen'. The German 'Christstollen' (page 18), a rich fruit loaf, is also very popular. The traditional Rumanian cake is the 'turte' – layers of thin dough sandwiched together with melted sugar or honey and walnuts – and the Russians traditionally tuck into pastries called 'hvarost' or 'branches' and a fruit cake called 'mazurka'. Hungarians usually make 'Beigli', a rich pastry-dough filled with walnuts or poppy seeds and Poland also has a poppy-seed cake. In Czechoslovakia a fruit stew called 'masika' is served with a slice of plaited white Christmas bread. Gingerbread is common throughout Scandinavia at Christmas as is 'Julekake' (page 49), a rich, spicy, honey-flavoured fruit bread in an unusual twisted spiral shape, brushed with a honey glaze. Yugoslavians bake a ring-shaped coffee cake and place 3 candles in the centre, the first of which is lit on Christmas Eve, although the cake is actually eaten at Epiphany.

DIANA'S TRADITIONAL RICH FRUIT CAKE
(makes 1 × 23cm/9in cake)

This traditional Christmas cake recipe was given to me by the well-known actress, Diana Coupland. It was her grandmother's recipe and Diana says she bakes several cakes in October and cuts into the extra ones at any time during the following year; they seem to improve with age.

350g/12oz butter
350g/12oz soft brown sugar
6 eggs
450g/1lb plain flour
Pinch of salt
5ml/½tsp ground mixed spice
450g/1lb sultanas
450g/1lb currants
125g/4oz seedless raisins
175g/6oz candied peel, shredded
50g/2oz glacé cherries, halved
125g/4oz blanched almonds, chopped

30ml/2tbsp black treacle
1 wine glass brandy

Cream the butter and sugar together until fluffy. Add each egg separately, beating well all the time. Sieve the flour with the salt and mixed spice and fold into the mixture. Mix the fruit, candied peel, cherries and almonds together, then stir into the mixture gradually, adding the treacle and brandy towards the end to make a dropping consistency. Transfer the mixture into a well-prepared 23cm/9in round, or 20cm/8in square cake tin (page 8) and bake in a pre-heated cool oven (275°F; 140°C; Gas Mark 1) for about 6 hours.

Test by inserting a fine knitting needle or skewer into the centre of the cake; if it comes out clean, the cake is cooked. Otherwise, continue cooking for an extra 10–15 minutes, then test again. Remove the cake from the oven and leave in the tin until completely cold. Take out of the tin, strip off the lining papers and store and feed with brandy as recommended on page 8.

Individual Christmas Cakes as gifts (page 8)

TO PREPARE THE CAKE TIN

Butter the tin well and line with 3 sheets of greaseproof paper. Brush the greaseproof liberally with melted butter and tie a double band of brown paper around the outside of the tin to stand well above the rim. Place 2 sheets of brown paper or a baking sheet on the lower shelf of the oven for the cake to stand on. Cover the top of the cake with a double square of buttered greaseproof paper with a hole in the centre approximately 2.5cm/1in in diameter. All this sounds a bit fiddly, but it is essential to protect your cake as it is cooking for a long time in a slow oven. The longer the baking period, the thicker the insulation should be, to prevent the bottom and the sides of the cake from darkening too much and sticking. Lining papers are left in place until the cake has cooled down completely.

☆ If you wish, this cake can be left to rest overnight in the fridge before being baked the following day. It is rather a mammoth task preparing the mixture and baking it the same day, so relax and take it in stages.

☆ Sprinkle the surface of the cake mixture with a little water, before baking. This will keep the top of the cake soft and is a good tip for any large cake which has a fairly long cooking time.

TO STORE THE CAKE

Wrap the cake tightly in two sheets of greaseproof paper, finish with a thick rubber band followed by a secure layer of kitchen foil. Place in an airtight container in a cool dry place. Each week unwrap the cake and make a few holes in the top and bottom with a skewer or thin knitting needle. Sprinkle with a little more brandy or rum before re-wrapping and placing back in the airtight container. This type of cake keeps for several months un-iced.

☆ INDIVIDUAL CHRISTMAS CAKES

The quantity of rich fruit cake mixture for a 20cm/8in round or 18cm/7in square tin will be enough for 4 small cakes cooked in 10cm/4in tins. As it is difficult to find small tins which are deep enough, make a collar from 2 thicknesses of foil and tie around each tin. Line the tins in the usual way and wrap a band of brown paper round the outside of the foil.

Divide the fruit cake mixture evenly between the tins and level the tops with the back of a spoon. Bake in the centre of a pre-heated cool oven (300°F;

150°C; Gas Mark 2) for 1¾–2 hours, or until cooked. Cool before removing the brown paper and foil. Marzipan and ice as normal. Finished with a satin ribbon and packed in a pretty gift box lined with greaseproof or waxed paper, individual cakes make ideal gifts for relatives and friends living on their own.

SOFT ALMOND PASTE
(makes 550g/1¼lb)

This quantity of paste is sufficient to cover a 20cm/8in round or 18cm/7in square cake. For other cake sizes see 'Quantity guide' opposite. The paste can be wrapped in a polythene bag or clingfilm and stored for up to 2 days, which means that you can make the paste when you have 10 minutes to spare, but leave the longer job of putting it on the cake until you have more time.

This particular recipe gives a soft paste which is rolled over the top of the cake. If you prefer to follow the more conventional method and roll the paste out on a board, use the next recipe, but I find this one much easier.

150g/5oz caster sugar
150g/5oz icing sugar
300g/10oz ground almonds
1 egg
15ml/1tbsp lemon juice
15ml/1tbsp brandy
10ml/2tsp orange-flower or rose water
2.5ml/½tsp vanilla essence
1.25ml/¼tsp almond essence

Sieve the two sugars into a mixing bowl and stir in the ground almonds. Make a well in the centre. Whisk the egg with the lemon juice and other flavourings and add to the dry ingredients. Mix to a paste, pounding lightly to release a little of the almond oil. Knead with your hands until the paste is smooth, but try not to handle it too much or it will become oily.

Christmas Cake with Cheese

An old Yorkshire custom is to serve a slice of Wensleydale or Cheshire cheese with Christmas cake – try it. Any crumbly cheese with a 'bite' will be successful; it counteracts the sweetness of the cake.

FIRM ALMOND PASTE
(makes 450g/1lb)

This quantity of paste is sufficient to cover an 18cm/ 7in round or 15cm/6in square cake and again, can be made and stored in a polythene bag or clingfilm for up to 2 days. Use lemon juice, orange-flower or rose water (available from grocers and chemists) for flavouring.

125g/4oz caster sugar
125g/4oz icing sugar
225g/8oz ground almonds
5ml/1tsp lemon juice, orange-flower or rose water
2–3 drops almond essence
2 egg yolks, beaten

Sieve the sugars together into a mixing bowl. Stir in the ground almonds. Make a well in the centre and add the chosen flavouring, almond essence and sufficient egg to make a firm but pliable dough. Beat together with a wooden spoon, then turn onto a lightly sugared (with sieved icing sugar) board or work surface and knead until very smooth. Wrap in clingfilm and chill for about 30 minutes before using.

☆ QUANTITY GUIDE

Some recipes may specify a quantity of almond paste, ie 450g/1lb. This is calculated by adding up the weight of the dry ingredients, ie 225g/8oz ground almonds and 225g/8oz sugar, usually half icing sugar and half caster sugar. This quantity will cover a 18cm/7in round or 15cm/6in square cake.

For a 20cm/8in round or 18cm/7in square cake you will need 550g/1¼lb almond paste using 275g/ 10oz ground almonds etc. For a 23cm/9in round or 20cm/8in square cake you will need 675g/1½lb almond paste using 350g/12oz ground almonds, etc. For a 25cm/10in round or 23cm/9in square cake you will need 800g/1¾lb almond paste using 400g/14oz ground almonds, etc.

TO MARZIPAN A CAKE

A cake should be covered with marzipan at least 7 days before it is iced if it is to be kept for a while before being eaten, to give the marzipan time to dry out. Otherwise the oil from the almonds can seep through and discolour the icing. If you are going to ice the cake and eat it very soon afterwards, 2 days drying will be enough.

APRICOT GLAZE

225g/8oz apricot jam
15ml/1tbsp lemon juice
30ml/2tbsp water

Put the jam into a saucepan with the lemon juice and water. Bring slowly to the boil and simmer for 5 minutes, then sieve.

METHOD 1

Brush the cake thinly with hot apricot glaze and place the almond paste on top of the cake. Roll it with a rolling pin over the top, over the edges and down the sides of the cake. Dust your hands with icing sugar or cornflour and smooth the paste firmly and evenly on to the sides of the cake. Turn the cake upside down, press to flatten the paste on the top and roll round the sides with the rolling pin or a straight-sided jar to give a clean, sharp edge to the paste. Leave the cake, uncovered, in a warmish place for at least 24 hours, then store in a double sheet of greaseproof paper for at least 7 days before icing.

METHOD 2

Divide the almond paste into 2. Roll out half the paste evenly on a board or working surface dusted with sieved icing sugar or cornflour, approximately 2.5cm/1in larger than the top of the cake using the cake tin as a guide.

Brush the top of the cake with warm apricot glaze, then pick up the whole cake and invert it on the prepared circle of almond paste. Press it gently but firmly so that it sticks well all over. Using a palette knife press the paste up around the edge of the cake. Turn the cake back again on to the right side and, using a rolling pin, lightly roll across the top to smooth out any irregularities and any excess paste over the top edge onto the side.

Measure the depth and circumference of the cake and cut 2 lengths of string, one for each measurement. Roll out the remaining almond paste into a rectangle and, using the string as a guide, cut into strips the same width and circumference as the cake.

Brush the sides of the cake with warm apricot glaze, then pick it up gently and roll it carefully over the ready-prepared paste strips. Smooth over the joins gently with a rolling pin or straight-sided jar and leave the cake as before for a few days before icing.

☆ MARZIPAN TOPPING

Marzipan makes an attractive finishing layer on its own without icing on top. Criss-cross the top of the marzipan decoratively with a small sharp knife or toast under the grill if you wish and tie a wide satin ribbon or cake frill (page 14) around the sides of your cake. A glacé fruit and nut topping may also be placed on a marzipanned cake if you wish (page 14).

ROLLING OUT

It is helpful to fix a sheet of greaseproof or silicone paper firmly to a board or working surface with masking tape. Dust the paper with sieved icing sugar or cornflour, place your almond paste on top and cover with another sheet of sugared greaseproof or silicone paper. Roll out the paste between the two layers of paper. This makes the job much easier and the fixed paper stops the almond paste slipping about while it is being rolled out.

☆ USING LEFT-OVER MARZIPAN TO MAKE SWEETS

If you have a little marzipan left over from your cake make a few sweets – they make an ideal gift or can be served with coffee at the end of a meal.

Divide the marzipan into pieces and colour each piece by adding a few drops of colouring. Roll out the marzipan pieces and sandwich different colours together, then cut into shapes, eg squares, triangles, diamonds, or roll up like a Swiss roll and cut into slices. Leave to dry, before storing between layers of waxed paper in an airtight container.

☆ MARZIPAN-STUFFED FRUITS AND NUTS

Fill the stone cavities of fresh or dessert dates and dried prunes which do not need soaking, halved glacé cherries, small halved glacé apricots and walnut halves with small balls of marzipan. Colour the marzipan first if you wish and try kneading in a few extra drops of brandy, rum or liqueur to give additional flavour. Criss-cross the top of the marzipan decoratively with a sharp knife or top with a small sliver of crystallised fruit or a blanched almond.

The stuffed fruits may be rolled in granulated or caster sugar for a crunchy sweet covering, or in icing sugar. Marzipan-stuffed dates are also excellent dipped in melted chocolate or a little melted chocolate can be drizzled or piped over them. Place in petits fours paper cases and serve. Only use fresh dates if they are going to be eaten on the day they are made.

These stuffed fruits and nuts also make excellent presents, packed in a pretty box between layers of waxed paper.

☆ MARZIPAN-COATED DATES

Dessert dates
1 whole blanched almond to each date
12g/½oz soft almond paste to each date
Caster sugar or melted chocolate to finish

Make a slit in the date lengthways and remove the stone. Lightly toast the almonds in a moderate oven and fill each date cavity with a cold toasted almond. Mould the almond paste around each date covering it completely. Roll in caster sugar or dip in melted chocolate, and pack in a pretty box between layers of waxed paper for an unusual and attractive present.

TO COLOUR MARZIPAN

Use edible food colourings, mixing the colours beforehand if you wish. Add the colouring on the end of a skewer to small pieces of almond paste so that you don't add too much, and knead the colour into the paste until it is evenly coloured. Make sure that you wash your hands before handling a new colour or the colouring will be transferred. If a deep colour is required and the colouring makes the paste too soft, mix a little icing sugar with the colouring and add it as a paste. For extra colour depth, the finished marzipan decorations can be painted with food colourings, which can be diluted with egg white if necessary.

TO MAKE DECORATIONS

Roll out the various colours of almond paste to about 3mm/⅛in thick, then with the aid of templates cut from stiff paper or card, cut out whichever decorations you choose. Mould into shape and leave to dry. Holly leaves and berries, ivy leaves, Christmas roses, Christmas trees and poinsettias are traditional and very attractive. Mark the veins of holly, ivy and poinsettia leaves on the surface of the paste

The Story of Marzipan

Almonds have been popular in cooking since early medieval days and at the end of every Elizabethan banquet worthy of note, a great marzipan sculpture called a 'sotelte' or subtlety was brought in. It would be an elaborate confection in the shape of a crowned panther or lion, an eagle with wings outspread, a dragon or a unicorn – no wedding, funeral, crowning or christening was complete without marzipan. Indeed, it was the most coveted gift amongst the nobility and even considered worthy of a gold-leaf covering. Its popularity continued in the seventeenth century as 'marchpane', when it was still offered as a special treat at the end of a banquet. After this, marzipan fell from favour in England and today now remains only as a topping for a festive cake or is moulded into single flowers, leaves or figures. However, marzipan confectionery is still popular in Germany while Spain and Italy specialise in a sort of almond nougat called 'turron' or 'turrone' at Christmas time.

with the back of a knife and dry over the handle of a wooden spoon or rolling pin (depending on their size) face upwards to give the leaves a curve.

To make flowers, cut out the individual petals, then mould them with your fingers dipped in cornflour. Attach the petals to each other at the base, but leave the top loose to show the centre of the flower.

Dry marzipan decorations on non-stick silicone paper or on upturned egg boxes for up to 1 week before storing carefully between layers of silicone or waxed paper in an airtight container. Store for up to 2 months.

ROYAL ICING
(makes 675g/1½lb)

This icing should be spread over a marzipan base. It is used for rich festive and wedding cakes and for piped decoration. Royal icing is not suitable for flat icing on sponge cakes because it would be too hard.

It can be kept for up to 7 days in the fridge. To prevent it from hardening, cover with a layer of clingfilm on the actual surface of the icing and with another layer covering the top of the bowl.

675g/1½lb icing sugar
4 egg whites
15ml/1tbsp lemon juice, strained or 5ml/1tsp orange-
    flower or rose water
10ml/2tsp glycerine (optional)

Finely sieve the icing sugar. In a large mixing bowl beat the egg whites until frothy, then gradually add the icing sugar a tablespoon at a time beating thoroughly between each addition to ensure a white icing. Add the lemon juice, orange-flower or rose water and glycerine and continue beating until the mixture stands in soft peaks. This can be done in an electric mixer. Cover the bowl with a damp cloth or transfer to an airtight container and leave for 1–2 hours to allow any air bubbles to come to the surface.

☆ QUANTITY GUIDE
When recipes specify an amount of icing, ie 450g/1lb royal or fondant icing, this refers to the amount of sugar used in the icing.

For an 18cm/7in round or 15cm/6in square cake you will need 450g/1lb icing sugar and 2½ egg whites. For a 20–23cm/8–9in round or 18–20cm/7–8in square cake you will need 675g/1½lb icing sugar and 4 egg whites. For a 25–28cm/10–11in round or 23–25cm/9–10in square cake you will need 900g/2lb icing sugar and 6 egg whites.

☆ COLOURINGS AND FLAVOURINGS
You should always use edible colouring for icing. Take great care when adding a colour because one drop too many can change a subtle shading into a gaudy one. A skewer dipped in the bottle of colouring is the best method of adding a colour. Flavourings are varied but are not meant to over-power and spoil the taste of the cake. Always try and use natural flavourings. A squeeze of lemon juice helps to counteract the sweetness of royal icing.

Add a tiny spot of blue colouring on the point of a skewer and beat it in very thoroughly; too much blue gives the icing a greyish tint.

TO COVER THE CAKE
A palette knife, a long kitchen knife or a ruler may be used to ice your cake and an icing comb and turntable certainly make the work much simpler. An upturned plate can be used instead.

TO ICE TOP OF A ROUND OR SQUARE CAKE
Mix the icing with a wooden spoon again just before starting and use a little to stick the cake to a cake board. The cake board needs to be 5–7.5cm/2–3in larger than your cake to allow for the marzipan and icing. Place the cake on the board in the centre of the turntable or upturned plate. Drop a large spoonful of icing onto the centre of the cake and with a palette knife, spread it over the top of the cake using a 'paddling action'. At the same time keep turning the turntable slowly or moving across the cake if it is on a plate.

Draw an icing ruler or long palette knife carefully and evenly across the cake, holding it at an angle of about 30°. Take care not to press too heavily for this first coat. Remove the surplus icing from the top edge of the cake with a palette knife held parallel to the sides. Clean the ruler and palette knife before using again.

Leave the top to dry for at least 1 hour before icing the sides.

TO ICE SIDES OF A ROUND CAKE
With the cake on the turntable or upturned plate, spread a small quantity of icing all round the sides, again using a paddling action to push out as much air as possible. Hold an icing comb, scraper or palette knife at an angle of about 45° to the side of the cake. Starting at the back of the cake, slowly rotate the cake with your free hand, at the same time moving the comb slowly and evenly round the sides of the cake. Remove the comb fairly quickly at an angle, so

that the join is hardly noticeable.

Remove the small ridge of icing from the top edge of the cake with a palette knife held at 45° and revolve the turntable in an anti-clockwise direction. Leave to dry overnight in a dry room.

TO ICE SIDES OF A SQUARE CAKE

Use a similar method as above but ice 2 opposite sides first and leave to dry for about 1 hour before icing the remaining 2 sides. Remove the surplus icing from the top edge and corners of the cake as each side is iced, forming sharp corners and edges. Leave to dry overnight.

Add a second and third layer of icing in the same way to the top and sides of your cake, making sure each layer is thoroughly dry before adding the next. 2 or 3 thinner coats of royal icing are better than 1 thick one if you want a very smooth finish ready for decorating, particularly if you are piping.

TO ICE THE CAKE BOARD

When your cake has been completely iced, coat the cake board with a thin layer of icing. Hold the icing comb or scraper at an angle on the icing and turn the turntable 1 revolution to smooth the surface. Remove the surplus icing on the edge of the cake board with a palette knife.

The Legend of the Poinsettia

A charming Mexican legend is attached to the poinsettia; a small peasant boy was standing by the doors of the village church on Christmas Eve watching as people took in gifts to put beside the crib. He had nothing to give but an angel told him to pick some of the plants which grew by the side of the road and take them in as his offering. He did this but the congregation laughed at him for taking in a bunch of 'weeds'. As he blushed, the leaves of the plants turned scarlet too and appeared to turn into beautiful flowers. People were amazed at this miracle. The Mexicans called it the Flower of the Holy Night and it is said to resemble the Star of Bethlehem. The Americans named it after the man who introduced it to the United States, Dr Poinsett.

Actually, the plant reacts to light and the leaves turn red if exposed to 11 hours of light every day for 70 days, but I prefer the legend, don't you? The poinsettia is now one of the most popular Christmas plants all over the world.

Diana's Traditional Rich Fruit Cake (page 6) with Moulded Icing (above) and Marzipan decorations (page 10)

Use this same method for a square cake board, but coat 2 opposite sides of the board, then leave for 1 hour before coating the 2 remaining sides. Cover the cake board with 2 coats of icing.

☆ PIPING

Royal icing is very versatile and ideal for piping. Most designs are made with writing and star tubes. The small tubes need fairly soft icing, the large tubes, stiffer icing. Keep the bowl of icing covered with a clean damp cloth or in an airtight container during use to prevent drying out.

MOULDED ICING
(makes 450g/1lb)

This is an alternative to royal icing and is used to cover rich fruit cakes over a base of almond paste. This quantity is sufficient to cover a 20cm/8in round or 18cm/7in square cake. Glucose liquid or syrup can be obtained from specialist cake-icing shops.

450g/1lb sieved icing sugar
1 egg white
1 rounded 15ml spoon/1 rounded tbsp
   glucose liquid or syrup

Place the icing sugar in a bowl. Add the egg white and glucose and mix together with a wooden spoon. Knead well with your fingers until the mixture forms a ball.

Turn the icing onto a board or work surface sprinkled with cornflour or icing sugar and knead until smooth and pliable. If the icing is too firm, add a few drops of water and knead well.

TO COVER THE CAKE

Place your marzipanned cake on a cake board. Roll out the prepared icing on a board or work surface sprinkled with cornflour or icing sugar into a circle or square 5cm/2in larger than your cake. Support the icing on a rolling pin and place over the top of a cake. Press the icing onto the sides of the cake working the surplus icing to the base of the cake board. Dip your hands in cornflour or icing sugar and rub the surface of the icing in a circular movement. Cut off any excess icing and use this to mould decorations if you wish. It can be coloured as required (page 11).

☆ Keep the icing in a well-sealed polythene bag to prevent it drying out. If it does become dry on the surface, dip quickly into hot water, replace in the bag and leave for 1 hour. Knead again before using.

☆ USING LEFT-OVER ICING TO MAKE SWEETS

Make little sweets from surplus icing by adding chocolate powder, edible food colouring, a little liqueur, or peppermint essence. Roll out the icing to about 6mm/¼in thick and cut out with a small 2.5cm/1in cutter. Dry for 24 hours in a warm place on a baking tray covered with waxed or greaseproof paper. Pack in airtight containers.

These simple sweets could easily be made by young children and would make an attractive gift if packed in a pretty box between layers of waxed paper and tied up with a satin ribbon.

SIMPLE CHRISTMAS-CAKE DECORATIONS: GLACÉ FRUIT AND NUT TOPPING

For a change from icing your rich fruit cake, or if you are in a hurry, try a topping of glacé and crystallised fruits and nuts. It looks just as festive and attractive, but is much simpler and quicker.

Brush the top of your cake while it is still warm with warmed apricot jam glaze (page 9), clear honey or golden syrup. Arrange glacé fruits and nuts in patterns, diagonal rows, or at random on the top of the cake and brush again with apricot glaze, honey or syrup.

Try glacé pineapple rings, cherries, apricots, angelica, crystallised ginger, orange rings (page 16 for how to crystallise your own fruit), brazil nuts, walnut halves, pecans and almonds. Finish with a wide satin ribbon tied around your cake. If you wish, just before serving the cake, drizzle a little white glacé icing over the topping.

TO MAKE A CAKE FRILL

A homemade cake frill is very simple to make and much cheaper than buying one. It is also much more fun. Use crêpe paper, metallic paper or Christmas wrapping paper; there is such a wide variety of lovely papers to choose from. Cut a strip of paper approximately 18cm/7in wide, depending on the depth of your cake, and long enough to wrap generously around your cake. Fold the 2 edges 4.5cm/1¾in into the centre of the paper and fasten with sellotape or glue. Cut the top and bottom edges at 3mm/⅛in intervals and approximately 2.5cm/1in deep to make a fringe. Cut the top of the fringe on the fold if you wish to make a more decorative frill. Wrap the frill around the cake and secure with a pin or glue. Finish by tying a brightly coloured satin ribbon around the frill with a flamboyant bow or decorate the frill by glueing on gold or silver leaves, bows, tiny fir cones, dried flowers or shapes cut from paper doilies.

CHRISTMAS TREE BAUBLES

Ice your cake in the normal way, then attach gold or silver leaves to the edge of the cake with little blobs of icing curving them over the edge a little. Tie a cake frill made from gold, silver, red, green or blue metallic paper around the cake or use a plain white frill finished with a wide ribbon.

Finish the cake by piling a few plain Christmas tree balls to match the cake frill or ribbon in the centre. These can be fixed with a little icing and are a really effective way of decorating a cake, which can be done last thing on Christmas Eve.

CRYSTALLISED FLOWERS AND LEAVES

Flowers, leaves and roots have been crystallised since Tudor times as a method of preservation. They were once added to salads, used to decorate puddings and tarts and served as sweetmeats at the end of a meal.

A great variety of flowers and leaves can be crystallised but do make sure they are not poisonous if you plan to eat them – err on the safe side! Those suitable for Christmas decorations would be carnations, Christmas roses, ordinary roses either whole or as individual petals, winter-flowering jasmine, primulas, rose leaves, mint leaves and sprigs of rosemary. Make sure the blooms are dry before you crystallise them.

Sprinkle a little gum arabic (12–25g/½–1oz will be plenty unless you are crystallising a large number of flowers) into the bottom of a small jam jar. Pour over enough rose water to just cover the gum arabic and seal with a lid. Leave to dissolve for 24 hours.

Next day, carefully paint the dissolved gum over each flower petal or leaf with a fine paint brush. Make sure that the petals are completely coated on both sides or they will go brown later. Sprinkle all over with caster sugar, preferably using a sugar sifter for an even coating. Place carefully on a sheet of greaseproof or silicone paper sprinkled with a little caster sugar. If you rest the greaseproof on a cake cooling rack, the flowers are less likely to stick. Dry in a warm place for at least 24 hours, until dry and crisp.

Store carefully between layers of greaseproof paper in an airtight container until needed. Crystallised flowers and leaves will keep for several months without losing their colour.

☆ WHERE TO BUY GUM ARABIC

Gum arabic is sold as a white powder by most good chemists, but if you have trouble obtaining it, use a lightly beaten egg white instead and omit the rose water although this will not give such a good result.

The Yule Log

Almost all the superstitions and ceremonies connected with bringing in and lighting the great Yule log, once the centre-piece of Christmas in many parts of Europe, are overtly pagan. The Viking Yule was a celebration of the triumph of light over darkness and the rebirth of the sun at the winter solstice. It was celebrated with drinking and feasting and fertility rites to ensure a good harvest and a high birth-rate among men and beasts. As part of the festivities, oak logs were lit in honour of the god Thor and to frighten away evil spirits. The Christians took over the custom and the Yule log came to symbolise the light Jesus brought to the world.

In the feudal period with its huge and hungry open fireplaces, the bringing in of the Yule log became the most important Christmas custom and until the advent of the Christmas tree it continued to play a leading role in the British Christmas. A great log or gnarled root of oak, pine, ash or birch was dragged in on Christmas Eve with great ceremony. The log was supposed to burn for the full twelve days of Christmas and it was considered very unlucky if it went out by itself. The ashes and charcoal from the log were thought to have many magical properties and curative powers.

Similar practices and beliefs could be found in many parts of Europe, with interesting regional variations. The Yule log was particularly important to the French, hence the chocolate Bûche de Noël. It was cut from a plum or cherry tree and carried into the house by the whole family singing a carol asking for blessings on the house, family and farm. The youngest child would pour wine onto the log as it was thrown on the fire.

In parts of Italy the Yule log was lit by the blindfolded children of the house who then beat it with tongs, while the whole family sang a hymn. In Spain, the lads of the village would drag the Yule log through the streets, also beating it soundly; they were given presents of nuts and chocolate as they went. Bulgarians used to beat the blazing Yule log to drive out evil spirits and in Greece, the Yule log was burned to scare away the spirit-souls of the dead thought to take the visible form of imps called Kallikantzaroi at Christmas time. In parts of Germany the Yule log, or 'Christbrand', was taken off the fire as soon as it was slightly charred and rekindled whenever a storm threatened, as protection against lightning. On Christmas Eve in Yugoslavia oak logs were felled before sunrise and decorated by the women with red silk, leaves and flowers. They were carried home in candle-lit processions at twilight and, as they were lifted over the threshold, corn or wine was thrown over the first log which was then received into the house with great honour.

Nearly all these superstitions and practices belonged to rural farming communities, so they have faded away over the years, but most of us still like to sit by a good log fire at Christmas if possible. Nothing can beat its comforting warmth, cheerful crackle and old-fashioned smell of burning wood.

CRYSTALLISED FRUIT CAKE
(makes 1×20cm/8in round or 18cm/7in square cake)

If you would like a change from the rich dark traditional Christmas cake try this recipe which can still be made in October as it keeps very well. A recipe like this which is not too dark is particularly suitable for un-iced cakes. This one has a nut and crystallised fruit decoration which can be put on immediately the cake is cooked.

225g/8oz sultanas
60ml/4tbsp brandy or sherry
125g/4oz crystallised pineapple
50g/2oz crystallised ginger
125g/4oz glacé apricots
175g/6oz glacé cherries, washed and dried
225g/8oz unsalted butter
225g/8oz caster sugar
Grated rind and juice of 1 lemon
Grated rind of 1 orange
4 eggs
50g/2oz ground almonds
225g/8oz plain flour
2.5ml/½tsp salt
125g/4oz walnuts, chopped
50g/2oz angelica
125g/4oz candied peel
A little extra brandy

Soak the sultanas in the brandy or sherry for several hours or preferably overnight. Prepare your 20cm/8in round or 18cm/7in square cake tin as recommended on page 8.

Chop the crystallised fruits and glacé apricots into smallish pieces and quarter the cherries. Cream the butter and sugar with the lemon and orange rind until soft and fluffy. Beat the eggs really hard and add to the creamed mixture a little at a time, beating well between each addition. When all the egg has been added, lightly fold in the ground almonds.

Sift the flour with the salt and gently fold into the creamed mixture. Stir in the lemon juice and then add the prepared fruit, nuts, angelica, candied peel, and the sultanas soaked in the brandy, a little at a time. The mixture should be moist enough to drop off a spoon if given a good shake. Add more brandy or sherry if it is not. Turn the cake mixture into the prepared tin and smooth the top making a hollow in the centre.

Bake in a preheated oven at 325°F; 170°C; Gas Mark 3 for 1 hour on the shelf below the centre of the oven. After 1 hour, place a double sheet of greaseproof paper over the top of the tin and turn

the oven down to 300°F; 150°C; Gas Mark 2 for a further 2–2¼ hours. The cake is done when it is evenly risen and brown and has shrunk a little from the sides of the tin. Leave the cake to cool in the tin for 10–15 minutes, then turn on to a wire rack. Make a few holes in the top and bottom of the cake with a fine skewer or thin knitting needle and pour over a little brandy. Leave to get completely cold before storing (page 8).

The cake may be marzipanned and iced in the normal way (pages 9, 11 and 13).

☆ INDIVIDUAL CRYSTALLISED FRUIT CAKES

The quantity of cake mixture given in the recipe will be sufficient to make 4 small cakes in 10cm/4in tins. Make as before and decorate with crystallised fruits and nuts.

TO PRESERVE ANGELICA

Growing your own angelica in the garden or collecting it from the hedgerow and preserving it for cooking and decorating cakes and puddings is a very satisfying thing to do. It is so expensive to buy and although like any candying or crystallising the process takes several days, it is extremely simple. Don't expect your homemade crystallised angelica to be bright green like the shop-bought variety which is artificially coloured. You can of course, colour your own with a little green food colouring, but I prefer the natural colour which is a delicate shade of green.

Angelica stems
Granulated sugar

Choose young stems of angelica and wash them well. Cut them into even lengths to fit your chosen saucepan, cover with water and boil gently until tender. Drain, reserving the cooking liquor and strip off the outer skin of the stems. Return to the pan with the cooking liquor and simmer very gently until green. (You can add a little green food colouring at this point if you wish.) Drain and dry well with absorbent kitchen paper, then weigh. Place the angelica in a shallow dish and measure out your sugar allowing 450g/1lb sugar to each 450g/1lb angelica. Sprinkle the sugar over the angelica stems, cover and leave for 2 days.

After 2 days, place the angelica and its syrup into a saucepan and bring to the boil. Continue boiling for a few minutes, then remove the angelica and add an extra 50g/2oz granulated sugar to the existing syrup. Bring this gently to the boil, then replace the angelica and boil for a further 5 minutes.

Drain the angelica and spread it out on a baking tray in a cool oven (300°F; 150°C; Gas Mark 2) to dry. Wrap in greaseproof or silicone paper and store in an airtight container until needed.

TO MAKE CANDIED, CRYSTALLISED AND GLACÉ FRUITS

These fruits have been very popular at special banquets since Tudor times. They were eaten at the end of a meal and also offered as refreshment to callers at other times of the day. Nowadays we tend to eat candied, crystallised and glacé fruits only at Christmas in our cooking, or as a special treat. They are very expensive to buy, but so delicious. The answer is obviously to make your own!

Only perfect, firm, ripe fruit should be used and you get the best results by candying each type of fruit separately to keep the individual flavour. Some of the most successful are whole apricots, cherries, grapes, both whole and segmented mandarins and satsumas, quartered pears, halved peaches and wedges of pineapple. What a marvellous extravagant present they would make!

CANDIED FRUIT

450g/1lb suitable fruit, prepared
125g/4oz powdered glucose
60g/2½oz granulated sugar for initial boiling
Extra granulated sugar for later boilings

Place the prepared fruit in a large saucepan and cover with boiling water. Simmer over a gentle heat until the fruit is just tender, but not broken up. This will vary with the type of fruit used. Remove the fruit carefully from the cooking liquor with a slotted spoon and place in a heatproof dish. Reserve the cooking liquor. Put 300ml/½pt of this in a saucepan with the glucose and sugar. Heat very gently, stirring all the time, until the sugar has dissolved. Then bring to the boil and pour the hot syrup over the fruit making sure that it is completely immersed. Cover and leave for 24 hours.

Place a sieve over a saucepan and carefully drain the syrup from the fruit into the saucepan. Return the fruit to the ovenproof dish. Add another 50g/2oz sugar to the syrup, stir over a gentle heat until this has dissolved, then bring to the boil. Pour over the fruit, cover and leave for a further 24 hours. Repeat

Crystallised Fruit Cake (page 15)

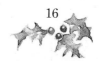

the process 3 more times adding another 50g/2oz sugar each time.

Carefully drain the syrup from the fruit into a saucepan as before. Add 75g/3oz sugar to the syrup, place saucepan over a gentle heat and stir until the sugar has dissolved, then add the fruit and simmer for 3 minutes. Return the fruit and syrup to the heatproof dish. Cover and leave for 48 hours. Repeat the process. The syrup should now be as thick as clear honey.

If the syrup is too thin at this stage, add another 75g/3oz sugar to the syrup, dissolve the sugar over a gentle heat, then add the fruit and simmer for 3 minutes. Leave the fruit to soak in the thick syrup for 4 days. Remove the fruit carefully from the syrup with a slotted spoon and lay it on a wire rack, placed over a baking tray to catch the drips.

To dry off the fruit, place the tray in a warm place, turning the fruit occasionally during the drying process. The fruit is candied when the surface is no longer sticky.

CRYSTALLISED FRUIT

Candied fruit, dried (see recipe, page 16)
Granulated sugar

Sprinkle some granulated sugar on greaseproof or waxed paper. Lift up each piece of candied fruit on a fine skewer and quickly dip it into boiling water. Allow to drain for a couple of seconds, then roll each piece in sugar until it is evenly, but not thickly coated. Leave to dry on a wire rack.

GLACÉ FRUIT

450g/1lb granulated sugar
150ml/¼pt water
Candied fruit, dried (see recipe, page 16)

Put the sugar and water into a saucepan. Dissolve the sugar over gentle heat, then bring to the boil. Boil for 1 minute. Pour a little of the syrup into a hot cup, keeping the remaining syrup hot, but not boiling. Lift up each piece of candied fruit with a fine skewer and quickly dip the fruit into boiling water, allow it to drain for a few seconds, then quickly dip into the hot syrup. Lay the fruit on a wire rack placed over a baking tray to drain.

When the syrup in the cup becomes cloudy or too diluted replace it with fresh hot syrup from the saucepan. Continue until all the fruit has been processed. Place the tray of fruit in a warm place to dry, turning it occasionally. The fruit is finished when its surface is no longer sticky.

TO STORE CANDIED, CRYSTALLISED AND GLACÉ FRUIT

Store in a cool dry place in cardboard or wooden boxes which have been lined with waxed paper. The fruits should be placed well apart and between layers of waxed paper and are best eaten within 6 months which shouldn't present a problem!

☆ USES FOR CANDIED, CRYSTALLISED AND GLACÉ FRUIT

Apart from using these delicious fruits in cooking, they are ideal for decorating puddings, cakes and homemade sweets and chocolates. Served with coffee they make a delicious sweetmeat at the end of a meal, but also try serving them as a dessert with whipped cream or yoghurt. A table centre-piece of the brightest fresh and crystallised fruits looks wonderful.

CHRISTSTOLLEN
(makes 2 large loaves)

This is the famous German Christmas bread filled with dried and candied fruits, peel and nuts. The traditional oval shape of this bread is said to represent the Baby Jesus wrapped in swaddling clothes. Try serving on Christmas Eve with a warming glass of mulled wine, cider or ale.

1kg/2lb 3oz strong plain flour
75g/3oz fresh yeast
210ml/7fl oz warm milk
250g/9oz caster sugar
350g/12oz butter
Grated rind and juice of 1 lemon
2 egg yolks
2.5ml/½tsp salt
Pinch of ground mace
Pinch of grated nutmeg
300g/10oz raisins
225g/8oz sultanas
125g/4oz glacé cherries, washed and dried
 and chopped
125g/4oz candied orange and lemon peel,
 finely chopped
50g/2oz angelica, finely chopped
150g/5oz flaked almonds
125g/4oz unsalted butter, melted
Icing sugar, sieved

Sieve the flour 2 or 3 times into a large mixing bowl and warm in the oven for a few minutes. Blend the yeast with the warm milk, 5ml/1tsp of the sugar and 50g/2oz of the flour. Leave on one side to froth.

Melt the 350g/12oz butter and cool slightly. Mix into the remaining flour with the lemon juice, then add the yeast mixture. Beat together, then add the remaining sugar, egg yolks, lemon rind, salt and spices. Continue beating and then knead until the dough is very firm and elastic and starts to come away from the sides of the mixing bowl. Cover with a damp cloth or place the bowl in an oiled polythene bag and stand in a warm place to rise until doubled in size.

Knock back the risen dough, knead for a few minutes, then pull the sides to the centre, turn it over and cover once more. Stand in a warm place to rise for a further 30 minutes or until it has doubled in size again.

Mix all the fruit, peel, angelica and nuts together in a large bowl and warm in the oven for a few minutes. Turn the risen dough out onto a floured board and scatter the warmed fruit mixture over. Knead it in carefully and divide the dough into 2 equal pieces. Return 1 to the bowl and cover it to prevent it drying out while the other piece is being finished.

Roll out the dough into a slightly flattened pointed oval shape, large enough to fit on to a greased baking tray, but allowing enough room for the loaf to expand again while it is proving. Lay the dough on the baking tray. Roll it with a rolling pin, pressing lightly across the full width from the centre outwards, on one side only. Brush this thinner half with a little water and fold over the other half leaving a margin of about 5cm/2in as a border, which also allows the dough to rise. Press well together, the water will seal it. This rolling and folding is essential to this bread to give its traditional shape. Prepare the remaining piece of dough in the same way. Cover both stollens and leave to prove in a warm place and to double in size again.

Carefully brush over the surface of both loaves with 50g/2oz of the melted butter before placing them in a preheated oven at 375°F; 190°C; Gas Mark 5. Bake for 45–60 minutes depending on the size of the loaves until well risen and brown. Remove from the oven and while still warm brush again with the remaining 50g/2oz butter and sprinkle with sieved icing sugar until the butter cannot absorb any more and a sugary crust is formed. Allow to cool on a wire rack before wrapping in greaseproof paper and storing.

Just before serving, dredge with a little sieved icing sugar and serve cut into fairly thin slices. Christstollen will keep fresh for several weeks wrapped tightly in greaseproof paper and stored in an airtight tin, or it can be frozen for up to 3 months.

☆ ALTERNATIVE TOPPINGS
The traditional topping for stollen is butter and icing sugar, but a good variation is to drizzle 30ml/2tbsp clear honey over each loaf and sprinkle with 30ml/2tbsp light soft brown sugar mixed with a pinch of cinnamon 5 minutes before the end of the cooking time. Replace the stollen in the oven to finish cooking. Yet another variation is to drizzle white glacé icing over the cooled loaves and decorate with glacé cherries and angelica.

ICED CHRISTMAS WREATH
(makes 1 wreath)

A feature of Dutch Christmas fare is the Christmas wreath made from a rich dough. The main meal generally takes place in the evening when families gather around their candle-lit tables decorated in traditional colours and eat roast hare, goose, venison or turkey followed by the wreath.

225g/8oz strong white flour
Pinch of salt
100ml/3½fl oz warm milk
12g/½oz fresh yeast
50g/2oz butter
125g/4oz caster sugar
1 egg, beaten
25g/1oz softened butter
50g/2oz stoned raisins
5ml/1tsp ground cinnamon

FOR THE TOPPING
White glacé icing
25g/1oz walnut halves or pecan nuts
25g/1oz glacé cherries
25g/1oz angelica or citron peel

Sieve the flour with the salt into a large mixing bowl. Add the yeast and 50g/2oz butter to the warm milk and stir until dissolved. Add 50g/2oz sugar to the yeast mixture followed by the beaten egg.

Make a well in the centre of the flour, pour in the liquid ingredients and mix until smooth with a wooden spoon followed by your hand. When the dough comes clearly away from the sides of the bowl, turn it out onto a floured board and knead until elastic. Place the dough back in the bowl, cover with

a damp tea-towel or greased polythene, and leave to rise in a warm place until double in size. Knock the dough back, knead again, turn it over, cover and let it rise again for about 30 minutes.

Turn onto a floured board and roll out to an oblong approximately 25cm/9in × 15cm/6in and 6–12mm/¼–½in thick. Cover the surface of the dough with knobs of the softened butter, sprinkle with the remaining 50g/2oz caster sugar and the raisins and cinnamon. Roll up the dough tightly beginning at the wide side and seal by pinching the edges together. Curl the dough round into a ring, joining the edges together well and place on a greased baking tray. Cut the ring at 2.5cm/1in intervals with scissors, making each cut two-thirds through the ring. Cover with a cloth and prove for about 15–20 minutes before baking in a pre-heated fairly hot oven at 400°F; 200°C; Gas Mark 6 for about 25 minutes. Pierce the roll with a fine skewer to test if it is done.

Brush glacé icing over the wreath while it is still warm. Decorate lavishly with nuts, red and green glacé cherries and leaves cut from angelica or citron peel, then lightly brush again with icing. Serve on a plate decorated with sprigs of holly or other evergreen.

☆ TABLE DECORATION

Double the quantity of dough to make 2 wreaths and use 1 as a table decoration. Place a tall red, green or white candle in the centre of the wreath and decorate with holly and ivy.

☆ SINTER KLAAS INITIALS

These Santa Claus initials are made for Dutch children from the same rich dough as the Christmas wreath. Roll the dough into long snakes and use to form initials. Place on a greased baking tray and leave to prove, then bake in a hot oven for 15–20 minutes. Use as place cards or pile around the wreath.

The legend of the robin

There are various stories as to how the robin got his beautiful red winter plumage. The most popular is that he was present in the stable when Jesus was born. Joseph had to go out to find wood for the fire and Mary was worried that the baby would get cold while he was gone. Down flew some small birds and fanned the dying embers of the fire back to life, singeing the feathers on their breasts. Mary was so grateful that she turned the breast feathers to a beautiful red as a reminder of their kindness.

BÛCHE DE NOËL

Instead of a rich fruit Christmas cake French families enjoy the chocolate Bûche de Noël, or Christmas log. The cake is traditionally iced with chocolate or coffee crème au beurre and can be as elaborate and realistic as you like. This particular recipe is filled with chestnut purée and cream, but chocolate or coffee butter cream, or just whipped cream would be equally delicious. Try serving it on Christmas Eve as a pudding or on Christmas Day for tea instead of rich fruit cake.

FOR THE CAKE
90g/3½oz plain flour
12g/½oz cocoa
Pinch of salt
4 eggs
125g/4oz caster sugar
25g/1oz melted butter, cooled
2–3 drops vanilla essence

FOR THE CHESTNUT FILLING
1 × 250g/8¾oz tin sweetened chestnut purée
60ml/4tbsp double cream

FOR THE CRÈME AU BEURRE AU CHOCOLAT
60g/2½oz caster sugar
60ml/4tbsp water
2 large egg yolks
150g/5oz unsalted butter
50g/2oz plain chocolate
15ml/1tbsp water

FOR THE DECORATION
175g/6oz firm almond paste (page 9)
Icing sugar
Crystallised flowers and leaves (page 14)

Sieve the flour, cocoa and salt together twice. Put the eggs and sugar into a bowl and stand this over hot water. Whisk the mixture hard until it is pale and thick enough to retain the impression of the whisk for a few seconds, then remove the basin from the heat. Sieve one-third of the flour mixture over the surface of the egg mixture and fold in very lightly, using a metal spoon. Add the rest of the flour in the same way and stir in the melted and cooled butter and the vanilla essence.

Pour the mixture into a greased and lined Swiss roll tin making sure that there is plenty of mixture

Bûche de Noël (above)

in the corners. Bake in a preheated oven at 375°F; 190°C; Gas Mark 5 for about 15–20 minutes, or until well risen and springy to the touch. Have ready a clean tea-towel wrung out in hot water covered with a sheet of greaseproof paper. Turn the cake upside down onto this and peel off the lining paper. Trim the side edges of the cake with a sharp knife, then roll up the cake with the paper and tea-towel inside and leave to cool on a wire rack.

TO MAKE THE FILLING

Whip the cream until stiff, then fold into the chestnut purée. If the filling is too thick, add 15ml/1tbsp milk to thin it a little.

Unroll the cake carefully, remove the paper and tea-towel and spread evenly with the chestnut filling. Re-roll carefully. Trim one end straight, then cut the other end diagonally across the roll to look like a log. Attach this cut off piece to the side of the roll with a firm strip of angelica or a piece of macaroni and place on a cake board.

TO MAKE THE CRÈME AU BEURRE

Place the sugar and the 60ml/4tbsp water into a small heavy saucepan and slowly bring to the boil. Make sure that the sugar has completely dissolved before it comes to the boil. Simmer gently for 10–15 minutes or until the mixture forms a thin thread when pressed between thumb and forefinger. To do this, take some on a teaspoon, cool it a little and dip your finger in cold water before testing. If you have a cooking thermometer the temperature should be between 218°F (103°C) and 220°F (105°C).

Whisk the egg yolks in a bowl, then pour on the sugar syrup in a thin steady stream, whisking all the time. Continue to whisk, adding the butter about 25g/1oz at a time, until you have a smooth fluffy cream. Melt the chocolate with the tablespoon of water in a small bowl over a pan of hot water. Stir continuously until smooth. Cool, then beat into the syrup mixture.

TO DECORATE THE CAKE

Roll the almond paste into small sausages and wind them round like a catherine wheel to form knots for the log. Form 2 ends for the cake in the same way using larger sausages of almond paste and 1 end for the small branch.

Spread the cake with a thin coating of chocolate butter cream, then attach the almond paste knots and ends. Pipe the remaining butter cream on to the log using a fine star tube, running the length of the cake but around the knots. The piping should be uneven to represent bark.

Sprinkle the top of the cake and the cake board with icing sugar to give the effect of snow and decorate as you wish. Crystallised flowers and leaves would look attractive (page 14) while a candle and robin are very traditional.

☆ Instead of making the ends and knots of your chocolate log from almond paste, cover the cake with chocolate butter cream as before and pipe rings of white royal or glacé icing at all ends of the log to represent the grain of the wood. Sprinkle icing sugar on top and decorate with sprigs of holly and a robin.

ITALIAN CHRISTMAS PANETONE
(makes 2 loaves)

This is the most popular Christmas cake in Italy and is a dome-shaped fruit loaf studded with sultanas, peel and flaked almonds.

125g/4oz sultanas
25g/1oz citron peel, shredded
25g/1oz candied orange and lemon peel, shredded
Grated rind and juice of 1 lemon
450g/1lb strong white flour
5ml/1tsp salt
50g/2oz sugar
25g/1oz fresh yeast
90–120ml/3–4fl oz warm water
3 eggs, beaten
125g/4oz softened butter
50g/2oz flaked almonds
Generous pinch of grated nutmeg
25g/1oz melted butter, to finish

Soak the sultanas and peel in the lemon juice for at least 1 hour. Sieve the flour together with the salt into a large mixing bowl. Stir in the sugar. Dissolve the yeast in the warm water. Add the beaten eggs, the yeast mixture and the softened butter to the dry ingredients and mix well to a firm dough.

Turn the dough out onto a floured board and knead in the drained fruit and peel, the lemon rind, almonds and nutmeg. If the dough is too stiff add the lemon juice. Continue kneading until the dough is smooth and elastic, then put in a large oiled polythene bag, cover with a cloth and allow to rise in a warm place until doubled in size. (This will take 1–1½ hours depending on the temperature.)

Divide the dough into 2 and put each piece in a lined and greased 15cm/6in round cake tin. Tie a collar of greased double-thickness foil around each tin to come 6–7.5cm/2½–3in above the top of the

tin. Cover the tins with greased clingfilm or poly-thene and allow the dough to rise well up in the tins.

Brush the tops of each loaf with melted butter and bake in a moderate oven 350°F; 180°C; Gas Mark 4 for 40–50 minutes. Allow to cool in the tins until the sides shrink slightly, then gently remove and leave to cool on a wire rack. Serve with mulled wine, cider or ale on Christmas Eve.

HANSEL AND GRETEL'S SPICED GINGERBREAD HOUSE

In 1893 Engelbert Humperdinck wrote a new opera, based on the fairy tale written by the Brothers Grimm. The German gingerbreadmakers, the Lebzelter, were quick to produce Hansel and Gretel spiced pepper cake houses as a follow-up to the opera and they appeared everywhere. The house was decorated with white icing and long icicles hung from the eaves, and sweets and chocolates were used for shutters and decorations. Even the figures of the wicked witch and the two children were included.

Today, spiced gingerbread houses can still be bought in Germany around Christmas time, although they are not nearly as elaborate as in the past. A gingerbread house makes a lovely centrepiece for a Christmas table, so have a go at making your own. It would make an ideal present for a family of small children.

450g/1lb plain flour
10ml/1dsp ground ginger
2.5ml/½tsp ground cinnamon
75g/3oz butter or margarine
75g/3oz soft dark brown sugar
120ml/8tbsp golden syrup
15ml/1tbsp bicarbonate of soda
30ml/2tbsp water
1 egg, beaten
1 egg yolk

FOR THE DECORATIONS
White royal icing (page 11)
Blanched almonds
Chocolate buttons
Silver cake decorating balls
Glacé cherries
Coloured chocolate dragées
Angelica
Candied peel

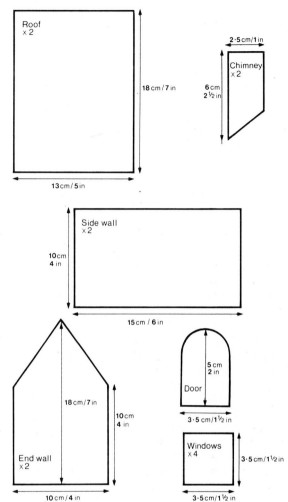

Following the diagrams, cut out shapes in thin card for the roof and walls of the house. Sieve the flour and spices together into a mixing bowl. Put the butter or margarine, sugar and syrup in a saucepan and stir over a low heat until the sugar has dissolved. Dissolve the bicarbonate of soda in the water, then add to the dry ingredients with the syrup mixture followed by the egg and the egg yolk. Mix together to form a soft dough. Divide the dough into 2 and put 1 piece into a polythene bag. Roll out the other half to about 6mm/¼in thick.

Cut out the roof, end and side wall from the dough using your templates. Arrange on a baking tray lined with silicone paper, then bake just above the centre of a pre-heated moderate oven 375°F; 190°C; Gas Mark 5 for 8–10 minutes or until risen and golden brown. Leave to cool on the baking tray for a few minutes, then transfer to a wire rack to cool completely.

Knead the remaining dough with the trimmings from the first piece and roll out to a thickness of 6mm/¼in. Cut out another roof, end and side wall and bake as before.

Knead together all the trimmings and cut out 1 door, 4 square windows and 2 chimney pieces. Bake these as before for 5–8 minutes, then cool on a wire rack.

TO ASSEMBLE HOUSE

Spread a little royal icing on all edges of the sides and end walls. Put together like a box on a 25cm/10in cake board and press the pieces lightly together. Fill the inside with sweets if you wish.

Spread icing along the remaining top edges of the house where the roof is fixed, and underneath the roof about 2.5cm/1in in from the edge where the roof joins the walls and along the top edge of the roof. Carefully place both roof pieces in position using more icing along the top of the join if necessary. Hold in position or place supports underneath the roof. Leave to dry overnight before decorating.

Next day, place the windows in position (2 on each side wall) and secure with a little icing. Put the door in position on an end wall and secure with icing. Cover the roof, tops of windows and the door with icing, pulling points of icing down with a small knife to represent snow and icicles. Sandwich the chimney pieces together with icing, place in position on the roof and secure with a cocktail stick, if necessary.

Cover the top and sides of the chimney with icing. Arrange chocolate buttons, dragees, glacé cherries etc all over the roof and around the windows and door. Spread more icing over the cake board and arrange more cherries, nuts, etc around the edge of the board. The children will love helping you with this cake!

The Story of the Christmas Rose

The Christmas rose has a beautiful creamy white flower and blooms between December and March, even in the snow. The flowers were once considered to be sacred and were used to ward off the plague and all sorts of evil spirits.

Legend has it that a little girl from Bethlehem wanted to give the Baby Jesus a present, but as she had no money, she searched the fields all day for a flower to give him, with no luck. She returned to the stable weeping, but a ray of light from within shone on a clump of pure white flowers which she gathered and took to the Baby; these were the first Christmas roses to bloom on earth.

GINGERBREAD PEOPLE
(makes about 20)

Gingerbread was often shaped into dolls for festive occasions in the past. At Christmas they were given to children to represent Jesus. Gingerbread cookies shaped like Christmas trees, pigs, stars, moons, angels, hearts and people are common throughout Scandinavia at Christmas time and, offered to visitors with a warming drink, what could be more welcoming?

Various shaped cutters are available, or you can make templates out of stiff card and cut around them. The biscuits can be decorated as you wish with cloves, currants, peel, glacé cherries, nuts or icing or they can be gilded while they are still warm; either use pure gold leaf in sheets which is edible (this was used in days gone by – hence the expression 'the gilt on the gingerbread'), or a gold powder mixed with egg white available from cake-icing centres.

30ml/2tbsp golden syrup
15ml/1tbsp black treacle
75g/3oz soft light brown sugar
7.5ml/1½tsp ground ginger
2.5ml/½tsp ground cinnamon
Pinch of ground cloves
Grated rind of ½ small orange
15ml/1tbsp water
90g/3½oz butter or margarine
2.5ml/½tsp bicarbonate of soda
225g/8oz plain flour

FOR DECORATION
Egg white
Currants and cloves
Glacé cherries
Glacé icing or royal icing
Narrow brightly coloured or gold ribbon
Silver cake-decorating balls
Gold paper shapes

Place the syrup, treacle, sugar, spices, orange rind and water into a large saucepan. Bring slowly to the boil making sure that the sugar is completely dissolved before boiling point is reached. Stir all the time, then remove the pan from the heat. Stir in the fat in pieces and the bicarbonate of soda. Next stir in the flour gradually, until you have a smooth dough (add a little more flour if the dough is too soft to manage). Cover and leave the dough in a cool place

Hansel and Gretel's Spiced Gingerbread House (page 23)

for about 30 minutes to become firm.

Roll out the dough on a lightly floured board to about 3mm/⅛in thick and cut out gingerbread men and women or whatever shapes you want. Brush with egg white and decorate with cloves, currants, glacé cherries and silver balls, then arrange on greased baking trays. Bake for 10–15 minutes in a pre-heated moderate oven 350°F; 180°C; Gas Mark 4 or until the biscuits feel firm when lightly pressed with your fingers. Leave the biscuits to cool on the trays for a few minutes before transferring to a wire cooling rack.

When cold, pipe icing on the biscuits to represent hair, eyebrows, shoes, cuffs, collars, ties, and clothes generally, or pipe names on the biscuits for each visitor. Finish by tying ribbon around their necks. Alternatively, decorate with gold paper shapes attached to the biscuits with a little icing or beaten egg white. Serve on a large platter decorated with sprigs of holly.

☆ TO MAKE DIFFERENT COLOURED GINGERBREAD MEN

Darker biscuits can be made using dark brown sugar and all black treacle. Lighter biscuits can be made using caster sugar and all golden syrup. The best effect is to make a quantity of both dark and light biscuits and serve them as an assortment. They also look good as a centrepiece on the table standing in a wreath of evergreen.

☆ TO MAKE GINGERBREAD SHAPES FOR THE CHRISTMAS TREE

Use the basic gingerbread dough and cut into different shapes. Before baking, make a hole in the top of each biscuit with a skewer, for hanging. When the biscuits have been cooked, but are still soft, run a skewer through the holes again. Leave to get cold, then decorate as you wish and thread narrow ribbon or gold thread through the holes. Hang on the Christmas tree (see photograph on front cover).

☆ HOMEMADE COOKIES AS PRESENTS

Home-baked cookies and cakes are a popular gift wherever Christmas is celebrated. Pack between layers of greaseproof or waxed paper in pretty airtight containers, or cover suitable tins with attractive Christmas wrapping paper. Tie with a festive bow and use one of the cookies as a name tag.

SUGAR-FREE CHRISTMAS CAKE
(makes 1 × 20cm/8in round or 18cm/7in square cake)

There is no added sugar or honey in this cake; it is sweetened by dried and candied fruit. If you are unable to eat sugar for health reasons, omit the candied peel and glacé cherries and add extra dates and chopped dried apricots. Polyunsaturated margarine may be used instead of butter.

This cake is lovely un-iced, but you can ice it in the normal way if you wish. It keeps very well.

175g/6oz cooking dates
60ml/4tbsp water
175g/6oz butter or margarine
5 eggs
175g/6oz plain wholemeal or white flour
5ml/1tsp mixed spice
75g/3oz ground almonds
Grated rind and juice of 1 lemon
125g/4oz glacé cherries, washed and dried
   and roughly chopped
225g/8oz currants
175g/6oz raisins
175g/6oz sultanas
125g/4oz candied peel, finely chopped
50g/2oz blanched almonds, chopped
30ml/2tbsp brandy or rum

Break up the dates and remove any stones and stalk. Place in a small saucepan with the water and cook gently until very soft. Remove from the heat and leave to cool. Prepare a 20cm/8in round or 18cm/7in square cake tin in the normal way for a rich fruit cake (page 8).

Put the cooled dates into a large mixing bowl with the butter or margarine and beat together until light and creamy. Beat in the eggs one at a time. Sieve the flour and spice together then add to the creamed mixture. Add all the remaining ingredients except the brandy and mix together well. Spoon into the prepared tin and bake in a preheated oven at 300°F; 150°C; Gas Mark 2 for about 3 hours.

Cool the cake on a wire rack, then when it is cold remove the lining papers. Prick the top and bottom of the cake with a fine skewer or knitting needle and pour the brandy or rum over it.

The Christmas Pudding

The last Sunday after Trinity and the Sunday before the first one in Advent is the traditional day for the Christmas pudding to be stirred before it is cooked and has come to be called 'Stir-up Sunday'. The name, however, comes from the Collect for the day which begins 'Stir up, we beseech Thee, O Lord, the wills of Thy faithful people'. Schoolboys apparently went round the houses singing

Stir up we beseech thee,
The pudding in the pot
And when we get home
We'll eat the lot.

The pudding must be stirred from east to west by every member of the family in honour of the Three Kings and to bring good luck for the coming year.

TRADITIONAL DARK PLUM PUDDING
(makes 2 puddings in 1 litre/2pt basins or 4 puddings in 600ml/1pt basins)

No English Christmas scene would be complete without the blazing plum pudding, traditionally spherical but now, for convenience, pudding-basin shaped and topped with a sprig of holly. Try and make your puddings as early as possible; by Stir-up Sunday at the latest.

125g/4oz self-raising flour
5ml/1tsp mixed spice
5ml/1tsp ground cinnamon
2.5ml/½tsp grated nutmeg
225g/8oz shredded suet
225g/8oz soft white breadcrumbs
450g/1lb soft dark brown sugar
350g/12oz stoned raisins
350g/12oz currants
225g/8oz sultanas
25g/1oz shredded citron peel
75g/3oz shredded candied orange and lemon peel, mixed
125g/4oz blanched almonds, chopped
Grated rind of 1 orange
Grated rind of 1 lemon
125g/4oz grated apple
125g/4oz grated carrot
4 standard eggs
60ml/4tbsp dark rum
150ml/¼pt stout
150ml/¼pt sweet brown ale or barley wine

Sieve the flour together with the spices into a large mixing bowl. Stir in the suet, followed by the breadcrumbs, followed by the sugar. Gradually mix in all the dried fruit, peel and nuts, followed by the orange and lemon rind, the grated apple and the carrot.

Beat the eggs in a separate bowl with the rum, stout and ale. Pour this over the dry ingredients and mix really well. This is where you get the rest of the family and any visiting neighbours to give the pudding a really good stir, because it is very hard work! Add any lucky charms and coins at this point, then cover with a clean tea-towel and leave overnight.

Next day, grease 2 or 4 pudding basins and pack the mixture into them right to the top. Cover the top of each basin with buttered greaseproof paper, followed by a pudding cloth or piece of kitchen foil. Tie securely with a piece of string making a loop of string to form a handle across the basin. This can be used for lifting the basin in and out of the saucepan.

Steam the puddings for 8 hours if they are large, or 6 hours if they are small, making sure that the water does not boil away or go off the boil. Store in a cool dry place and, when ready to eat, steam for a further 3 hours before serving.

To serve, place the pudding on a warm plate and sprinkle the top with sieved icing sugar. Put a sprig of holly on top or surround the base with holly, then flame with brandy or rum. Carry the pudding, still flaming, to the table. Accompany with a suitable sauce (pages 32–3) or whipped or clotted cream.

TO STORE THE PUDDING

Many people still like to keep a rich Christmas pudding a year before serving it and a well-stored pudding will keep as long as this if it contains enough alcohol and is stored in the correct way. The flavour does improve if it is kept for several months, however. After cooking leave your pudding to cool before removing the greaseproof paper and pudding cloth or kitchen foil. Replace carefully with fresh buttered greaseproof paper and a new pudding cloth or foil. Store in a cool dry place.

TO SET THE PUDDING ALIGHT

Make sure your pudding is heated right through and place it on a warm serving dish. Warm some rum or brandy in a metal ladle or small saucepan, before pouring it over the pudding. Ignite with a match and carry the flaming pudding to the table. Burning holly will only add to the fun, but be careful.

☆ HOW TO FROST HOLLY

Lightly beat an egg white until frothy. Paint it all over a sprig of holly with a fine paint brush, covering both the back and front of the leaves. Sprinkle with caster sugar and leave to dry in a warm place for 24 hours. The Victorians used to coat the holly with melted butter before sprinkling with caster sugar.

☆ INDIVIDUAL CHRISTMAS PUDDINGS

Individual puddings make lovely presents for relations or friends living on their own. Make them in small basins or cups and cook for 3 hours. Cover with a circle of pretty material tied with a festive ribbon, or remove from the basin and wrap in clingfilm. Tie with ribbon.

☆ CANNONBALL CHRISTMAS PUDDING

Divide the pudding mixture into equal quantities (450g/1lb or 900g/2lb). Scald the appropriate number of large squares of white cotton cloth (old sheeting or tea-towels will do). Wring out the cloths and lay out on a board or work surface. Rub all over with butter, then dredge generously with flour and brown sugar.

Have ready several very large saucepans full of boiling water. Turn the pudding mixture into a cloth and tie up securely with string, leaving room for the pudding to swell. Plunge each pudding into a pan of water and tie the string to the upturned lid of the pan or place a wooden spoon across the pan and tie the string to this so that the pudding will be cannonball shaped. If you are happy to have a flat-bottomed pudding, let it stand freely on a trivet in the saucepan. Boil steadily, topping up with boiling water as necessary, for 4 hours (450g/1lb quantity) or 6 hours (900g/2lb quantity).

A round pudding can also be cooked in a rice steamer. Wrap the mixture in a cloth as before or a piece of kitchen foil, then place in a rice-steaming ball. Cook as before.

SUGAR-FREE CHRISTMAS PUDDING
(makes 1 pudding in a 1 litre/2pt basin or 2 puddings in 600ml/1pt basins)

This recipe is for a beautiful dark Christmas pudding which is sweet and spicy, but without sugar or suet. If you are unable to eat sugar for health reasons, leave out the black treacle as well.

225g/8oz cooking dates
150ml/¼pt dark rum
225g/8oz butter or margarine
2 eggs, beaten
15ml/1tbsp black treacle
Grated rind and juice of 1 lemon
125g/4oz stoned raisins
225g/8oz currants
125g/4oz sultanas
125g/4oz candied peel, shredded
25g/1oz blanched almonds, chopped
125g/4oz plain wholemeal flour
2.5ml/½tsp ground ginger
7.5ml/1½tsp mixed spice
2.5ml/½tsp grated nutmeg
125g/4oz soft wholemeal breadcrumbs

Chop the dates, removing any stones and hard stem. Put them in a small saucepan with the rum and heat gently until very soft. Remove from the heat and cool. Cream together the butter or margarine and the dates in a large mixing bowl until soft and fluffy.

Beat in the eggs followed by the treacle and the lemon rind and juice. Stir in the dried fruit, peel and almonds. Sieve the flour with the spices and mix into the other ingredients. Lastly, stir in the breadcrumbs. Mix really well until all the ingredients are well combined.

Grease a pudding basin or basins and fill with the mixture to about 2.5cm/1in from the top. Cover with greased greaseproof paper and a pudding cloth or foil. Tie securely with string and steam for 4 hours, topping up with more boiling water as necessary. Store in a cool dry place until needed.

When required, steam for a further 3 hours before serving with low-fat cream or yoghurt.

CRYSTALLISED FRUIT CHRISTMAS PUDDING
(makes 2 puddings in 1 litre/2pt basins or 4 puddings in 600ml/1pt basins)

A little goes a long way with this very rich, fruity and alcoholic pudding!

125g/4oz self-raising flour
125g/4oz fresh brown breadcrumbs
125g/4oz ground almonds
225g/8oz dark brown sugar
175g/6oz cold unsalted butter
175g/6oz sultanas
175g/6oz stoned raisins
175g/6oz whole glacé cherries
25g/1oz angelica, chopped
50g/2oz crystallised apricots, roughly chopped
50g/2oz crystallised chestnuts, chopped
3 eggs
Grated rind and juice of ½ lemon
Grated rind and juice of 1 orange
300ml/½pt sweet brown ale, eg barley wine
1 miniature bottle of Benedictine

Mix the flour, breadcrumbs, ground almonds and sugar together in a large mixing bowl. Grate the butter into the dry ingredients using the coarse side of the grater. Stir in all the fruit and the chestnuts. Don't chop up the apricots and chestnuts too small.

Beat the eggs and add to the bowl. Mix the lemon rind and juice with the orange rind and juice and the ale and liqueur. Pour into the other ingredients and mix thoroughly. Pack into buttered basins, cover with greaseproof and foil, secure tightly with string and steam for 5 hours. Cool, and store in a cool dry place. On the day of eating, steam for a further 3 hours. Serve with a suitable sauce (pages 32–3).

CRYSTALLISED CHESTNUTS

These days crystallised chestnuts seem only to come from France as 'marrons glacés' and are extremely expensive. They take experts a long time to prepare with endless syrup boiling, but the following method gives a good result and would make a luxurious present for the friend or relative who has everything.

450g/1lb large fresh chestnuts, peeled
450g/1lb granulated sugar
150ml/¼pt water
2.5ml/½tsp vanilla essence

Cook the nuts in boiling water until tender (about 20 minutes). Dissolve the sugar in the water in a saucepan over gentle heat, then bring to the boil. Add the vanilla essence, then the drained chestnuts. Boil briskly for 10 minutes. Remove the nuts with a slotted spoon and drain on a wire rack over a baking tray. Leave in a warm dry place for 24 hours. Re-boil the syrup, put the nuts back and simmer gently until thickly coated with the syrup. Drain as before and allow to dry before packing in wooden or waxed boxes between layers of waxed paper. Don't store for too long before eating.

TO MAKE YOUR OWN CANDIED PEEL
(makes 16 pieces)

This rather long-winded procedure takes 2 days, but the result is quite delicious and of course much cheaper than shop-bought candied peel. It is also a way of making use of orange and lemon skins after you have used the fruit and juice.

4 oranges
4 lemons
12g/½oz bicarbonate of soda
675g/1½lb granulated sugar

Quarter the fruit and remove all the pulp and juice. Dissolve the bicarbonate of soda in 150ml/¼pt hot water and pour over each piece of peel. Add sufficient boiling water to cover the peel completely. Allow to stand for 20 minutes, then rinse off very well. Cover the peel with cold water and bring to the boil. Simmer gently until tender, then drain well, reserving the liquor. Place the peel in a heatproof dish. Make a sugar syrup from 450g/1lb of the sugar and 450ml/¾pt cooking liquor and water by dissolving the sugar in the liquid over gentle heat, then bringing to the boil. Pour this hot syrup over the peel, making sure that it is completely immersed. Cover and leave for 48 hours. Place a sieve over a saucepan and carefully drain the syrup from the peel into the saucepan. Add the remaining 225g/8oz sugar to the syrup and bring slowly to the boil making sure that the sugar is completely dissolved before the syrup reaches the boil. Simmer the peel in this gently until it looks clear. Lift the peel out with a draining spoon and dry it slowly on a baking tray in a cool oven 300°F; 150°C; Gas Mark 2.

Reduce the syrup by boiling it gently for 30 minutes. Dip the dried peel into the reduced syrup and dry again in the oven. Boil up the remaining syrup until it is cloudy and thick. Pour a very little into each cap of dried peel. Allow to dry again, then store in airtight containers until needed.

We all want some Figgy Pudding

Plum or figgy pudding started life in medieval days as plum porridge, or potage, made from meat broth thickened with breadcrumbs and flavoured with dried plums (prunes), raisins, currants, wine and spices. In the eighteenth century it became more solid and was boiled in a cloth. By the early nineteenth century meat was no longer an ingredient and the plum pudding we know and love today, rich with nuts, fruit and alcohol, emerged. However, it did not become associated particularly with Christmas until the mid-nineteenth century when Prince Albert introduced it as part of the royal Christmas Day dinner because he was so fond of heavy rich puddings. The palace always set the fashion for the rest of the country, so the Christmas pudding became one of the main ingredients of the Victorian Christmas feast and today is the dish which symbolises a Victorian Christmas more than any other.

LAST MINUTE FIGGY PUDDING
(makes 1 pudding in a 1 litre/2pt basin)

225g/8oz dried figs, chopped
225g/8oz cooking dates, chopped
125g/4oz stoned raisins
75g/3oz stem ginger, chopped
45ml/3tbsp brandy or rum
225g/8oz self-raising flour
Pinch of salt
175g/6oz fresh white breadcrumbs
175g/6oz shredded suet
3 eggs, beaten
Grated rind and juice of 1 lemon
A little milk (optional)

Place the prepared fruit and ginger in a bowl. Sprinkle with the brandy or rum and leave to stand for at least 1 hour. Sieve the flour with the salt into a mixing bowl and stir in the breadcrumbs and suet. Mix the beaten eggs into the dry ingredients with the lemon rind and juice followed by the fruit mixture. Mix thoroughly adding a little milk if necessary to make a dropping consistency.

Turn into a well-greased 1 litre/2pt basin, cover with greaseproof paper and foil or a pudding cloth and steam for 4 hours. Reheat when you want to serve the pudding and accompany with a hard sauce (page 32).

Cannonball Christmas Pudding (page 28)

TUTTI-FRUTTI SPONGE PUDDING
(serves 6)

This is a light sponge pudding studded with glacé and dried fruit, which can be varied as much as you like. It makes a delicious alternative to a rich fruit pudding and can be made the day before and heated up, or indeed on Christmas morning if you have the time and energy!

Natural glacé cherries ie with no artificial colouring, can be obtained from good grocers and health shops.

125g/4oz large prunes
75g/3oz glacé cherries (without artificial colouring)
75g/3oz dried apricots, chopped
50g/2oz angelica, chopped
175g/6oz butter or margarine
175g/6oz caster or soft brown sugar
Grated rind and juice of 1 lemon
3 eggs, beaten
125g/4oz self-raising flour
50g/2oz soft white breadcrumbs
50g/2oz ground almonds (optional)
30–45ml/2–3tbsp apricot jam

Place 3 of the prunes in a saucepan with water to cover and simmer for 10 minutes, then leave on one side to soak. Remove the stones from the other prunes with scissors and cut off the flesh. Halve 3 of the glacé cherries and set aside. Chop the remainder of the cherries and mix with the chopped prunes, apricots and angelica.

Cream the butter or margarine and sugar with the lemon rind until pale and fluffy. Gradually beat in the eggs a little at a time, then fold in the sieved flour, breadcrumbs and ground almonds, if you are using them. Lastly, fold in the prepared fruit and the lemon juice. The mixture should be of a soft dropping consistency; add a little water if it is too stiff.

Butter a 1 litre/2pt pudding basin and coat the base with apricot jam. Cut the reserved prunes in half and discard the stones. Arrange the prunes on the jam with the reserved cherries. Spoon over the pudding mixture. Cover the basin with buttered greaseproof paper and kitchen foil, making a pleat to allow the pudding to rise. Secure tightly with string and steam for 2–2½ hours or until the pudding is firm to the touch.

Unmould on to a warm serving dish and serve with Hot Sabayon or Brandy Sauce (pages 32–3) or whipped cream.

BRANDY AND LEMON BUTTER

This hard sauce can be made 2 or 3 weeks before Christmas and kept in the fridge until needed, or it can be frozen. Serve with steamed puddings, fruit pies, tarts and mince pies.

125g/4oz unsalted butter
125g/4oz caster sugar
Grated rind of ½ lemon (optional)
15ml/1tbsp boiling water
5ml/1tsp lemon juice
30–45ml/2–3tbsp brandy or rum

Cut the butter into small pieces and place in a warmed bowl with the sugar and lemon rind. Beat hard until creamy, then add the boiling water. Continue to beat until every grain of sugar has dissolved, then add the lemon juice and brandy gradually, beating thoroughly all the time to prevent curdling. When completely blended, press into lidded wax or plastic cartons and store in the fridge until needed.

Serve cold, sprinkled with a little extra grated lemon rind.

BRANDY AND LEMON BUTTER WITH GLACÉ FRUIT

Try adding a few chopped glacé cherries and a little chopped angelica to the finished butter. Red, green, yellow and natural-coloured glacé cherries are now widely available and make the butter look very colourful and taste even more mouth-watering.

RUM AND ORANGE BUTTER

Like Brandy and Lemon Butter, this can be made early and stored for 2–3 weeks in the fridge, or can be frozen.

125g/4oz unsalted butter
125g/4oz soft brown sugar
Generous pinch of ground cinnamon
5ml/1tsp grated orange rind
15ml/1tbsp boiling water
15ml/1tbsp orange juice
30–45ml/2–3tbsp dark rum or brandy

Make in exactly the same way as Brandy and Lemon Butter, beating the cinnamon with the butter and sugar. Serve chilled and sprinkled with a little extra grated orange rind to accompany Christmas pudding or mince pies.

TRADITIONAL CUMBERLAND RUM BUTTER

Serve with rich fruit puddings, mince pies or spread on scones as they do in Cumberland. Adjust the amount of nutmeg to taste.

125g/4oz unsalted butter
225g/8oz dark brown sugar
30–45ml/2–3tbsp dark rum
2.5ml/½tsp grated nutmeg

Melt the butter gently in a saucepan. Stir in the sugar, rum and nutmeg. Pour into a bowl and leave to set.

Until very recently in Cumberland, rum butter was spread on oatcakes and given to friends and relatives who called at the house to see a new baby. In turn, they would leave a 'silver coin' and on the day of the christening when the butter bowl was empty, the coins were placed in it. A bowl with plenty of coins sticking to it meant that the child would never be wanting.

BRANDY OR RUM SAUCE
(makes 300ml/½pt)

If you, like myself, prefer a pouring sauce with a rich Christmas pudding, then try this recipe.

10ml/2tsp cornflour
2 egg yolks
15ml/1tbsp caster sugar
300ml/½pt milk
12g/½oz unsalted butter
45ml/3tbsp brandy or rum

Blend the cornflour with the egg yolks and sugar. Add a little of the milk and put the rest in a saucepan. Bring to the boil, then pour gradually on to the egg mixture stirring continuously. Return to the pan and heat gently until slightly thickened. Stir in the butter and brandy or rum and taste, adding extra spirit if you wish.

Serve hot with Christmas pudding.

TO KEEP THE SAUCE WARM

Keep the sauce warm in a basin over hot water or in the top of a double saucepan making sure that the water is not in contact with the bottom of the basin. Sprinkle the surface of the sauce with caster sugar and cover closely with greaseproof paper or clingfilm to prevent a skin forming.

HOT SABAYON SAUCE
(serves 4)

This classic French sauce is delicious served with Christmas pudding, fruit pies, sponge puddings and ice-cream.

3 egg yolks
15ml/1tbsp caster sugar
150ml/¼pt sweet sherry
Strip of lemon rind

Put all the ingredients into a small basin and stand it over a small saucepan quarter-filled with simmering water. Whisk with a balloon whisk or electric hand whisk until the sauce becomes very frothy and starts to thicken. Remove the lemon rind and serve at once.

☆ Sabayon is the French corruption of zabaione (or zabaglione), the Italian sweet which can be served as a sauce for a pudding, or on its own in a warmed glass, with Savoy fingers or thin slices of sponge cake. In Italy, it is made with Marsala or white wine instead of sherry.

VALENCIA SAUCE
(serves 6–8)

This delicious and refreshing sauce, based on a very old recipe, can be served with Christmas pudding instead of Brandy or Rum Sauce (page 32). Clementines, satsumas or tangerines can be used instead.

1 large orange
40g/1½oz unsalted butter
40g/1½oz plain flour
600ml/1pt milk
30ml/2 level tbsp Demerara sugar
1 miniature bottle of Cointreau or Grand Marnier

Finely grate the rind from the orange and reserve. Remove all the pith and cut the orange into segments. Cut each segment into small pieces. Melt the butter in a saucepan and stir in the flour. Cook gently for a few minutes, then remove from the heat and slowly stir in the milk. Return to the heat and cook gently until the sauce has thickened. Stir in the orange rind, sugar and orange liqueur. Taste and add more sugar or liqueur if necessary.

Just before serving, stir in the orange pieces and heat gently for 2–3 minutes. Serve hot.

FLUFFY BRANDY CREAM
(serves 4–6)

As an alternative to brandy or rum butter, try this sauce which is lighter in texture and not so rich. It is very good with any rich fruit pudding or pie. Rum can be used instead of brandy.

1 egg, separated
125g/4oz icing sugar, sieved
45ml/3tbsp brandy
150ml/¼pt double cream

Whisk the egg white until thick, then whisk in 50g/2oz of the icing sugar, a little at a time, until the mixture stands in peaks. In a second basin, beat the egg yolk and remaining 50g/2oz icing sugar until the mixture thickens. Fold into the egg white mixture.

Whisk the cream until it is thick and fold into the egg mixture together with the brandy. Serve chilled.

BRANDY OR RUM CREAM SAUCE
(serves 6)

600ml/1pt double cream
Pinch of salt
150ml/¼pt brandy or rum

Gently heat the cream and salt in a large saucepan to boiling point. Continue cooking for about 45 minutes without burning until the cream is pale brown and thick. Meanwhile reduce the spirit to a tablespoon by boiling, then stir in the cream. Serve with rich fruit puddings, mince pies and fruit pies.

Lucky charms

Lucky charms and coins are traditionally added when all the family gather to stir the pudding mixture on Stir-up Sunday. This idea probably came from the earlier tradition of burying beans and lucky charms in the Twelfth Night cake (page 125). Wealthy Victorians baked their Twelfth Night cake with silver charms inside and between the two World Wars the poor copied this custom by burying a threepenny joey, a tiny silver coin worth half a sixpence, inside the Christmas pudding. Somehow a 5p piece doesn't sound so romantic, but ideally a coin, a ring and a thimble should be pushed into your pudding; the coin is to bring worldly fortune, the ring a marriage and the thimble a life of blessedness.

Christmas Eve Dinner

Today Christmas Eve in Britain is mainly seen as a time for last-minute preparations for Christmas Day, but in the past it had its own traditions and superstitions. Mummers' plays were usually performed on Christmas Eve, as was the lively ceremony of hauling home the Yule log, in England usually ash, because the shepherds were supposed to have lit a fire for the infant Jesus at a moment's notice and ash is the only wood which will burn while it is still green. In Scotland the Yule log was birch stripped of its bark, hence the proverb 'He's as bare as a bark on Yule e'en' (ie he's very poor).

Christmas Eve is also the traditional day for decorating the house and for dressing the Christmas tree. Last, but certainly not least, comes the excitement of hanging up the Christmas stockings for Santa to fill.

SMOKED OYSTER MOUSSES
(serves 6–8)

Fresh oysters are a traditional part of the French 'Le Réveillon', the Christmas Eve feast. This is a very easy starter, which can be prepared well in advance.

3×100g/3⅔oz cans of smoked oysters
225ml/7½fl oz dry white wine
Salt and freshly milled black pepper
20g/¾oz powdered gelatine
30ml/2tbsp cold water
450ml/¾pt double cream
225ml/7½fl oz sour cream
Black or red lumpfish roe, to garnish
Watercress to garnish

Drain the oysters from their oil and place in a blender or processor with the white wine. Blend until smooth and season to taste.

Sprinkle the gelatine over the water in a small bowl and leave to soak for 5 minutes. Place the bowl over a saucepan of simmering water and stir until dissolved. Remove the bowl from the saucepan and leave until lukewarm. Whip the cream until it starts to form soft peaks, but is not stiff. Gradually add the dissolved gelatine to the oyster mixture, then stir in the lightly whipped cream. Spoon into small greased moulds, such as castle pudding or dariole moulds, and chill until set.

Carefully unmould each mousse onto a small serving plate. Stir the sour cream and pour a little around each mousse. Garnish with a little black or red lumpfish roe and a few sprigs of watercress. Serve with thin brown bread and butter.

CREAM OF ARTICHOKE SOUP
(serves 8)

This soup is also called Palestine soup because of the myth of the vegetable's connection with the ancient city of Jerusalem. Actually, the Jerusalem artichoke is related to the sunflower, Italian for which is girasole, so 'Jerusalem' is just a misinterpretation.

900g/2lb Jerusalem artichokes
Juice of 1 lemon
50g/2oz butter
2 medium onions, sliced
¼ cucumber, chopped
1 litre/2pt chicken stock
300ml/½pt single cream
Salt and freshly milled black pepper
Freshly grated nutmeg
Finely chopped parsley and bronze chrysanthemum
  petals to garnish

Scrub the artichokes under cold running water with a stiff brush. Scrape or peel them if necessary, quickly dropping them into water acidulated with the lemon juice to prevent the artichokes discolouring.

Melt the butter in a large heavy-based saucepan and add the onions. Cook gently until soft, but not coloured. Drain and dry the artichokes thoroughly and slice them. Add to the onions, then add the cucumber and stir to coat with butter. Cover with a lid and simmer gently for about 5 minutes, shaking the pan frequently. Pour on the stock and bring slowly to the boil. Cover again with a lid and simmer very gently for about 20 minutes, or until the artichokes are very soft. Purée or process the soup,

then return to the saucepan. Stir in the cream and season to taste with salt, pepper and nutmeg. Reheat gently and serve garnished with a little chopped parsley and a few chrysanthemum petals.

PEARS STUFFED WITH STILTON
(serves 8)

4 large ripe dessert pears
Juice of 1 lemon
50g/2oz cream cheese
125g/4oz ripe Stilton cheese
30ml/2tbsp port or brandy
Freshly milled black pepper
50g/2oz pistachio nuts or walnuts
   (25g/1oz if not making sauce)

FOR THE SAUCE (optional)
150ml/5fl oz sour cream
15ml/1tbsp walnut oil
15ml/1tbsp dry sherry
Salt and freshly milled black pepper
Paprika to garnish
Watercress sprigs and/or celery leaves to garnish

Peel, halve and core the pears. Immerse in water, acidulated with lemon juice, to prevent them from discolouring.

To prepare the filling, blend the cream cheese with the Stilton and port or brandy until smooth. Season to taste with black pepper, then mix in 25g/ 1oz of finely chopped nuts. Drain and dry the pears thoroughly, then place each pear half, cut side down, on a small plate. Pipe a decorative 'frill' of cheese mixture around each pear.

To make the sauce, if required, beat all the ingredients together and season well. Pour a little sauce over each pear and sprinkle with a dusting of paprika. Coarsely chop the remaining 25g/1oz nuts and sprinkle over the cheese 'frill'. Garnish with watercress and/or celery leaves.

Serve chilled with brown bread and butter.

Père Noel

The children of France leave wooden clogs on the hearth to receive presents from Père Noel, but adults give each other presents at New Year. The tradition harks back to the days when French children wore wooden peasant shoes called 'sabots'. French candy and pastry shops make replicas out of chocolate and fill them with candy.

Christmas Eve Feasts

In many European countries Christmas Eve is the time for eating the main Christmas meal, although in Catholic countries it is also time for fasting, so meat is not eaten until after midnight.

In areas of Germany around the Black Forest, an extra place is laid at the table for the Virgin Mary because there was no room for her in Bethlehem. In France three masses are held during the night in beautifully lit churches and cathedrals, then the family returns home and breaks their fast with a meal called Le Réveillon. This is a generous spread, often cold, consisting of oysters, pâtés, boudins (special black or white sausages), goose or turkey with chestnuts and foie gras, baked ham, a salad, cheeses and desserts. When the festivities are over and the family has gone to bed, it is customary to leave a fire burning, candles lit and food and drink on the table in case the Virgin Mary passes by.

Das Christkind

In Germany a table near the Christmas tree ('Tannenbaum') is set with soup plates, one for each child of the house, which are filled with sweets overnight by the silently passing Christ Child ('das Christkind'). The children write him letters and leave them on the window sill so that He may read them and grant their wishes.

PHEASANT CASSEROLE WITH PORT, ORANGE AND CHESTNUTS
(serves 8–10)

Many supermarkets now sell oven-ready fresh or frozen pheasant during the season, from 1 October to 1 February (10 December in Scotland). Cock and hen birds may be sold singly or as a brace; an average hen bird will serve 2, a cock bird 3. Pheasant has a rich gamey flavour and makes a delicious and very special casserole for Christmas Eve.

3 oven-ready pheasants, jointed
25g/1oz butter
30ml/2tbsp vegetable oil
2 medium onions, sliced
350g/12oz peeled chestnuts
30ml/2tbsp flour
750ml/1¼pt chicken stock
210ml/7fl oz port
Finely grated rind and juice of 2 oranges
15ml/1tbsp redcurrant jelly

1 bouquet garni
1 bay leaf
Salt and freshly milled black pepper
Beurre manié, to thicken
Chopped fresh parsley to garnish

Wipe the pheasant joints with absorbent kitchen paper, then brown them all over in the butter and oil heated together in a large flameproof casserole. Remove the joints from the pan and put on one side.

Fry the onions and chestnuts in the remaining fat for a few minutes until brown, then sprinkle over the flour. Cook for 2–3 minutes, then gradually stir in the stock, port, orange rind and juice and redcurrant jelly. Bring slowly to the boil, stirring continuously until smooth, then replace the reserved pheasant joints in the casserole. Season to taste and add the bouquet garni and bay leaf. Cover the casserole and cook in a moderate oven 325°F; 170°C; Gas Mark 3 for 1–1½ hours, or until the pheasant is tender. Remove the bouquet garni and bay leaf and thicken with beurre manié if necessary. Check and adjust the seasoning before serving garnished with chopped parsley.

Accompany with jacket potatoes, Julienne Potato Cake, Casserole of Potatoes and Leek (page 70) Leeks with Ginger or Gratin Dauphinois (page 121), Braised Red Cabbage with Pears (page 71) and a green vegetable or salad.

LEEKS WITH GINGER
(serves 8)

These leeks can be cooked without the ginger.

900g/2lb leeks, trimmed
50g/2oz butter
2 garlic cloves, finely chopped
10ml/2tsp fresh ginger, grated
½tsp dried thyme
½ chicken stock cube
Freshly milled black pepper

Cut the leeks into 2.5cm/1in lengths. Melt the butter in a heavy-based saucepan and fry the garlic, ginger and thyme very gently for 2 minutes. Stir in the chicken stock cube until dissolved, then add the leeks and black pepper. Stir well until the leeks are buttery, cover with a lid and cook very gently for about 10 minutes until the leeks are tender. Remove the lid and continue cooking on a higher heat until the moisture has completely evaporated. Adjust the seasoning if necessary. Serve immediately.

Snapdragon

This was one of the most popular Victorian Christmas games traditionally played on Christmas Eve and the subject of many Victorian Christmas cards. A quantity of raisins and nuts was placed in a large shallow bowl and brandy or rum was poured over. The lights in the room were put out before the spirit was ignited, then players tried to grab a raisin or nut by plunging their fingers into the flames and the Song of Snapdragon was sung.

> *Here he comes with flaming bowl,*
> *Don't he mean to take his toll*
> *Snip! Snap! Drago.*

In the west of England, a similar game of Flapdragon was played. A lighted candle was placed in a container of cider and the contents drunk by the players without, if possible, burning themselves!

JULIENNE POTATO CAKE
(serves 8)

1–4kg/2½lb potatoes, peeled
75g/3oz butter
Salt and freshly milled black pepper

Cut the peeled potatoes into Julienne strips (matchsticks). Dry well in a tea-towel, or kitchen paper.

Rub a thick, even coating of butter over the base and sides of two small frying pans or sandwich tins. Press in the potatoes and season between the layers. Dot with any remaining butter, then cover tightly with foil with a plate on top. Cook for 10 minutes on top of the stove over a very gentle steady heat, then transfer to a moderate oven 350°F; 180°C; Gas Mark 4 for a further 30 minutes. Test to see if the potatoes are cooked with the point of a knife. The cakes should be golden brown.

☆ BEURRE MANIÉ

This 'kneaded butter' is used to thicken sauces and casseroles, etc, at the end of cooking time. Work 25g/1oz plain flour into 50g/2oz softened butter. Place a small piece on the end of a balloon whisk and whisk it into the simmering liquid. Add more in the same manner until the required thickness is reached. It makes a lovely rich sauce. Store leftover beurre manié in a covered jar in the fridge for up to 1 month. It can also be frozen.

Pheasant Casserole with Port, Orange and Chestnuts (page 35)

Christmas Fish Dishes

Catholic pre-Christmas fasting traditions rarely led to actual suffering. The Polish 'wigilia', the Christmas Eve meal, is meatless because Advent is a period of fasting, but is none the less opulent. It consists of an odd number of dishes, nine or eleven, which should all represent hard work and the produce of the farmer's land. Mushrooms, wheat or millet, dried fruit, peas and cabbage, herring and carp, together with sweet dishes are commonly served. Fasting Hungarians tuck into grilled or jellied carp or a fried fish. Stuffed baked carp in a sweet, spicy sauce is common in Czechoslovakia and cured hake or ling was eaten in Ireland.

Fish also features on the Christmas Eve menus further south, where a wider variety of seafood is available. Coastal Italians, for instance, may feast on eels, octopus and squid.

CHESTNUT STUFFED SOLE
(serves 6)

In many countries fish is served on Christmas Eve as a reminder of the old Christmas fast. It makes a change to eat fish for Christmas lunch, too.

6 medium Dover or lemon sole
75g/3oz butter, melted
Orange slices to garnish
Fresh dill, fennel or parsley to garnish

FOR THE STUFFING
175g/6oz chestnuts, boiled and peeled
25g/1oz butter
50g/2oz streaky bacon, very finely chopped
1 medium onion, finely chopped
1 garlic clove, crushed
50g/2oz celery, very finely chopped
50g/2oz fresh wholemeal breadcrumbs
15ml/1tbsp chopped parsley
Grated rind and juice of 1 orange
Salt and freshly milled black pepper
Pinch of ground mace

Prepare the fish for stuffing.

To make the stuffing, roughly chop the chestnuts and place in a mixing bowl. Melt the butter and fry the bacon until crisp. Transfer to the bowl using a draining spoon, then fry the onion, garlic and celery until soft. Tip the mixture into the bowl and stir in the breadcrumbs, parsley and orange rind. Season

well with salt, pepper and mace and stir in enough orange juice to bind the mixture together. Divide the stuffing between the fish and place the fish in shallow buttered ovenproof dishes. Brush with melted butter and season well. Bake in a preheated moderate oven 350°F; 180°C; Gas Mark 4 for 20–30 minutes.

Arrange the fish on a large warmed serving platter, decorated with orange slices and fresh dill, fennel or parsley. Serve with Château Potatoes (page 110) or Gratin Dauphinois (page 121), Cauliflower and Lemon Roll (page 40), and a green vegetable or salad. Accompany, if you wish, with Orange Cream Sauce or Orange Hollandaise (see following recipes).

BONING A SOLE FOR STUFFING

Leaving the head and tail on, place the fish on a board, dark side up and run a sharp knife down the backbone of the fish. Insert your knife into the flesh and rest the tip against the backbone and on top of the rib bones. Slide the knife right down the backbone, then work with long, slicing motions across the ribs to the outer edge of the fish. Gently lift away the fillet on either side of the bone, exposing the ribs. Snap or cut the backbone in several places with kitchen scissors, or by bending back the fish until the bone snaps. Remove these sections of the backbone and ribs with the help of a small sharp knife. The fish now has a pouch-like cavity, which can be stuffed.

☆ FISHY SLIMMER

White fish is ideal to eat for Christmas lunch if you are on a diet. Make the stuffing without the bacon and breadcrumbs – chestnuts are low in calories.

Serve the sole with a green vegetable and salad, but without a sauce.

ORANGE CREAM SAUCE
(serves 6)

175g/6oz butter
300ml/½pt double cream
Salt and pepper
Orange juice

Just before serving the fish, melt the butter in a frying pan over gentle heat. Stir in the cream and cook over moderate heat for about 5 minutes until the sauce is thick. Season with salt, pepper and orange juice. Serve separately with the fish.

ORANGE HOLLANDAISE
(serves 6)

45ml/3tbsp white wine vinegar
30ml/2tbsp water
10 white peppercorns
½ bay leaf
3 large egg yolks
175g/6oz unsalted butter, cut into small pieces
Grated rind of 1 small orange
Salt
Orange juice to taste

Put the vinegar, water and peppercorns and ½ bay leaf into a small pan. Boil down to about 15ml/1tbsp of liquid. Leave to cool, then strain.

Beat the egg yolks in a basin and add the reduced vinegar. Pour into the top of a double saucepan, or set the basin over a pan of barely simmering water on a low heat. Cook slowly without letting the water boil or the sauce will get too hot and curdle. Add the butter, piece by piece, stirring all the time. The sauce is finished when it coats the back of a spoon and looks thick. Stir in the orange rind and season to taste with salt and orange juice. Keep warm on a very low heat until ready to serve.

BUTTERED BROAD BEANS WITH PARSLEY
(serves 6–8)

The beans can be prepared in advance, ready for heating through in the butter and seasoning just before serving.

2 × 350g/12oz packets frozen baby broad beans
Salt
50g/2oz butter
Freshly milled black pepper
2.5ml/½tsp ground mace
½ clove of garlic, crushed
15ml/1tbsp chopped parsley

Cook the broad beans in boiling salted water for 4–5 minutes, then drain and cool under cold running water. Drain again, then remove and discard the pale green skins revealing the bright green beans underneath.

Melt the butter in a saucepan or frying pan and toss the beans in this until hot right through. Dredge with black pepper and stir in the mace, garlic and parsley just before serving.

CABBAGE AND CELERY CASSEROLE
(serves 8–10)

75g/3oz butter
1 medium onion, finely chopped
1 garlic clove, crushed
1 head of celery, washed and sliced
900g/2lb white cabbage, shredded
50g/2oz butter
50g/2oz flour
600ml/1pt milk
Salt and freshly milled black pepper
50g/2oz fresh wholemeal breadcrumbs
Grated nutmeg
25g/1oz butter

Melt the 75g/3oz butter in a large heatproof casserole and add the onion, garlic and celery. Cook gently for about 5 minutes, stirring from time to time, then add the cabbage and continue cooking for a further 5 minutes. Season to taste.

Melt the 50g/2oz butter in a small saucepan and stir in the flour. Cook for a few minutes, then gradually add the milk, stirring continuously until the sauce is smooth. Season well, then pour over the vegetables in the casserole. Sprinkle with the breadcrumbs and a little grated nutmeg and dot with butter. Cook in a preheated moderate oven 350°F; 180°C; Gas Mark 4 for about 30 minutes, until the crumb topping is golden brown.

Midnight on Christmas Eve – Beliefs and Superstitions

Midnight on Christmas Eve has always been thought to be a magical and mysterious time because people believe that Jesus was born then. It was thought to be a time when ghosts and witches had no power to harm and, according to an Irish story, the gates of Paradise open so that anyone who dies at that hour goes straight to heaven.

As Jesus was born in a stable surrounded by animals, many of the beliefs were about animals. It was thought that the cattle and sheep in the fields and the wild animals of the forest knelt down in prayer at midnight to worship the New Baby and had the gift of human speech for a few minutes, although great misfortune was said to befall anyone foolish enough to listen to their conversation! Bees were also supposed to wake up from their winter hibernation to hum the Hundredth Psalm in their hives.

Midnight on Christmas Eve is, of course, primarily the time for Midnight Mass and for the tolling of bells announcing the death of the devil and the coming of Christ.

CAULIFLOWER AND LEMON ROLL
(serves 6–8)

This makes a delicious vegetable accompaniment to most fish dishes, or a vegetarian meal for 3–4 with a salad.

1 large cauliflower, broken into florets
Finely grated rind of ½ lemon
50g/2oz cream cheese
5 eggs, separated
Salt and freshly milled black pepper
30ml/2tbsp chopped parsley

FOR THE FILLING
150ml/¼pt sour cream
15ml/1tbsp chopped parsley
15ml/1tbsp capers

Grease a 33×23cm/13×9in Swiss roll tin and line with greased greaseproof paper or non-stick baking parchment. Cook the cauliflower in boiling salted water until just tender. Drain and dry off over a gentle heat thoroughly. Purée in a blender or processor with the lemon rind, cheese and egg yolks. Season to taste.

Whisk the egg whites until stiff but not dry, then fold lightly into the cauliflower mixture with a large metal spoon until evenly incorporated. Gently fold in the parsley and spread the mixture evenly in the prepared tin. Bake in a moderate oven 400°F; 200°C; Gas Mark 6 for 15–20 minutes, until firm but spongy to the touch.

Meanwhile, make the filling. Stir the parsley and capers into the sour cream. Season to taste.

When the roll is cooked, turn it out onto a sheet of greaseproof paper and peel off the lining paper. Spread quickly with the filling and roll up by gently lifting the greaseproof paper. Serve hot, cut into thick slices.

SPINACH AND PEAR PURÉE
(serves 6)

The combination of pears or apples with spinach is very good, either as a vegetable or a soup with the addition of stock and cream.

900g/2lb fresh or frozen spinach
4 ripe pears
75g/3oz butter
Salt and freshly milled pepper
Freshly grated nutmeg

Wash and trim the spinach if using fresh. Drain well. Peel, core and dice the pears. Melt 50g/2oz of the butter in a large saucepan and cook the pears gently for a few minutes. Add the spinach and cook over a high heat, turning the leaves over frequently until tender and all the liquor has evaporated. Press out the excess juices and reserve for soup or casseroles. Purée in a blender or processor and season with salt, pepper and nutmeg. Reheat gently with the remaining 25g/1oz butter.

Saint Nicholas

Twas the night before Christmas, when all thro' the house
Not a creature was stirring, not even a mouse;
The stockings were hung by the chimney with care;
In hopes that Saint Nicholas soon would be there.

Saint Nicholas, the original saintly bishop and friend of children, is honoured for his true self in Holland. December 6 is his day and a great one for children, although Saint Nicholas' parties are usually held on Christmas Eve.

Children all over the world hang up their stockings or put out their shoes for Santa Claus, Father Christmas, or another gift-bringer to fill. The stocking tradition is followed in Britain, Australia, New Zealand and the USA, while in Holland children fill their shoes with hay and a carrot for the saint's white horse and Saint Nicholas puts a present there in return. Hungarian youngsters carefully shine their shoes before putting them near the door or window sill for the saint to fill. In the morning they find a toy, candy and a small bundle of twigs as a warning to behave during the coming year. The gift-bringer, whoever he may be, is the last and most important visitor to arrive on Christmas Eve.

The Christmas Tree

Christmas trees twinkle and blaze with light in the squares of German towns and cities on Christmas Eve. For it was Germany that gave the world the custom of lighting and decorating small fir trees. Some people believe that its origins lay in the pagan worship of vegetation; others associate it with the story of St Boniface, an English missionary in Germany during the eighth century. One Christmas Eve in Germany, he was said to have chopped down a sacred oak beneath which human sacrifices had been offered. As the oak fell, a young fir tree miraculously appeared in its place and the saint suggested the fir tree as an emblem of the new faith he had brought to Germany. The Germans also believed that Martin Luther first decorated the Christmas tree to symbolise the starry heavens from which Christ came to save us.

In England the tradition of a tree at Christmas is only about 140 years old. Prince Albert popularised it as the central feature of a family Christmas and it has remained so ever since.

CHRISTMAS GINGER MERINGUES
(serves 8)

Make the basic meringue shells up to 2 days before you need them and store in an airtight container.
Meringue shells also freeze very well if you pack them carefully in rigid containers. Serve with or without the caramel sauce.

4 large egg whites
225g/8oz caster sugar
5ml/1tsp ground ginger
Extra caster sugar for dredging

FOR THE FILLING
300ml/½pt double cream
12g/½oz caster sugar
15ml/1tbsp brandy or preserved ginger syrup
25–50g/1–2oz preserved stem ginger, grated
Extra slivers of stem ginger to decorate

FOR THE SAUCE (optional)
225g/8oz caramels
300ml/½pt double cream

Line 2 baking sheets with non-stick silicone paper. Whisk the egg whites until stiff peaks form, then whisk in 20ml/4tsp of the caster sugar and the ground ginger. Fold in the remaining sugar with a metal spoon. Place dessertspoonfuls of the meringue mixture on the prepared baking sheets, spacing them well apart, or use a piping bag with a large plain nozzle. Place in a pre-heated, very cool oven 250°F; 120°C; Gas Mark ½ for about 1 hour, changing the baking trays round halfway through. When meringues are set, carefully lift them from the sheets and peel off the non-stick paper. Gently press the soft undersides of the meringues to form hollows, put back on the sheets on their sides and replace in the oven for a further 20–30 minutes, or until the undersides are dry. The meringues should be delicate beige in colour, crisp in texture and slightly sticky. Cool on a wire rack.

To make the filling, whip the cream, add the brandy or ginger syrup and the stem ginger and sandwich the meringues together in pairs. Serve within 1–2 hours of filling, piled up on a cake stand or pretty serving dish and decorated with slivers of stem ginger and small gold paper leaves.

If you want to serve the meringues with a caramel sauce, place the caramels and cream in a saucepan and heat very gently, stirring until melted. If the sauce is too thick, add a little milk. Pour over the meringues just before serving.

GINGER ICE-CREAM FILLING
(serves 8)

The ginger meringues can also be filled with homemade ginger ice cream, which is very easy to make. This recipe is my mother-in-law's and I use the base for all my ice creams.

Beat 4 egg yolks with 125g/4oz caster sugar, 5ml/1tsp ground ginger and 30ml/2tbsp preserved ginger syrup. Whip 450ml/¾pt double cream and fold into the mixture, followed by 4 stiffly beaten egg whites. Freeze until almost set, then mix 6 pieces of chopped preserved stem ginger evenly into the ice cream. Return to freezer until completely set. Remove from the freezer 20 minutes before serving and place in the fridge.

Sandwich the meringues together with the ice cream at the last minute.

SPICY MINCEMEAT AND BRANDY CRUMBLE
(serves 8)

A crumble is very easily prepared and ideal for serving on Christmas Eve when there are so many other things to do. The crumble topping can be prepared beforehand and frozen; it is always a useful mixture to have in the freezer.

900g/2lb cooking apples
625g/1½lb mincemeat (page 52)
30ml/2tbsp brandy
125g/4oz plain flour
125g/4oz wholemeal flour
5ml/1tsp ground cinnamon
Pinch of ground cloves
½tsp grated nutmeg
125g/4oz butter
50g/2oz caster or soft brown sugar
Extra sugar to finish

Peel, core and chop the apples roughly. Layer them in a deep 1.5 litre/3pt buttered ovenproof dish with the mincemeat. Pour over the brandy.

To make the crumble, sieve the flours and spices together into a mixing bowl. Rub in the butter until the mixture resembles fine crumbs, then stir in the sugar. Sprinkle over the apple and mincemeat mixture and press down gently. Bake in a moderate oven 375°F; 190°C; Gas Mark 5 for 30–40 minutes until pale golden and crisp. Sprinkle with extra sugar before serving with Foaming Lemon Sauce (page 124), one of the butters or sauces on pages 32–3, chilled whipped cream or yoghurt.

MARBLED CHOCOLATE CHEESECAKE
(serves 12)

A very rich luscious pudding, which is most people's idea of heaven. Serve cut into modest slices.

225g/8oz digestive biscuits
125g/4oz butter, melted
25g/1oz soft brown sugar
350g/12oz low-fat cream cheese
350g/12oz full-fat cream cheese
225g/8oz vanilla-flavoured sugar
3 large eggs, beaten
150ml/5fl oz double cream
90g/3½oz Menier, or similar-quality chocolate

FOR THE TOPPING
300ml/10fl oz sour cream or natural yoghurt
30ml/2tbsp soft brown sugar

Crush the biscuits and mix together with the melted butter and brown sugar. Use the mixture to line the bottom of a 23cm/9in spring-form, or flan tin with a removable base. Chill while preparing the filling.

Beat together the cream cheese, vanilla-flavoured sugar and beaten eggs until smooth. Stir in the cream. Pour half this mixture into the chilled crust.

Melt the chocolate in the top of a double saucepan, or in a basin set over a saucepan of hot water, then stir it into the remaining filling. Add spoonfuls of this chocolate mixture to the vanilla mixture, marbling the two mixtures together with a knife. Bake in the centre of a moderate oven 350°F; 180°C; Gas Mark 4 for about 1 hour until the filling is set. Cool the cheesecake until it is just warm, then make the topping. Mix the sour cream with the sugar, then spread evenly over the cake. Bake in a hot oven 425°F, 220°C; Gas Mark 7 for 7 minutes to form a glaze. Remove from the oven and leave to cool.

Chill well for several hours in the fridge, then remove a couple of hours before serving. Decorate with gold or silver-covered almonds or dragees, small gold or silver paper leaves and stars.

☆ TO MAKE VANILLA-FLAVOURED SUGAR

Caster sugar which has been impregnated with a vanilla pod may be used for making custard instead of the vanilla pod itself. Place caster sugar in a storage jar containing a vanilla pod, cover with a lid and leave for several weeks for the flavour to transfer. The sugar can be replaced as you use it.

A vanilla pod which has been used to flavour sauces can be washed and used again several times.

BETTY TODD'S FUDGE
(makes 2 × 18cm/7in square tins)

Homemade fudge is a year-round favourite, but an absolute must at Christmas. This treasured recipe was given to me by a friend, who remembers the passing round of Betty's delicious fudge as being the high spot of Christmas Day as a child in Kenya.

225g/8oz butter
1 × 410g/14.5oz tin evaporated milk
1.3kg/2½lb granulated sugar
Few drops of vanilla essence

Heat the butter and milk together in a heavy-based deep saucepan until the butter has melted. Add the sugar and cook over a gentle heat, stirring occasionally, until the sugar has dissolved. Bring to the boil and continue boiling until the soft ball stage is reached, or a temperature of 240°F; 116°C if using a sugar thermometer. (To test for soft ball stage, drop a little of the mixture into a cup of cold water. If it forms a soft ball when rolled between finger and thumb, the correct temperature has been reached.)

Remove the pan from the heat and add the vanilla essence. Beat the fudge briskly with a wooden spoon as it cools for about 10 minutes, or until it is very thick and on the point of setting. Pour into 2 × 18cm/7in oiled or buttered square tins or 1 × 37.5× 30cm/15×12in greased oblong tin. Mark into squares or oblongs and leave to cool completely.

When cold, cut up the fudge and remove from the tins. Store in waxed paper in an airtight container for up to 2–3 weeks.

☆ HOMEMADE SWEETS AS PRESENTS

Before storing, wrap sweets in waxed paper or foil and keep in airtight containers. Leave the gift packing of sweets until the last moment, as once transferred from an airtight tin, toffee is inclined to become sticky and fudge a bit hard on the outside.

Buy new boxes, or pretty up old cartons and boxes with coloured decorative paper, fabric and ribbons. Line with waxed paper. Transfer the sweets to individual paper or foil cases, or wrap in coloured tissue paper or Christmas wrapping paper. Pack into the prepared boxes and tie with ribbons. Decorate the boxes as you wish with bows, small sprigs of evergreen and fir cones.

(clockwise) Rich Chocolate Rum Truffles (page 44), Coconut Ice (page 44), Betty Todd's Fudge (above), Rose Turkish Delight (page 44)

RICH CHOCOLATE RUM TRUFFLES
(makes about 350g/12oz)

Traditionally, these mouth-watering sweets have been associated with Christmas, but are delicious as an after-dinner sweet at any time. This particular recipe contains fresh cream, so they should be eaten up quickly. Some people don't like the flavour of rum, so replace it with brandy, Grand Marnier or any favourite liqueur.

175g/6oz good-quality plain chocolate
175g/6oz good-quality milk chocolate
30ml/2tbsp rum
150g/5oz unsalted butter
15ml/1tbsp double cream
Cocoa powder or grated chocolate to finish

Melt all the chocolate with the rum in a bowl over a saucepan of hot water. Slowly work in the butter with a wooden spoon, followed by the cream. Allow the mixture to cool until it thickens. Spoon onto greaseproof or non-stick silicone paper.

When cold, shape into balls and roll tightly in cocoa powder or grated chocolate until coated. Place in small paper cases and refrigerate until needed.

COCONUT ICE
(makes about 575g/1¼lb)

Store for a short time only because these sweets go stale quickly. If you are giving them as presents make just before the festive season.

450g/1lb vanilla-flavoured sugar
150ml/¼pt single cream or milk
150g/5oz desiccated coconut
Few drops of pink food colouring

Oil or butter a 20.5×15cm/8×6in tin.

Dissolve the sugar in the cream or milk in a heavy-based saucepan over a gentle heat. Bring to the boil and boil gently for about 10 minutes, until the mixture reaches soft ball stage or reaches a temperature of 240°F; 116°C on a sugar thermometer. Remove the pan from the heat and stir in the coconut. Pour half the mixture quickly into the prepared tin, then colour the second half with a few drops of pink colouring. Pour quickly on top of the white layer. Leave until half-set, then mark into bars.

When completely cold and set, cut or break into pieces. Store in an airtight tin.

ROSE TURKISH DELIGHT
(makes about 450g/1lb)

25g/1oz powdered gelatine
15ml/1tbsp rose water ⎫ to dissolve gelatine
45ml/3tbsp cold water ⎭
450g/1lb granulated sugar
270ml/9fl oz cold water
15ml/1tbsp rose water
Few drops pink food colouring
50g/2oz icing sugar ⎫ to finish
25g/1oz cornflour ⎭

Sprinkle the gelatine on 15ml/1tbsp rose water mixed with 45ml/3tbsp cold water and leave to sponge. Heat the granulated sugar and 270ml/9fl oz water gently in a heavy-based saucepan until the sugar has dissolved. Add the gelatine mixture to the pan, stirring constantly. Simmer gently until the gelatine has dissolved, then bring to the boil. Boil gently for 20 minutes, then remove from the heat and add the extra rose water and pink food colouring. Pour the mixture into a wet 20×15cm/8×6in tin and leave in a cool place for 24 hours until completely set.

Sieve the icing sugar and cornflour together and sprinkle it evenly over a piece of greaseproof paper. Turn the Turkish delight out onto this paper and cut it into 2.5cm/1in squares with a sharp knife. Toss well in the sugar mixture, then pack in an airtight container lined with waxed paper.

IRISH OR GAELIC COFFEE
(serves 1)

1 part Irish whiskey
5ml/1tsp brown sugar (to taste)
4 parts double-strength black coffee
15–30ml/1–2tbsp double cream

Gently warm a suitable glass and pour in the whiskey. Add the sugar, then pour in the black coffee. Stir to dissolve the sugar and taste, adding more sugar if necessary. Pour the chilled cream over the back of a spoon into the glass and allow to stand for a few minutes.

☆ LIQUEUR COFFEES

Experiment with Cointreau, Grand Marnier, Curacao, Tia Maria (Calypso coffee), vodka (Russian coffee), rum (Caribbean coffee), Calvados (Normandy coffee) and Kirsch (German coffee). Make as for Irish coffee.

Carol-singers' Supper

In England, convivial wassailers used to carry the wassail bowl of steaming ale from house to house and sing seasonal songs in the hope that their neighbours would replenish the contents. The custom was continued in the eighteenth and nineteenth centuries by 'waits' or watchmen who serenaded householders at Christmas and then returned on Boxing Day for their tips.

Visiting carol singers continued to be called waits and as Christmas approached, children and sometimes even adults took to the streets with their lanterns and mufflers in ever-increasing numbers in order to sing carols. Generally it was the custom to invite wassailers into the house for a glass of punch and a mince pie.

Today most carol singing is done on a large scale and is well organised, although in some villages it still takes place in the traditional manner. Whether the carol singers are well organised or not, inviting them in for a warm drink and something tasty to eat is lots of fun and a sociable way to start the Christmas festivities. If the carol singers don't visit you, there is nothing to stop you and the family singing your own carols round the Christmas tree, followed by a carol-singers' supper in front of the fire!

GLÖGG
(serves 10–12)

Glögg is the Scandinavian mulled red wine served with almonds and raisins. Traditionally, Swedes and Finns gather around the decorated Christmas tree and drink a cup of Glögg on Christmas Eve.

2 bottles red wine
150ml/¼pt vodka
2 whole dried ginger roots
12.5cm/2×5in cinnamon sticks
5ml/1tsp cardamom seeds
12 whole cloves
90ml/6tbsp seedless raisins
45ml/3tbsp blanched almonds

Pour the wine and vodka into a saucepan and add the spices. Allow to stand and infuse for several hours, then heat the wine mixture gently until very hot but not boiling. Divide the raisins and almonds between the required number of warmed glasses, then strain the wine into the glasses. Serve piping hot with spiced Yule bread, mince pies, buns or savouries.

The Yule Candle

Decorate the house with candles for your carol-singers' supper to give welcoming light. Candles have always played an important part in Christmas festivities particularly on Christmas Eve. Apart from being a source of illumination, the candle symbolised the coming of spring and with it, longer days, while Christians saw the candle as a symbol of Jesus as the 'Light of the World'. In quite recent years it was usual for chandlers or grocers to make gifts of special large candles to their customers at Christmas.

In many European countries it was the custom for each member of the congregation to carry a candle to church for the Midnight Mass and at the end of the service, the priest would light the candle of the person nearest to him, who in turn would light his neighbour's. When everyone present held a lighted candle, the people would carry them homeward so that the snowy darkness glittered with a galaxy of tiny flames.

In many countries, a lighted candle is placed in the window of every room in honour of Christ's birthday and in the hope that He will bless the house. If the candle goes out by accident, bad luck will surely follow. Candles lit on Christmas Eve in Norway are extinguished the following morning, but are re-lit every evening until New Year's Day. This custom is also followed in Ireland where the candles are re-lit until Twelfth Night.

GLÜHWEIN
(serves 10–12)

This is the traditional hot spiced wine served in Austria on Christmas Eve with spicy fruit bread.

1 litre bottle dry red wine
125–175g/4–6oz dark soft brown sugar
12.5cm/2×5in cinnamon sticks
2 lemons
12 whole cloves
300ml/½pt brandy

Place the wine, sugar and cinnamon in a large heavy saucepan. Stick the cloves into the lemons and add these to the pan. Heat very gently until the sugar has dissolved, then continue to heat for 5–10 minutes without boiling. Remove from the heat and stir in the brandy. Taste for sweetness, then strain into a warmed bowl and serve hot in heatproof wine glasses or stoneware goblets, with chunks of Scandinavian Julekake (page 49), mince pies, Revel Buns (page 48) or Christmas Eve Wigs (page 47).

LAMBSWOOL
(serves 10)

In the past this was a standard English Christmas drink. The custom of making it has been revived in some City of London taverns where the ceremony of Hoisting the Ale Garland takes place. Lambswool used to be a mixture of ale, roasted apples, sugar, spices, eggs, thick cream and small pieces of toast and was often carried around in a wassail bowl.

6 baked eating apples
2.4 litres/4pt strong brown ale
600ml/1pt sweet white wine
1×12.5cm/5in cinnamon stick
5ml/1tsp ground ginger
10ml/2tsp grated nutmeg
2 strips lemon rind
Soft dark brown sugar to taste

Heat the ale, wine, spices and lemon rind in a large pan. Skin the apples, remove the pulp and mash it well in a large bowl. Pour over the spiced ale removing the cinnamon stick and lemon rind. Mix together well, then pass through a sieve pressing down well. Add sugar to taste and reheat.

Serve steaming from a punch bowl into 300ml/½pt glass, pewter or earthenware tankards. Accompany with Yule bread, buns, mince pies or savouries.

WESTCOUNTRY EGG-HOT
(serves 10–12)

The origin of this warming drink is the sixteenth-century English sack posset, a mixture of milk ale, or sack and spices thickened with eggs. Posset was the old word for a mixture which could be eaten with a spoon.

In Devon and Cornwall, egg-hot, a mixture of cider heated with eggs and spices, was traditionally drunk on Christmas Eve while the Yule log blazed. Egg nog is also the traditional American Christmas drink. The Americans adapted the English recipe for sack posset to include rum, bourbon and cider.

2.4 litres/4pt dry cider
4 eggs
60ml/4tbsp caster sugar
Freshly grated nutmeg

Heat the cider in a large pan, but don't bring to the boil. Beat the eggs with the sugar in a large jug. When the cider is hot, pour some on to the beaten eggs, then pour back into the pan. Transfer some of the mixture back and forth into the jug and the pan until the whole drink becomes frothy. Serve in warmed glasses and sprinkle the frothy top with freshly grated nutmeg.

Carol-singing Customs Round the World

In Britain, carol singers are traditionally pictured gathered round a lantern, but in many parts of Europe from Italy to Iceland, 'star singers' sing from house to house. They carry a great star in memory of the Star of Bethlehem and sometimes dress up as the Magi and other figures from the Nativity. In Poland the cardboard star is made to revolve like a pinwheel and one or two of the boys may wear a goat mask. A goat figure, originally the personification of the devil, also appears in Sweden, where the rest of the star boys, dressed in white, act out short biblical scenes and sing songs. Tyrolean star singers had to stamp on the snowy fields to promote a good crop before they received any hospitality and in Hungary carol singers used to walk in procession to church on Christmas Eve, led by three young girls wearing beautifully embroidered white robes and tall mitres representing the Three Kings. Throughout Scandinavia, the medieval meaning of carols as ring dances is still upheld by many families who circle the tree on Christmas Eve to sing traditional songs.

NON-ALCOHOLIC MULLED GINGER BEER
(serves 10)

2 large oranges
12 whole cloves
2 bottles good-quality ginger beer
2×12.5cm/2×5in cinnamon sticks

Push the cloves into the oranges and bake in a moderate oven 350°F; 180°C; Gas Mark 4 for 30 minutes. Put the ginger beer into a large saucepan with the cinnamon sticks and the baked oranges cut into slices. Bring almost to the boil, then remove from the heat and leave to cool slightly. Serve from a warmed punch bowl or pour immediately into warmed glasses.

CHRISTMAS EVE WIGS
(makes about 16)

These are the small cakes of spiced dough always offered to guests on Christmas Eve in the past. They were dipped in mulled ale or elderberry wine and eaten instead of mince pies. Yule spice cakes have always been a Yorkshire speciality. Eat these buns very fresh, preferably warm from the oven.

450g/1lb self-raising (or wholemeal flour plus 20ml/4 level
    tsp baking powder)
5ml/1tsp ground mixed spice
Pinch of salt
175g/6oz butter
175g/6oz caster or brown sugar
50g/2oz candied peel, shredded
50g/2oz sultanas
50g/2oz currants
15–20ml/3–4tsp caraway seeds (optional)
2 standard eggs
30ml/2tbsp milk

Sieve the flour with the spice and salt into a mixing bowl. Rub in the butter, then stir in the sugar, peel, sultanas, currants and caraway seeds if you wish. Whisk the eggs and milk together, then stir into the dry ingredients. Mix quickly with a fork to a stiff dough. Put small heaps of the mixture into greased bun tins or onto greased baking trays and bake in a pre-heated moderately hot oven 425°F; 220°C; Gas Mark 7 for 15–20 minutes or until golden. Serve warm with Lambswool (page 46) or mulled wine.

HERBY SAUSAGE ROLLS
(makes about 20)

Sausage rolls are best frozen unbaked and then cooked as needed. Try sausage meats other than pork for a change and vary the pastry – use wholemeal, shortcrust with herbs, cheese, puff or rough puff. A little chopped sweet pickle or tomato sauce added to the sausagemeat is very good.

FOR THE PASTRY
225g/8oz plain flour
Pinch of salt
175g/6oz block margarine
Approx 150ml/¼pt cold water

FOR THE FILLING
450g/1lb good-quality pork sausagemeat
1 small onion, very finely chopped
15ml/1tbsp chopped parsley
5ml/1tsp dried sage
Salt and freshly milled black pepper
1 egg, beaten with a little salt

To make the pastry, sieve the flour and salt together into a mixing bowl. Put the margarine into the freezer for about 30 minutes, then coarsely grate into the flour. Cut into the flour with a palette knife until the mixture looks like crumbs. Add enough water to form a smooth dough which leaves the sides of the bowl clean, then wrap in clingfilm and chill in the fridge for 30 minutes.

Mix the sausagemeat with the onion, parsley and sage and season well. Roll out the pastry thinly on a floured board to form a rectangle. Cut into 3, then divide the sausagemeat into 3. With floured hands roll the meat mixture into 3 long sausages the same length as the pastry, then place one down the centre of each piece of pastry. Brush along one edge with the beaten egg. Fold the pastry over and press the edges together well to seal them. Lift up each roll and turn so that the join is underneath, then cut into individual rolls about 5cm/2in in length. Brush with beaten egg, then make 2 or 3 diagonal slashes across the top of each roll to allow the steam to escape.

Place on a baking tray and bake near the top of a pre-heated oven at 425°F; 220°C; Gas Mark 7 for 20–25 minutes, or until the pastry is golden brown. Remove from the oven, transfer to a warmed serving platter and serve warm.

PAM'S FINGER PASTIES
(serves 10)

Individual pasties used to be served in Cornwall for high tea, or a special Sunday afternoon tea. They are a delicious couple of mouthfuls, ideal for a party, especially if you follow Pam Pascoe's family recipe which she has been kind enough to share with me. Pam recommends that the pastry is not too rich so that it is easier to handle. The pasties may be prepared in advance and cooked later, or can be cooked and reheated, or cooked and frozen.

300g/10oz plain flour
Pinch of salt
50g/2oz lard
50g/2oz margarine or butter
Cold water to mix

FOR THE FILLING
300g/10oz good chuck steak
Potato
Piece of swede
Onion
Salt and freshly milled pepper
Beaten egg to glaze

Sieve the flour and salt into a mixing bowl, then cut the fat into small pieces and add to the flour. Rub in the fat until the mixture resembles crumbs, then mix with enough water to form a smooth dough that will leave the bowl clean. Leave to rest in a cool place for 20–30 minutes, wrapped in polythene.

To prepare the filling, cut the meat into small pieces. Peel and cut the potato and swede into thin slivers or flakes. Chop the onion finely.

Roll out the pastry thinly and cut into circles using a plain 9cm/3½in pastry cutter. Pile 25g/1oz meat on each circle of pastry and pad out with vegetables. Fill the pasties really well because the contents shrink during cooking. Season well, then fold over each pastry circle, dampen the edges of the pastry, then crimp from corner to corner, making sure that the seam lies to one side of the pasty and not across the top. Make a small hole in the top of each pasty and place on a greased baking sheet. Brush with a little beaten egg and bake in a moderate oven 375°F; 190°C; Gas Mark 5 for about 30 minutes or until the meat is tender.

Serve warm straight from the oven or heat up as needed. Alternative fillings can be made from a combination of vegetables, herbs, cheese, fish and other meats. In Cornwall they say anything can be put in a pasty!

SAFFRON REVEL BUNS
(makes about 16)

Revel buns were always made for special occasions in Cornwall as tokens of goodwill; they are still very popular today. Saffron buns and bread are also popular in Scandinavia at Christmas time. The dough can also be baked in a round cake tin to make saffron cake. Soak the saffron overnight if possible. You may of course omit the saffron if you have difficulty obtaining it.

2.5ml/½tsp saffron strands
30ml/2tbsp boiling water
25g/1oz fresh yeast
50–75g/2–3oz caster sugar
Approx 300ml/½pt warm milk and water, mixed
450g/1lb strong white flour
2.5ml/½tsp salt
125g/4oz butter or half butter and half lard
125g/4oz currants
50g/2oz candied peel, shredded (optional)

Dry the saffron strands gently on a piece of greaseproof paper in a cool oven, then fold the paper over the crush the saffron with a rolling pin. Put the saffron into a cup and cover with the boiling water. Leave to steep overnight. Next day, cream the yeast with 5ml/1tsp of the sugar and about 150ml/¼pt of warm liquid. Leave to froth in a warm place for about 10 minutes.

Sieve together the flour and salt into a warm mixing bowl. Rub in the butter, then add the remaining sugar, currants and peel. Make a well in the centre of the dry ingredients and pour in the yeast mixture, steeped saffron and enough of the remaining milk and water mixture to form a smooth dough which will leave the sides of the bowl clean. Knead well, then cover with a clean cloth or oiled polythene bag and leave in a warm place until the dough has doubled in size. Knead well again on a floured board, then shape the dough into round buns. Arrange them on a greased baking tray allowing plenty of room for expansion, then leave to rise again in a warm place, covering with a cloth or oiled polythene. Bake in a pre-heated moderately hot oven 375°F; 190°C; Gas Mark 5 for 15–20 minutes. If you want to make a loaf rather than buns, shape the dough to fit a greased 450g/1lb loaf tin or a 20cm/8in cake tin. Bake at 350°F; 180°C; Gas Mark 4 for about 1 hour. Serve in slices either spread with butter or clotted cream, or warm as they are.

CAROL-SINGERS' TURNOVERS
(makes about 24)

*Any filling can be baked in these delicious little cheese
turnovers. Try mushroom, spinach, smoked
mackerel, salmon or crab for a change.*

FOR THE PASTRY
175g/6oz plain flour
5ml/1 level tsp salt
Good pinch of cayenne
Freshly milled black pepper
225g/8oz margarine
225g/8oz grated Parmesan cheese
2 large egg yolks
Approx 60ml/4tbsp milk

FOR THE FILLING
12g/½oz butter
1 small onion, very finely chopped
225g/8oz mushrooms, finely chopped
30ml/2tbsp dry sherry
25g/1oz walnuts, chopped
175g/6oz smooth chicken liver pâté
Salt and freshly milled pepper
1 beaten egg to glaze
Sesame or poppy seeds

To make the pastry, sieve the flour with the
seasonings into a mixing bowl. Add the margarine
roughly cut in lumps and rub it into the flour until the
mixture resembles breadcrumbs. Stir in the grated
cheese and mix with the egg yolks and enough milk
to make a smooth dough. Knead lightly to get rid of
any cracks. Make sure that your pastry is not too
dry or it will be difficult to make into turnovers.
Chill the pastry while you prepare the filling.

Melt the butter in a small saucepan and fry the
onion gently until soft and transparent. Stir in the
mushrooms and sherry and cook for a few minutes
until soft. Remove from the heat, stir in the chopped
walnuts and leave to cool a little before mixing in the
pâté. Season to taste with salt and pepper.

Roll the cheese pastry as thinly as possible and
cut out circles, using a 9cm/3½in plain cutter. Place
a teaspoonful of the filling on one side of each pastry
circle and brush the pastry edges with beaten egg.
Fold over and seal each turnover firmly. Brush with
egg and sprinkle with sesame or poppy seeds.

Line 2 baking trays with greaseproof paper so that
the cheese pastry does not burn and transfer the
turnovers onto them. Bake in a pre-heated fairly hot
oven 425°F; 220°C; Gas Mark 7 for about 12
minutes, or until golden brown. Serve warm.

SCANDINAVIAN JULEKAKE
(makes 1 loaf in a 23cm/9in cake tin)

*This is a rich, spicy, honey-flavoured fruit Yule
Bread baked in an unusual twisted spiral shape,
served on Christmas Eve with mulled wine.*

225g/8oz strong plain flour
225g/8oz rye flour
2.5ml/½tsp salt
50g/2oz sultanas
50g/2oz candied peel, shredded
Grated rind and juice of 1 orange
10ml/1dsp crushed cardamom seeds
25g/1oz caster sugar
20g/¾oz fresh yeast
180–240ml/6–8fl oz warm water
25g/1oz butter
45ml/3tbsp clear honey
1 egg, beaten

FOR THE GLAZE
15ml/1tbsp clear honey
15ml/1tbsp water

Sieve the flours and salt together into a large warm
mixing bowl. Add the sultanas, peel, grated orange
rind, crushed cardamom seeds and sugar. Dissolve
the yeast in 60ml/2fl oz of the warm water and leave
to froth. Melt the butter and honey together in a
small saucepan and allow to cool. Add this with the
yeast mixture, orange juice and beaten egg to the
flour. Mix together with enough warm water to
make a manageable dough. Turn onto a floured
board and knead until the dough is smooth and
elastic. Place in an oiled polythene bag and leave to
rise in a warm place until doubled in size.

Knock back and knead the dough again, then
divide it into 2 pieces. Roll each piece into a long
sausage, then starting at the edge of a well-greased
23cm/9in spring-sided cake tin, coil the two snakes
of dough round and round to the centre, joining the
second piece to the end of the first with a little warm
water. Cover with oiled clingfilm and allow to rise
again until almost level with the top of the tin.

Bake in a pre-heated moderately hot oven 375°F;
190°C; Gas Mark 5 for 10 minutes, then reduce the
oven to 325°F; 170°C; Gas Mark 3 and continue
cooking for a further 40–50 minutes. Remove from
the tin and place on a wire rack. Glaze the loaf with
honey mixed with a little water and leave to cool.
Serve in thick slices, buttered if you wish, or with
chunks of cheese and generous glasses of Glögg
(page 45), cider or wine.

SILENT NIGHT, HOLY NIGHT,
SON OF GOD, LOVE'S PURE LIGHT:
RADIANCE BEAMS FROM THY HOLY
FACE—
WITH THE DAWN OF REDEEMING
GRACE,
JESUS, LORD, AT THY BIRTH,
JESUS, LORD, AT THY BIRTH.

"Silent Night" Verse 3

ORANGE AND ALMOND MINCE PIES
(makes about 20)

Hot mince pies are indispensable at Christmas. Most people have their favourite pastry for making them, but try this rich almond and orange one for a change.

FOR THE PASTRY
300g/10oz plain flour
25g/1oz ground almonds
175g/6oz butter, chilled
75g/3oz icing sugar, sieved
Grated rind of ½ orange
1 egg yolk
45–60ml/4–5tbsp orange juice

FOR THE FILLING
450g/1lb homemade mincemeat
1 egg white, lightly beaten
Caster sugar to dredge

To make the pastry, place the flour and ground almonds in a mixing bowl. Cut the butter into small pieces and rub into the flour until the mixture resembles breadcrumbs. Stir in the icing sugar and orange rind. Mix the egg yolk with the orange juice and gradually add to the mixture to make a soft, but not sticky dough. Turn onto a floured board or work surface, and knead gently until smooth. Wrap in clingfilm and chill for about 30 minutes, or until firm.

Divide the dough into 2 pieces. Roll out one piece of the pastry about 3mm/⅛in thick and cut out 20–24 circles with a 7.5cm/3in cutter. Roll out the second piece of pastry and cut into 20–24 slightly smaller circles using a 6cm/2½in cutter. Line greased patty tins with the larger circles of pastry and put a teaspoonful of mincemeat into each one. Brush the edges of the smaller circles of pastry with a little cold water and place them over the mincemeat pressing down lightly to seal the edges. Roll out any pastry trimmings and cut out stars, holly leaves or bells to decorate the lid of each mince pie. Make a small hole in the top of each pie and brush with egg white or a little milk and dredge lightly with sugar. Bake in a pre-heated fairly hot oven 400°F; 200°C; Gas Mark 6 for 15–20 minutes, or until golden brown. Leave to cool slightly in the tins, then

Carol-singers' Supper: (back) Glögg (page 45), Non-alcoholic Mulled Ginger Beer (page 47); (front) Saffron Revel Buns (page 48), Scandinavian Julekake (page 49), Carol-singers' Turnovers (page 49), Orange and Almond Mince Pies (above)

carefully transfer to a wire rack to cool completely.

Serve hot or cold sprinkled with extra icing or caster sugar on a serving plate or tray, or in a basket decorated with sprigs of evergreen, small Christmas tree baubles and satin ribbons. Serve with whipped cream, yoghurt or a suitable butter or sauce (pages 32–3) and mulled ale, cider or wine.

ADDITIONS TO MINCE PIES

(i) Mix the mincemeat with an extra 30–45ml/2–3tbsp brandy or rum before filling the mince pies. Dip each pastry lid into a little brandy, or brandy mixed with a little milk, before baking.

(ii) Just before serving, remove the lids of the mince pies and put a dollop of brandy or rum butter (see page 32) or clotted cream on top of the mincemeat. Replace the lids and serve.

(iii) Serve warm mince pies with Wensleydale or Cheshire cheese in the Yorkshire tradition.

MERINGUE-TOPPED MINCE PIES

Bake the mince pies as before without pastry lids. Whisk 3 egg whites until they stand in peaks. Add 175g/6oz caster sugar, a tablespoon at a time, and beat until the meringue is stiff. Top the mince pies with the meringue using a piping bag and bake in a cool oven 300°F; 150°C; Gas Mark 2 for a further 30 minutes or until the meringue is crisp and just tinged with brown. Serve warm or cold.

TRADITIONAL MINCEMEAT WITH BRANDY
(makes about 2.3kg/5lb)

50g/2oz blanched almonds or hazelnuts
125g/4oz candied peel or 30ml/2tbsp orange marmalade
450g/1lb Cox's apples or pears, cored
225g/8oz shredded suet, melted margarine or butter
350g/12oz seeded raisins
225g/8oz sultanas
225g/8oz currants
2 medium carrots, peeled
350g/12oz soft dark brown sugar
Grated rind and juice of 2 lemons
Grated rind and juice of 2 oranges
2.5ml/½tsp grated nutmeg
20ml/4tsp mixed spice
Pinch of salt
30ml/2tbsp black treacle
90ml/6tbsp brandy or rum

Chop the nuts and candied peel, then chop the unpeeled apples finely. Mix with the suet, butter or margarine. Halve the raisins if large, then keeping one-quarter of the fruit on one side, put the rest of the fruit and the carrots through the coarsest blade of the mincer. Mix everything together apart from the brandy very thoroughly in a large mixing bowl. Cover with a clean cloth and leave for 48 hours.

Place the uncovered mincemeat in a cool oven 250°F; 125°C; Gas Mark ¼–½ for 3 hours, then remove and allow to get completely cold. Stir in the brandy, then pack into sterilised jars and cover with circles of greaseproof paper dipped in brandy. Seal and label as for jam.

APRICOT AND HAZELNUT MINCEMEAT
(makes about 3kg/6lb)

If you don't like candied peel in mincemeat, this is the recipe for you. Many combinations of dried and crystallised fruit and nuts can be used to make mincemeat, so it is worth experimenting.

450g/1lb cooking apples
225g/8oz seeded raisins
225g/8oz cooking dates or dried figs
450g/1lb dried apricots
450g/1lb sultanas
125g/4oz glacé cherries, washed
50g/2oz angelica
50g/2oz crystallised ginger
125g/4oz hazelnuts
225g/8oz shredded suet
350g/12oz soft dark brown sugar
Grated rind and juice of 1 lemon
Grated rind and juice of 1 orange
5ml/1 level tsp ground mixed spice
5ml/1 level tsp ground cinnamon
5ml/1 level tsp ground mace
150ml/¼pt brandy

Peel, core and chop the apples roughly. Mix with the raisins, dates or figs, apricots and sultanas and push through a mincer or food processor. Finely chop the glacé cherries, angelica, ginger and hazelnuts and add to the minced fruit, followed by the other ingredients. Stir very well and cover with a clean cloth. Leave to stand overnight, then stir well again. Pack into sterilised jars and cover as for jam. Store in a cool dry place until needed.

VEGETARIAN MINCEMEAT
(makes about 2kg/4lb)

210ml/7fl oz dry cider
225g/8oz soft dark brown sugar
900g/2lb cooking apples
225g/8oz currants
225g/8oz seeded raisins
50g/2oz glacé cherries, chopped
50g/2oz blanched almonds, chopped
Grated rind and juice of ½ lemon
2.5ml/½ level tsp mixed spice
2.5ml/½ level tsp ground cinnamon
Pinch of ground cloves
30ml/2tbsp brandy or rum

Place the cider and sugar in a large saucepan and heat gently until the sugar has dissolved. Peel, core and roughly chop the apples and add to the pan, then stir in all the remaining ingredients except the brandy or rum. Bring the mixture slowly to the boil, stirring all the time, then half-cover with a lid and simmer gently for about 30 minutes or until the mixture has become a soft pulp. Stir from time to time, then turn off the heat and leave the mincemeat to get completely cold. Stir in the brandy or rum, then pack into sterilised jars and cover as for jam. Store in a cool dry place until needed.

The Story of the Mince Pie

Mince pies have been associated with Christmas since at least Tudor times and were known as 'shred', 'shredded' or 'minced' pies because of the minced or shredded meat in them, mixed with dried fruits and spices.

Their original shape was oblong to represent the manger and often there was a pastry baby inside. These crib-shaped pies were denounced by Oliver Cromwell as idolatrous and papist and the eating of mince pies was forbidden. They came back into favour when Charles II returned to the throne, but were now round without the pastry baby. Much later, in the nineteenth century, the meat was omitted and the modern mince pie was born with just a few ounces of suet to remind us of the original recipe.

Superstitions attached to mince pies vary from it being considered unlucky ever to refuse a mince pie, to whoever eats a mince pie every day from Christmas to Twelfth Night will have twelve happy months after. In Jamaica, instead of eating twelve mince pies for luck, twelve pieces of particularly rich and alcoholic Christmas pudding are consumed! Another traditional custom is to make a wish on the first bite of your first Christmas mince pie.

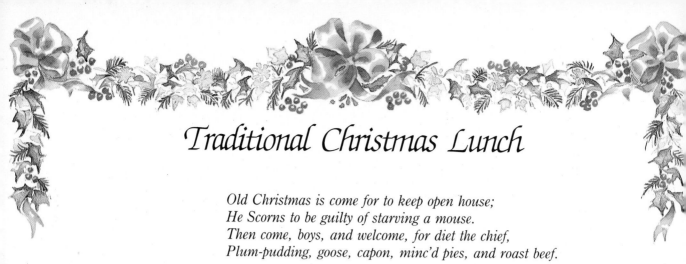

Traditional Christmas Lunch

Old Christmas is come for to keep open house;
He Scorns to be guilty of starving a mouse.
Then come, boys, and welcome, for diet the chief,
Plum-pudding, goose, capon, minc'd pies, and roast beef.

By the 1880s most well-off Victorian families in England would have had a
turkey on the Christmas Day menu with vegetable soup, oyster patties, boiled
leg of mutton and port wine jelly, plus traditional plum pudding and mince
pies, followed by nuts, fruit and port or hot toddy, wassail or mulled wine.
The traditional Christmas lunch has changed very little since then and as
Christmas Day is the climax of the Christmas season and a day of traditions,
most families still like to sit down to a meal steeped in history.

ROAST TURKEY

Turkey needs careful cooking or the meat, especially
the breast, can be dry and indigestible. Look for
traditionally hung fresh turkeys, free-range turkeys
and the old breeds of turkey like the Bronze and
Norfolk Black.

There are many ways of roasting a turkey, but I
have found the best is to start the bird in a hot oven
to seal the juices, then reduce the heat for the rest of
the cooking time allowing 15 minutes per 450g/1lb,
plus an extra 30 minutes. This size turkey is ideal for
the average family.

1 × 5.4–6.8kg/12–15lb oven-ready turkey
Chosen stuffing(s)
1 large onion, sliced
2 medium carrots, sliced
Salt and freshly milled black pepper
225g/8oz fat bacon rashers
175–225g/6–8oz butter
A double thickness of butter muslin large
   enough to cover the turkey

When you are ready to cook the turkey, wipe it
inside and out with a damp cloth or kitchen paper.
(Don't wash the turkey or the skin may not crisp
properly.) Stuff the neck end loosely (page 58) with
your chosen stuffing (pages 55–8) and truss (page
58). Weigh the bird to calculate the cooking time.
Place the sliced onion and carrots in the bottom of a
roomy roasting tin and sit the turkey on top, breast
side up. Prick the breast with a sharp cocktail stick

to help prevent the skin bursting during cooking,
then season well with salt and pepper. Arrange the
bacon rashers over the breast to protect it, then
melt the butter in a small saucepan. Soak the piece
of muslin in the butter, then fold in two and place
over the turkey. Place in a pre-heated oven at
425°F; 220°C; Gas Mark 7 for 30 minutes, then
reduce to 350°F; 180°C; Gas Mark 4 for the
remainder of the cooking time, basting the bird
every 30 minutes or so. The trussing threads around
the drumsticks can be cut after 1 hour by which time
the legs will have set in position.

Remove the muslin and bacon for the last 30
minutes cooking time, sprinkle the bird with flour,
baste well and continue cooking to crisp and brown
the skin. When the turkey is cooked, remove it from
the oven and discard the trussing threads and
skewers. Transfer to a hot meat platter, and leave
to rest for at least 10 minutes before carving (page
58). This will give you time to make the gravy (page
60).

Arrange bacon rolls and lovely brown pork saus-
ages around the turkey and garnish with watercress.
If you have time, make small paper frills to fit the
drumsticks in the same way as a ham frill (page 88).
Serve the turkey accompanied by thin gravy, Bread,
Celery or Chestnut Sauce and Cranberry Orange
Sauce (pages 61–3).

SIZES OF TURKEY (oven-ready weight)
3.6–5.4kg/8–12lb will serve 10–15
5.4–6.8kg/12–15lb will serve 15–20
6.8–9kg/15–20lb will serve 20–30

USING FROZEN POULTRY

Look for 'fresh-style' frozen and free-range frozen poultry, both frozen without added water. Make sure you allow plenty of time for a frozen bird to thaw out. Turkey is a high-risk food for salmonella food poisoning so it must be completely thawed before cooking. The more slowly a bird is defrosted, the better the flavour and texture. Thaw the frozen bird in its polythene bag on a plate preferably in a cool room or larder. You can thaw out in the fridge, although this is not recommended for very large turkeys, which will take so long you are likely to get impatient. Poultry can be defrosted in a microwave oven, according to the manufacturer's instructions. To hasten thawing if you are in a hurry, run cold water through the centre of the bird. Never thaw in hot water.

The bird is completely thawed when there are no ice crystals left in the body cavity and the legs are flexible. Remove the giblets as soon as you can. If they are still frozen it is likely that the inside of the bird is still frozen. When completely thawed, wipe the body cavity thoroughly with absorbent kitchen paper and dry the outside really well to ensure a crisp skin. Store in the fridge and cook within 24 hours.

RECOMMENDED THAWING TIMES

Oven-ready weight	Thawing at room temperature 65°F; 16°C	Thawing in refrigerator 40°F; 4°C
3.6–5.4kg/8–12lb	up to 24 hours	up to 36 hours
5.4–6.8kg/12–15lb	up to 30 hours	up to 48 hours
6.8–9kg/15–20lb	up to 36 hours	up to 60 hours
9–11kg/20–25lb	up to 48 hours	not recommended

No poultry, once thawed, should be re-frozen unless it is cooked first.

TO STORE POULTRY BEFORE COOKING

Fresh poultry should ideally be cooked within 2–3 days of buying and ready-packaged birds usually carry storage instructions on the pack. As soon as you get home, remove any polythene wrapping and, most importantly, the giblets if they are inside. Place the bird on a plate, cover loosely and store in the lower part of the fridge or in a cold larder. Cook the giblets as soon as possible to make stock (page 60). When storing frozen poultry, follow the pack instructions and freeze as quickly as possible to prevent thawing.

BASTING

This means moistening poultry, meat, vegetables or fish with pan juices during roasting, using a spoon or bulb baster. It is usually done every 20 minutes or so.

COOKING TURKEY IN KITCHEN FOIL

Many people like to roast turkey in foil, which helps to retain the natural juices and reduces the need for basting. Line the roasting tin with a large sheet of foil, bringing the edges over the rim. Place the stuffed turkey on its back in the centre of the tin, then rub it generously all over with butter as before. Season well and cover the breast with bacon. Cover the bird loosely with another large sheet of foil allowing an air space around the upper part of the body. Tuck the edges of the foil firmly inside the rim of the tin and cook as before, allowing 20 minutes per 450g/1lb. About 30 minutes before the end of the cooking time, remove the bacon rashers and the foil to allow the skin to brown. Sprinkle with flour and baste before continuing to cook.

'FRENCH ROASTING' A TURKEY

Place the turkey in a roasting tin and spread with butter as before. Pour in about 300ml/½pt giblet stock (see page 60) and cover the bird with a double sheet of buttered greaseproof paper or a sheet of foil. Cook according to weight, removing the paper or foil 30 minutes before the end of cooking time to brown the skin.

MA'S CHESTNUT STUFFING
(for a 5.4–6.8kg/12–15lb oven-ready turkey)

Chestnut stuffing is a classic accompaniment to all poultry and game birds and this particular recipe is made by the mother of a very good friend. On average, 450g/1lb of unpeeled chestnuts gives about 225g/8oz when shelled. Canned unsweetened or 'natural' chestnut purée can be used in this recipe.

450g/1lb chestnuts, peeled and skinned
Milk or a mixture of half milk, half stock
50g/2oz ham or grilled bacon, finely chopped
75g/3oz fresh white or wholemeal breadcrumbs
25g/1oz melted butter
Grated rind of ½ lemon or 1 orange
10ml/2tsp chopped parsley or 5ml/1tsp sage
Salt and freshly milled pepper
5ml/1tsp caster sugar
1 beaten egg

Place the chestnuts in a saucepan with enough milk or milk and chicken stock to just cover. Simmer gently for about 30 minutes or until the chestnuts are tender, then mash them. Pound the chestnuts with the ham, breadcrumbs, melted butter, lemon rind and parsley. Season to taste with salt, pepper and sugar, then bind together with the beaten egg.

SAUSAGEMEAT AND MUSHROOM STUFFING
(for a 5.4–6.8kg/12–15lb oven-ready turkey)

This is our family's favourite stuffing.

150ml/¼pt milk
6 whole cloves
1 bay leaf
1 small onion, finely chopped
450g/1lb pork sausagemeat
125g/4oz button mushrooms, chopped
125g/4oz fresh white or wholemeal breadcrumbs
10ml/2tsp dried sage
1 egg, separated
Salt and freshly milled black pepper

Put the milk in a saucepan with the cloves, bay leaf and chopped onion. Bring very slowly to the boil, then remove from the heat. Allow to stand and infuse for at least 10 minutes while you fry the sausagemeat gently in its own fat. When this is cooked through, remove it from the frying pan with a slotted spoon to a mixing bowl.

Fry the mushrooms gently in the remaining sausage fat and add these to the bowl with the breadcrumbs and sage. Remove and discard the cloves and bay leaf from the milk and add the milk with the onion to the sausage mixture. Beat the egg yolk, add to the mixture and mix together well. Season to taste and leave for at least 1 hour in a cool place. Just before stuffing the turkey, beat the egg white until stiff and fold in; this helps to keep the stuffing light and moist.

If you want to freeze the stuffing, omit the egg yolk and white and add after defrosting.

Alderman's Chain

This is the way sausages were served in Victorian times. They were cooked in a string, then draped over the turkey just before serving to look like an alderman's chain.

BACON AND SWEETCORN STUFFING
(for a 5.4–6.8kg/12–15lb oven-ready turkey)

12g/½oz butter
1 large onion, finely chopped
225g/8oz smoked streaky bacon
225g/8oz frozen or tinned sweetcorn
50g/2oz shredded suet
125g/4oz fresh white breadcrumbs
15ml/1tbsp chopped parsley
10ml/2tsp dried mixed herbs
1 egg, beaten
Salt and freshly milled black pepper

Melt the butter and fry the chopped onion gently until soft, but not coloured. Remove with a slotted spoon to a mixing bowl. Derind the bacon and cut into strips, then fry it in the remaining butter until crisp and golden. Meanwhile, if you are using frozen sweetcorn, cook it in boiling salted water for 5 minutes, then drain and add to the bowl. Tinned sweetcorn can just be drained before adding. Transfer the bacon to the bowl, then add the suet, breadcrumbs, parsley and herbs. Mix well and bind with the egg. Season to taste with salt and pepper.

DRIED APRICOT, RAISIN AND ALMOND STUFFING
(for a 5.4–6.8kg/12–15lb oven-ready turkey)

Hazelnuts, walnuts or brazil nuts can be used instead of almonds for a change.

225g/8oz good-quality dried apricots
50g/2oz butter
1 large onion, finely chopped
125g/4oz seedless raisins
50g/2oz blanched almonds, chopped
125g/4oz fresh white or wholemeal breadcrumbs
5ml/1tsp grated orange rind
5ml/1tsp ground allspice
5ml/1tsp brown sugar
Salt and freshly milled black pepper
30ml/2tbsp medium sherry or Madeira

Cover the dried apricots with water and leave to soak overnight. Next day, melt the butter and fry the onion until soft and golden brown. Transfer to a mixing bowl.

Drain the apricots and chop into small pieces. Add to the bowl followed by all the other ingredients. Mix thoroughly into a loose stuffing. Season to taste with salt and pepper.

The Christmas Turkey in Britain

The British tradition of eating turkey at Christmas began in the sixteenth century in the homes of the wealthy. Before this, the popular Christmas delicacies were bustard, goose, capon, peacock and the most prized of all, the mute swan, with gilded beak and elaborately garnished with its own feathers. Swans were difficult to rear; they bred in the wild and the cygnets had to be rounded up and taken to swan pits to be fattened for the table. From the moment the turkey arrived in Britain, it was successful as a domestic bird and swans declined in importance as food for feasts. Although turkey became associated with the Christmas dinner quite early on, it was just one of a mass of feathered creatures which were slain for great banquets and was not specifically a Christmas dish. The turkey was introduced into Europe by the Spanish conquerors on a return journey from the New World, which is where the birds came from. They were called turkeys in England because merchants from the Levant, or Turkey, first brought them over here. The French claim that the Jesuits were responsible for importing the turkey into Europe and breeding it in large numbers a century later, which is why a turkey is still called a 'jesuite' in parts of France.

Great flocks of turkeys were kept in Norfolk, Suffolk and Cambridgeshire and slowly driven to London from August onwards, stopping to graze and rest by the roadside verges on the way. They had small leather boots, rags or a coating of tar on their feet as protective wear for the long journey. By the late eighteenth century turkey was becoming the fashionable Christmas bird for the well-to-do in London and Norwich alone was sending a thousand turkeys a day up to London; even today, the Norfolk turkey has the reputation for being the best. During the nineteenth century, more and more were slaughtered at the farm and taken by stagecoach from Norwich to London, a three-day journey, but it was not until the latter half of the century that turkey was within the financial grasp of the majority of Christmas revellers. Then, the poulterers stayed open even on Christmas morning in the hope of selling one more turkey; it was the last prize turkey that Scrooge bought for the Cratchits on Christmas Day.

The Turkey in America

On Thanksgiving day, the fourth Thursday in November, most self-respecting citizens of the United States tuck into their roast turkey complete with an apple and onion stuffing, cranberry sauce and glazed sweet potatoes, possibly with a marshmallow topping. They probably do so again on Christmas Day, for wild turkey was among the bounties of nature that the early settlers found and first gave thanks for in 1623. Its size and magnificent plumage made it the perfect festal bird and turkey shoots were among the pre-Christmas activities in America, long before the bird became popular in Britain.

PEAR AND CELERY STUFFING
(for a 5.4–6.8kg/12–15lb oven-ready turkey)

50g/2oz butter
1 medium onion, finely chopped
4 celery sticks, finely chopped
2 firm, but ripe pears
Grated rind and juice of ½ large lemon
175g/6oz fresh white breadcrumbs
50g/2oz shredded suet
Salt and freshly milled black pepper
45ml/3tbsp chopped parsley
1 egg, beaten

Melt the butter in a saucepan and fry the onion until soft and light golden brown. Add the celery and cook until soft. Remove from the heat and cool. Peel and core the pears and cut into small pieces. Toss in the lemon juice.

Combine all the ingredients in a mixing bowl and season to taste. Bind together with beaten egg.

MY MOTHER'S GIBLET AND HERB STUFFING
(for 5.4–6.8kg/12–15lb oven-ready turkey)

This is another family favourite which produces delicious stock for soup. Cook the giblets as on page 60.

1 set of turkey giblets, cooked
25g/1oz butter
1 medium onion, finely chopped
1 celery stick, finely chopped (optional)
125g/4oz fresh white or wholemeal breadcrumbs
5ml/1tsp mixed herbs
15ml/1tbsp chopped parsley
Grated rind of 1 lemon
Salt and freshly milled black pepper
A little stock

Remove all the meat from the neck of the turkey and chop up the rest of the giblets roughly. Put all the giblets through the coarse blade of a mincer or chop finely in a food processor.

Melt the butter in a small saucepan and fry the onion and celery gently until soft. Place in a mixing bowl and add the breadcrumbs, herbs, lemon rind and minced giblets. Season well with salt and pepper and bind together with a little stock from the giblets.

SMOKED OYSTER STUFFING
(for a 5.4–6.8kg/12–15lb oven-ready turkey)

This is a luxurious stuffing and makes a delicious change. It is especially good with turkey, but can be used with chicken or veal.

175g/6oz butter
1 large onion, finely chopped
175g/6oz fresh white or wholemeal breadcrumbs
3 sticks of celery, finely chopped
2 garlic cloves, crushed
5ml/1tsp dried mixed herbs
15ml/1tbsp chopped parsley
2 tins smoked oysters
Salt and freshly milled black pepper
A little cream or milk to bind

Melt the butter and cook the onion until soft and golden brown. Add about ⅓ of the breadcrumbs and stir over heat until all the butter is absorbed. Tip the mixture into a mixing bowl, then add the remaining crumbs, celery, garlic and herbs. Drain the oysters, chop them roughly, then add them to the other ingredients. Season to taste and bind together with a little cream or milk.

TO STUFF A TURKEY

Stuffings are very important to keep the turkey moist and to add flavour. Traditionally, turkey was always stuffed from both the neck and the tail ends, but the British Turkey Federation now recommend that to be really safe you do *not* stuff the body cavity, particularly if cooking a large or a frozen turkey; the inside of the turkey may not be cooked properly especially if a dense stuffing is used, or the stuffing may not be cooked right through, or if it is, the breast meat may become too dry.

Before stuffing *any* poultry, bring both the stuffing and the bird to room temperature, then spoon the stuffing into the neck end, loosening some of the breast skin. Tuck the neck flap under the bird's back and secure it in place with a small skewer or fine string and a trussing needle. Place an apple, a cut orange or lemon and a peeled onion, plus a bundle of herbs, inside the body cavity instead of stuffing to add flavour.

Once a bird is stuffed, cook it immediately. Don't ever stuff it the night before, because fresh air should always be able to circulate in the carcass. Extra stuffing can be cooked separately in a greased ovenproof dish, or formed into balls and cooked.

Tradition of the Wishbone

A traditional custom is for two people to hold each end of the 'merry-thought', or wishbone, from the carcass of poultry or game birds, then wish and pull. As the bone breaks, the person with the longer piece – in some places, the shorter – will gain his wish, but only if he does not reveal his thoughts or laugh and talk during the proceedings.

TO MAKE STUFFING BALLS

Make up your chosen stuffing, then using your fingertips form into small balls. Roll in a little flour, then fry in butter and oil until crisp. Keep warm until needed, then arrange around the turkey on the serving platter.

TO TRUSS THE TURKEY

Sew up or skewer the vent end of the bird tightly to prevent the juices escaping. If you wish, cut off the ends of the wings to use for giblet stock. Tie the legs together with string and fasten the string around the parson's nose or tail.

After 1 hour of cooking, the string tying the bird's legs together should be cut to allow more even cooking. By this time the legs should be set in place.

TO TEST IF POULTRY IS COOKED

Insert a clean steel knitting needle or metal skewer into the thickest part of the thigh and into both the breast and thigh of large birds. If the juices run clear, the bird is cooked; if pink, continue cooking for a further 15 minutes or until the juices run clear when tested again.

When the juices are running clear, an additional test is to tug the leg of the bird gently away from the body; if it gives, the bird is cooked. For a whole unstuffed bird, tip it up and check that the juices from the body cavity are clear and not pink.

CARVING THE TURKEY

Allow at least 15 minutes (30 minutes for a very large turkey) between cooking and carving, to let the juices go back into the flesh and make carving easier. A really sharp knife is necessary to carve

Roast Turkey (page 54) with Pigs in a Blanket (page 61), Dried Apricot, Raisin and Almond Stuffing (page 56), Cranberry Orange Sauce (page 62) and Sweet Potatoes in Orange Shells (page 63)

successfully and it is helpful to provide a second warmed platter for the carver's use. Remove all the trussing strings and any skewers; this should be done in the kitchen.

To carve the turkey, first cut off the legs and wings by holding the bird firmly with a carving fork and cutting the skin around the leg. Insert the knife between the leg and body and press gently outwards to expose the joint. Cut through and remove the thigh and drumstick in one piece. Remove the wing on the same side, then carve the breast meat downwards in thick slices, or thin slices if the turkey is large. Serve everyone with some breast and some leg meat.

TURKEY GRAVY
(makes about 900ml/1½pt)

Medium dry sherry or Madeira is added to this gravy to make it very special. The basic giblet stock can be made on Christmas Eve or earlier.

FOR THE GIBLET STOCK
Turkey giblets
50g/2oz butter
1 litre/2pt chicken stock or water
1 onion, quartered
1 carrot, cut in chunks
1 stick of celery, chopped
1 bay leaf
6 black peppercorns
1 bouquet garni
2 blades of mace
Onion skins

Wash and dry the giblets, including the liver, unless you are using a stuffing which requires it. Cut the giblets into small pieces, then heat the butter in a frying pan. Fry the giblets until browned, then transfer to a saucepan and cover with stock or water. Add the vegetables, bay leaf, black peppercorns, bouquet garni and mace then bring to the boil. Remove any scum, cover with a lid and simmer for 1–1½ hours. Strain and leave to cool until ready for use. Remove any fat before adding to the gravy.

FOR THE GRAVY
45–60ml/3–4tbsp pan juices from roasting the turkey
5ml/1tsp tomato purée
25–40g/1–1½oz plain flour
900ml/1½pt giblet stock
150ml/¼pt medium dry sherry or Madeira
Salt and freshly milled pepper

When the turkey is cooked, transfer it to a warm serving platter and keep warm.

Remove all but the required amount of juices from the roasting tin, leaving the browned vegetables and any pieces of skin or stuffing which may have stuck to the bottom of the tin. Stir in the tomato purée and sprinkle over the flour. Cook over a moderate heat until a good colour, stirring continuously and scraping all the juices from the bottom of the tin. Remove from the heat and gradually stir in the giblet stock and sherry. Return to the heat and bring slowly to the boil. Continue boiling for 2–3 minutes, then strain into a smaller pan. Simmer for a further 5–10 minutes until smooth, glossy and a rich brown colour. Check the seasoning.

Serve in a warmed jug or gravy boat.

MAKING STOCK WITH THE CARCASS OF POULTRY

Any poultry carcass can be used to make stock which can be stored in the freezer for up to 3 months.

1 poultry carcass
1 large onion, quartered, including the onion skin
1 large carrot, roughly chopped
1 leek, chopped
1 celery stick, roughly chopped
5ml/1tsp black peppercorns
1 bouquet garni
1 bay leaf
3–4 blades of mace
Salt
Cold water to cover

Break up the carcass into pieces and place in a large pan. Add any odd pieces of skin, bone and juices,

The Turkey in other Countries

In spite of temperatures in the hundreds, many Australians tried to reproduce the Christmas they knew in an earlier homeland with hot roast turkey and all the trimmings. They persevered with the roast turkey, but many now prefer it cold with salad. Canadians of English extraction also roast a turkey, as do Parisians and Burgundians for the main dish of their Reveillon, the meal served after Midnight Mass on Christmas Eve.

In fact, many favourite national festive dishes are being replaced by the turkey.

the vegetables, herbs and seasoning. Cover with cold water, then bring slowly to the boil. Skim off any scum, cover the pan with a tight-fitting lid and simmer over a low heat for 1½–2 hours. Top up with boiling water as necessary.

Strain the stock through a fine sieve into a large mixing bowl and leave to cool. Remove the fat from the surface and season to taste.

BACON AND CHESTNUT ROLLS
(serves 6–8)

These are just a little bit different from the plain bacon rolls that are traditionally served with roast turkey. Try them for a change with roast chicken or pheasant at other times of the year. You can use tinned, frozen or dried chestnuts if you wish and the rolls can be cooked earlier and reheated for a few seconds under the grill just before serving.

175g/6oz smoked streaky bacon rashers, derinded
450g/1lb peeled and cooked chestnuts

Remove the rind from the bacon and stretch each rasher on a board with the back of a knife. Cut each rasher into 2 pieces and roll each piece around a cooked chestnut. Thread the rolls carefully onto skewers and grill for 5 minutes, or until golden brown. Serve immediately, arranged around the turkey.

MA'S BREAD SAUCE
(serves 8)

75g/3oz white breadcrumbs (approx 2 days old)
Salt and freshly milled pepper
300ml/½pt milk
12g/½oz butter
1 medium onion, peeled
5 cloves
A little single cream or extra milk

Place the breadcrumbs and seasoning in a double saucepan or in a basin over a saucepan of simmering water. Bring the milk and butter slowly to the boil, then pour over the breadcrumbs. Stick the cloves in the onion, then place in the middle of the mixture. Cover and cook over gentle heat for at least 2 hours until the onion is soft, stirring occasionally.

Before serving, remove the cloves and stir in a little cream or milk if the sauce is too thick. If you wish, the onion can also be removed.

BACON AND SAUSAGE KEBABS
(serves 6–8)

12–16 cocktail sausages
6–8 streaky bacon rashers, smoked

Stretch the bacon rashers with the back of a knife and cut in two. Roll up each piece and thread alternately with the cocktail sausage onto metal skewers. Grill or bake in a moderate oven until brown and crisp.

PIGS IN A BLANKET
(serves 6–8)

6–8 chipolata sausages
6–8 streaky bacon rashers, smoked

Stretch the bacon rashers a little with the back of a knife and wrap one around each sausage. Grill or bake in a moderate oven until brown and crisp.

CHESTNUT SAUCE
(serves 6–8)

This makes a change from chestnut purée and is excellent with roast chicken and game birds as well as turkey.

40g/1½oz butter
40g/1½oz flour
300ml/½pt chicken or turkey stock
150ml/¼pt milk
350g/12oz chestnuts, cooked and chopped
Salt and freshly milled black pepper
Large pinch of sugar (optional)
Large pinch of ground cinnamon (optional)

Melt the butter in a heavy saucepan and stir in the flour. Cook gently for a few minutes, then gradually stir in the stock and milk. Continue cooking gently until the sauce is smooth, then stir in the chestnuts. Season to taste with salt and pepper, and a little sugar and cinnamon if you wish. Cook very gently for a further 5–10 minutes, stirring occasionally. Taste and adjust seasoning if necessary. Serve hot.

RED CHESTNUT SAUCE

Make as before, but add 1 glass of red wine instead of the milk. The resulting sauce is particularly good with roast beef.

MY GRANDFATHER'S CHESTNUT PURÉE
(serves 6–8)

My grandfather was very interested in cooking and many of his specialities were cooked only at Christmas. He always made his purée to accompany the turkey.

350g/12oz chestnuts, peeled
450ml/¾pt turkey stock
2–3 strips of lemon peel
Salt and cayenne pepper
Grated nutmeg
225ml/7½fl oz double cream

Place the peeled nuts and lemon peel in a saucepan and cover with the stock. Simmer gently for about 30 minutes until the nuts are soft, then sieve or purée in a blender or food processor. Season with salt, cayenne pepper and nutmeg. Reheat gently, then stir in the cream. Serve either hot or cold.

☆ TO PEEL CHESTNUTS

(a) *By boiling*: Make a small slit on the flat side of their shells from the centre to the pointed end. Place in cold water to cover and bring to the boil. Simmer for 3–5 minutes then take the pan from the heat. Lift out a few nuts at a time and remove the shell and inner membrane. The water must not boil again but can be reheated; the skins come off easily if the chestnuts are hot, but not too cooked.
(b) *By roasting*: Slit the nuts as before then roast them in a moderate oven for 6–8 minutes. With a cloth wrapped around one hand use a sharp knife to peel off the shell and skin.
(c) *By frying*: To shallow fry, slit the skins of the chestnuts, then heat 45ml/3 tablespoons cooking oil in a wide heavy saucepan. Add enough chestnuts to make a single layer, then saute over a high heat for about 5 minutes, shaking the pan to keep the chestnuts from burning. Transfer the nuts to a colander with a draining spoon, then rinse briefly so that they are cool enough to handle. Peel and skin the chestnuts.
   To deep fry, heat the oil as usual, slit the chestnuts then add a few at a time. Fry for 2 or 3 minutes, then rinse and peel as before. Be careful because they are apt to spit a great deal.

☆ COOKING CHESTNUTS
If a recipe calls for cooked chestnuts, the nuts should be peeled, skinned, then boiled in water, milk or stock for 20–30 minutes.

CELERY SAUCE
(makes about 600ml/1pt)

50g/2oz butter
1 small onion, finely chopped
½ large head of celery, finely chopped
25g/1oz plain flour
450ml/¾pt chicken or turkey stock
1 bouquet garni
Salt and freshly milled pepper
2 egg yolks
150ml/¼pt double cream

Melt the butter in a heavy saucepan and soften the onion and celery in it. Stir in the flour and cook for a couple of minutes. Gradually add the stock and bouquet garni, stirring all the time, then bring slowly to the boil. Simmer for 10 minutes, then season to taste. Remove and discard the bouquet garni.
   Just before serving mix the egg yolks with the cream and stir into the sauce. Reheat gently, but do not bring to the boil again or it will curdle. Serve separately with roast turkey or any roast poultry.

CRANBERRY ORANGE SAUCE
(serves 6–8)

The British and Americans serve cranberry sauce with the Christmas turkey, although it is only in the last 25 years that Britain has acquired a taste for it. The Continentals use the sauce to accompany meat dishes of all kinds, especially game. It is also good with a vegetarian chestnut roast and will keep for up to a month in the fridge or can be frozen.

225g/8oz fresh or frozen cranberries
75g/3oz caster sugar
150ml/¼pt fresh orange juice
Grated rind of 1 orange
Good pinch of mixed spice
15ml/1tbsp orange liqueur (cointreau or Grand Marnier)

Put the cranberries in a saucepan with the sugar, orange juice, orange rind and mixed spice. Stir well and cook gently for 5–7 minutes until the fruit pops and softens. Cool completely, then chill in the fridge. Stir in the orange liqueur just before serving with roast turkey, game or pork.
   Cranberry sauce looks most attractive if served in fresh orange shells arranged around the bird or joint. Cut the edges of the orange shells into V-shapes. Another good idea is to serve the cranberry sauce in individual pastry tartlet cases baked blind.

CRANBERRY AND PORT SAUCE
(serves 6–8)

225g/8oz fresh or frozen cranberries
Approx 75g/3oz caster sugar
75ml/2½fl oz port or red wine

Dissolve the sugar in the port or red wine over a gentle heat, then add the cranberries. Simmer very gently for about 7 minutes until the cranberries pop. Taste and add extra sugar if necessary. Cool completely, then chill in the fridge before serving with roast turkey, game or pork.

CELERY BRAISED WITH GARLIC AND SPICES
(serves 8)

Celery is a traditional accompaniment to turkey and the flavours certainly compliment each other. This dish can be prepared in advance and cooked later.

3 large heads of celery
50g/2oz butter
30ml/2tbsp sunflower oil
2 medium onions, thinly sliced
2 garlic cloves, crushed
2 carrots, thinly sliced
5ml/1tsp celery seeds
5ml/1tsp ground allspice
330ml/½pt chicken stock
15ml/1tbsp dry white Vermouth
Salt and freshly milled black pepper
Chopped parsley, to garnish

Wash the celery thoroughly and trim each head to about 18–20cm/7–8in long. Blanch the celery by simmering it in boiling salted water for about 10 minutes. Drain very well and cut each head in half lengthways, then arrange in a large buttered oven-proof dish in a single layer. Melt the butter and oil in a saucepan and fry the onions and garlic very gently for a few minutes. Add the carrots and cook for another 5 minutes. Spread this mixture over the celery and sprinkle with the celery seeds. Mix the allspice with the stock and Vermouth and season to taste. Pour over the celery, cover with foil or buttered greaseproof paper and cook in a preheated moderate oven 350°F; 180°C; Gas Mark 4 for 1 hour. Turn the celery over, baste it, and continue cooking without the foil or greaseproof for a further 25 minutes.

SWEET POTATOES IN ORANGE SHELLS
(serves 6–8)

Sweet potatoes traditionally accompany the American roast turkey on Thanksgiving Day. Try them for a change with turkey, goose or duck.

900g/2lb sweet potatoes
30ml/2tbsp single cream
50g/2oz butter
Salt and freshly milled pepper
6–8 orange shells

Scrub the sweet potatoes and bake in a moderate oven 350°F; 180°C; Gas Mark 4 until soft. Scoop the potato out of the skins into a bowl and mash with the cream and butter. Season to taste, then pile into orange shells and serve surrounding the turkey.

BRUSSELS SPROUTS WITH BACON AND CHESTNUTS
(serves 8)

Brussels sprouts and chestnuts are a delicious combination, traditionally served at Christmas to accompany the turkey, but excellent with all poultry and game.
   The sprouts and chestnuts can be prepared the night before and kept in the fridge in polythene bags.

900g/2lb Brussels sprouts
50–75g/2–3oz butter
225g/8oz streaky bacon rashers, chopped (optional)
450g/1lb fresh or frozen chestnuts, peeled and cooked
Salt and freshly milled black pepper
Buttered wholemeal breadcrumbs (optional)

Trim the sprouts, then cook them in boiling salted water or chicken stock for 5–10 minutes, depending on their size, but they should still be crisp. Drain well and dry over a low heat. Keep hot. Melt 50g/2oz butter in a deep frying pan or saucepan and add the bacon. Sauté until the fat runs. Add the chestnuts and toss over a fairly high heat until thoroughly hot and lightly coloured, then add the sprouts. Toss together and season to taste. Serve immediately or the sprouts will lose their wonderful green colour. Garnish with buttered breadcrumbs.

   Toasted or fried almonds, walnuts and hazelnuts are all delicious added to sprouts.

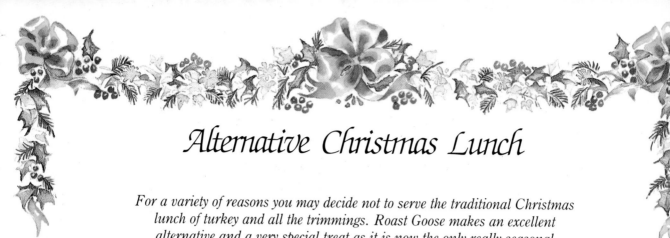

Alternative Christmas Lunch

For a variety of reasons you may decide not to serve the traditional Christmas lunch of turkey and all the trimmings. Roast Goose makes an excellent alternative and a very special treat as it is now the only really seasonal poultry, but remember that it provides a relatively small amount of meat; the chances of having any left over to serve cold are slim.
A large joint of beef is now a luxury and is also a good alternative to turkey for a large gathering of people. Fish also makes a change although it is sometimes difficult to buy fresh fish at Christmas if the weather is bad. Try serving Chestnut Stuffed Sole (page 38) or Poached Salmon (page 80) for a real treat.
If you want to serve a vegetarian Christmas lunch which still looks traditional, try a Brazil-nut Bake (page 73) served with roast potatoes and Brussels sprouts, or a Creamy Leek and Cheese Croustade (page 74) if you do not want to follow tradition.
The traditional Christmas Pudding is far too rich for many, particularly after a heavy main course, so try serving Vanessa's superb Bread Pudding (page 76), or Lime and Almond Ice Cream (page 76). For a very light alternative, try the Christmas Tangerine Soufflé (page 75) or a refreshing Pink Champagne Sorbet (page 75) to provide a truly celebratory conclusion to the meal.

ROAST GOOSE
(serves 6–8)

Although a goose can cost four times as much as the average turkey, it is considered by many to be the best of all poultry and is very rich with a slightly gamey flavour. Geese are not widely stocked, so you will probably have to order in advance for Christmas. Allow 450–575g/1–1¼lb oven-ready weight per serving and if you buy a frozen bird, make sure it is completely thawed before stuffing and cooking.

1 × 4–5kg/9–11lb oven-ready goose
Salt and freshly milled black pepper
Chosen stuffing
A little seasoned flour

Remove the goose and the prepared stuffing from the fridge and leave at cool room temperature for at least 3 hours before cooking.

Wipe the bird inside and out with kitchen paper and pull out the inside lumps of fat from the tail end and reserve. Spoon your chosen stuffing into the body cavity of the bird and sew up or skewer both ends. Wipe the outside of the goose again with kitchen paper to make sure the skin is perfectly dry;

this will ensure a very crisp skin which is half the beauty of a goose or duck. Prick the skin all over with a fine skewer or cocktail stick, making sure not to stab too deeply into the flesh which would encourage precious meat juices as well as fat to run out during cooking. Rub salt and black pepper all over the skin and weigh the bird to calculate the cooking time, allowing 15 minutes per 450g/lb.

Place the goose, breast up, on a wire rack in a roasting tin. Cover the breast with the reserved fat and roast in a preheated oven at 425°F; 220°C; Gas Mark 7 for 30 minutes. Pour off the fat from the tin, turn the goose over and reduce the oven temperature to 350°F; 180°C; Gas Mark 4. Continue roasting for 1½ hours, basting frequently. Turn the goose over again breast side up and discard the lumps of fat. Baste with the fat that has collected in the tin then pour off excess fat and continue roasting. 15–20 minutes before the cooking time is up, dredge the breast of the bird with seasoned flour and turn the oven up again to 425°F; 220°C; Gas Mark 7 to give the skin a final crisping. Test to see if the bird is cooked by piercing the thickest part of the thigh; if the juices run clear and not pink, it is cooked.

Remove the goose to a hot serving platter and

keep in a warm place for 10–15 minutes before bringing to the table. This will give you time to make the gravy using giblet stock (see page 60). Gravy made with half stock and half cider is excellent with goose.

Serve the roast goose surrounded by small baked apples or decorated with fried apple slices and garnished with watercress or parsley. Plain boiled, mashed, floury roast or casseroled potatoes go well with the richness of goose, as does a sharp fruit or onion sauce (see recipes on pages 66–70).

☆ If your goose is browning too much, especially the legs, protect with foil or a double thickness of butter-muslin soaked in melted goose fat. Remove before the final crisping.

HONEY-GLAZED GOOSE

Before roasting, rub the skin of the goose with salt, then brush with 30ml/2tbsp clear honey. Cook as before.

SPICED ROAST GOOSE

Mix a pinch of ground cinnamon or mixed spice with black pepper and salt. Rub into the skin of the goose and cook as before.

Goose as a celebratory bird

Christmas is coming the goose is getting fat,
Please put a penny in the old man's hat.
If you haven't got a penny, a ha'penny will do,
If you haven't got a ha'penny, then God bless you!

Ever since Elizabethan days, roast goose has been the traditional bird on the farmhouse table at Christmas. Even when Queen Victoria came to the throne in 1837, the traditional Christmas fare for the poor and for country folk in the south of England was still goose, usually eked out with rabbit to help feed large families. Goose Clubs had been introduced so that even the lowest-paid worker could enjoy a goose at Christmas by contributing a small part of his week's wages throughout the year to his local club, which was often organised in the pub. Bottles of whisky and port plus a goose were usually raffled, the draw being performed by a child to ensure fair play! On Christmas Day, bakers would keep their ovens alight to cook the local families' geese.

In Europe, the Austrians, Germans and Dutch enjoy a goose on Christmas Day and goose is eaten in some areas of France for Le Réveillon on Christmas Eve.

TO CARVE A GOOSE

Allow at least 15 minutes between cooking and serving. First, remove any trussing strings and skewers, then with a sharp knife, cut off the legs and the wings. Slice down through the breast in the centre and then cut thick, parallel slices. Serve each person with both breast and leg meat and some of the delicious crispy skin.

☆ GOOSE FAT

Reserve all the excess fat poured from the roasting tin when cooking a goose. It is excellent for frying, particularly potatoes and bread, and is also good for making pastry; use instead of lard. Farmers used to coat their boots with goose fat to protect them from wet and snowy weather and of course goose fat is well known as a protection for the chest from colds and 'flu'.

TRADITIONAL SAGE AND ONION STUFFING
(for a 4–5kg/9–11lb oven-ready goose)

This is the traditional stuffing for roast goose and goes exceptionally well with it. Goose is so rich that a stuffing with a definite herb, onion or fruit flavour is best.

50g/2oz butter or goose fat
450g/1lb onions, finely chopped
Goose liver, finely chopped (optional)
275g/8oz fresh white or wholemeal breadcrumbs
45ml/3tbsp chopped fresh sage or 15ml/1tbsp dried sage
5ml/1tsp chopped parsley
Salt and freshly milled black pepper
1 egg, lightly beaten

Melt the butter or goose fat and fry the onion until soft. Add the goose liver if using and continue cooking for a further 5 minutes. Transfer to a mixing bowl and add the breadcrumbs, sage and parsley. Mix thoroughly, then season to taste. Bind the mixture together with the beaten egg and allow to cool completely before using.

APPLE, SAGE AND PICKLED WALNUT STUFFING
(for a 4–5kg/9–11lb oven-ready goose)

Apples marry particularly well with roast goose as they counteract the richness. If you include apples in the stuffing, serve an alternative fruit sauce such as gooseberry, prune or plum.

25g/1oz butter
1 medium onion, finely chopped
125g/4oz fresh white or wholemeal breadcrumbs
1 medium cooking apple
10ml/2tsp dried sage
4 pickled walnuts or 50g/2oz shelled walnuts, roughly
    chopped
Grated rind and juice of ½ lemon
Salt and freshly milled black pepper
1 egg, beaten

Melt the butter and fry the onion until soft. Transfer to a mixing bowl, then add the breadcrumbs. Peel, then grate the apple and add to the bowl with the sage, pickled or shelled walnuts, lemon rind and juice. Season to taste, then bind together with beaten egg, adding a little extra stock or milk if necessary. Allow to cool completely.

PRUNE AND PORT STUFFING
(for a 4–5kg/9–11lb oven-ready goose)

25g/1oz butter
1 large onion, finely chopped
Goose liver, finely chopped
225g/8oz prunes, soaked overnight
60ml/4tbsp port
5ml/1tsp dried sage
125g/4oz fresh white or wholemeal breadcrumbs
Salt and freshly milled black pepper

Melt the butter and fry the onion until soft. Add the goose liver and cook for a further 2–3 minutes.
   Remove the stones from the soaked and drained prunes and chop the prunes roughly. Add to the onion with the port, then cover and simmer gently for about 5 minutes. Add the sage and breadcrumbs and mix together roughly. Season to taste and allow to cool before filling the goose.

SAUSAGEMEAT AND APPLE STUFFING
(for a 4–5kg/9–11lb oven-ready goose)

50g/2oz butter
2 medium onions, finely chopped
Goose liver, finely chopped
225g/8oz pork sausagemeat
2 large cooking apples
175g/6oz fresh white or wholemeal breadcrumbs
10ml/2tsp dried mixed herbs
Salt and freshly milled black pepper

Melt the butter and gently fry the onions until soft and golden. Add the liver and sausagemeat and cook until browned, breaking it up and stirring all the time. Peel, core and chop the apples and add to the pan. Continue cooking for about 5 minutes, then transfer to a mixing bowl. Stir in the breadcrumbs and herbs and season to taste. Mix well and cool before using to stuff the bird.

POTATO, BACON, HERB AND SAUSAGEMEAT STUFFING
(for a 4–5kg/9–11lb oven-ready goose)

In the past, roast goose was often cooked with a potato stuffing to soak up the fat and make the meat go further.

675g/1½lb potatoes, cooked and mashed
125g/4oz streaky bacon, diced
1 large onion, chopped
450g/1lb pork sausagemeat
15ml/1tbsp chopped parsley
5ml/1tsp dried thyme
5ml/1tsp dried sage
45ml/3tbsp double cream
Salt and freshly milled black pepper

Fry the bacon very gently until the fat runs, then add the onion. Cook until soft, then add the sausagemeat. Fry until golden, breaking it up and stirring continuously. Place the mashed potatoes in a mixing bowl and add the other ingredients. Mix thoroughly and bind together with the cream. Season to taste and allow to cool before using to stuff the goose.

BUTTERY APPLE SAUCE
(serves 6–8)

675g/1½lb Cox's apples
Approx 15ml/1tbsp dry cider or water
40g/1½oz butter
15ml/1tbsp caster sugar (optional)
Squeeze of lemon juice

Peel, core and slice the apples. Poach in a covered saucepan with a very little cider or water and the butter until very tender and fluffy. Stir in the sugar, if using, and the lemon juice. Pass through a blender or purée in a food processor, or just beat apples to a pulp with a wooden spoon.
   Keep warm until ready to serve, or serve chilled, to accompany roast goose, duck or pork.

SPICED APPLE AND ONION SAUCE
(serves 6–8)

50g/2oz butter
1 medium onion, finely chopped
675g/1½lb Cox's apples
15–30ml/1–2tbsp dry cider or water
3 or 4 whole cloves
15ml/1tbsp caster sugar (optional)
Pinch of grated nutmeg

Melt 25g/1oz butter in a saucepan and cook the onion in it for about 5 minutes until soft. Peel, core and slice the apples and add to the onion. Stir well, then add the cider or water and cloves. Cover the saucepan and leave the apples to cook until very tender and fluffy. Remove the cloves and stir in the sugar if using. Beat to a pulp with the remaining butter, then grate in a little nutmeg. Serve warm or chilled to accompany roast goose, duck or pork.

GREEN GOOSEBERRY SAUCE
(serves 6–8)

This sauce can be made well in advance and frozen. It makes a good alternative to apple sauce with the Christmas goose.

450g/1lb green gooseberries
25g/1oz butter
30ml/2tbsp cold water
Sugar to taste
½tsp ground ginger (optional)

Top, tail, and wash the gooseberries. Put in a saucepan with the butter and the water. Cover the pan tightly and cook very gently, shaking the pan occasionally, until the gooseberries are soft. Add sugar to taste – the sauce should be tangy – and add ginger if you wish. Purée in a blender or processor, or serve as it is.
   Serve warm or chilled with roast goose, chicken, turkey or pork.

APPLE AND ORANGE MARMALADE SAUCE
(serves 6–8)

675g/1½lb Cox's apples
25g/1oz butter
15–30ml/1–2tbsp orange marmalade
15ml/1tbsp orange liqueur

Cook the peeled and sliced apples with the butter in a covered pan until very soft. Beat in the marmalade to taste and stir in the orange liqueur. Serve warm or chilled.

APPLE AND REDCURRANT SAUCE
 (serves 6–8)

Serve with roast goose, duck or pork.

675g/1½lb Granny Smith apples
30ml/2tbsp lemon juice
50g/2oz sugar
150ml/¼pt dry white wine
150ml/¼pt water
150g/5oz redcurrant jelly
2 cinnamon sticks
Grated rind of 2 lemons

Put lemon juice into a heavy pan with the sugar, wine and water. Heat gently until the sugar has dissolved, then bring to the boil. Peel, core and slice the apples and add to the saucepan. Cook gently until tender, then transfer to a serving bowl using a draining spoon. Add the redcurrant jelly and cinnamon sticks to the saucepan and bring to the boil. Simmer until reduced by half, then add the lemon rind. Pour over the apples and stir gently.

☆ Apple sauce can be flavoured with anything that seems complementary to the dish it is intended to accompany from herbs like sage and rosemary, spices like cloves, cinnamon and nutmeg to grated orange and lemon rind, brandy, rum, sherry and fruit liqueurs. Grated horseradish can also be added for a change, as can chopped or ground nuts, dried fruit such as sultanas or raisins, and crisp vegetables such as celery.

PRUNE SAUCE
(serves 8)

This is a delicious sauce for serving with roast goose, duck, game or pork. Plums may also be used.

450g/1lb large prunes, soaked overnight in cold tea
4 plump garlic cloves
2.5ml/½tsp salt
Freshly milled black pepper
2.5ml/½tsp paprika
Approx 300ml/½pt chicken stock
45ml/3tbsp chopped parsley

Drain the soaked prunes, reserving the liquor, and remove the stones. Place the prunes in a small saucepan with the soaking liquor and simmer gently until soft. Crush the garlic with the salt and purée in an electric blender or food processor with the prunes, black pepper and paprika, adding enough stock to make a thick, creamy sauce.

Transfer the sauce back into the pan and stir in the chopped parsley. Taste and adjust seasoning if necessary. Bring to boiling point, stirring from time to time. Chill before serving.

CREAMY ONION SAUCE
(serves 6–8)

Onion sauce is a very good accompaniment to roast goose, duck or pork. Leeks may be used instead of onions. Serve in addition to a fruit sauce.

50g/2oz butter
4 medium onions, finely chopped
25g/1oz flour
Pinch of curry powder
150ml/¼pt milk
150ml/¼pt chicken stock
150ml/¼pt double cream
Salt and freshly milled black pepper
Pinch of grated nutmeg

Melt the butter in a saucepan and cook the onion very gently for about 10 minutes until soft but not coloured. Stir in the flour and curry powder to make a smooth paste. Cook for a few seconds, then gradually stir in the milk and stock stirring continuously, until you have a smooth sauce. Cook for a further 5 minutes, then stir in the cream. Remove from the heat and season to taste with salt, pepper and nutmeg. If you have to reheat the sauce, make sure you don't bring it to the boil again.

☆ Before adding the cream, the sauce can be puréed in a blender or food processor to give a much smoother result. A little fresh or dried sage is an excellent addition.

Honey-glazed Roast Goose (page 65) with Spiced and Stuffed Baked Apples (page 71), Green Peas with Hazelnuts (page 72) and Braised Red Cabbage with Pears (page 71)

BAKED APPLES STUFFED WITH APRICOT JAM
(serves 8)

These apples make a very good accompaniment to roast goose, duck and pork.

8 medium cooking apples
60ml/4tbsp brown sugar
Grated rind and juice of 1 large lemon
50g/2oz butter
A little cider or water
45ml/3tbsp good-quality apricot jam

Wipe the apples and remove the cores. Pare off about 1cm/½in of peel from the top of each apple. Mix together the sugar, lemon rind, juice and butter and pack into the apple cavities. Set the apples in a baking dish and pour in just enough cider or water to cover the bottom. Bake with the goose or in a moderate pre-heated oven for 30–40 minutes depending on size of apples.

When cooked, cool a little, then carefully scoop out about 15ml/1tbsp of soft apple, taking care not to break the skins. Put this pulp into a bowl and add the apricot jam. Taste and add more sugar or lemon juice if necessary. Fill the apples with this mixture and reheat. Serve hot arranged around the goose or joint of pork.

CASSEROLE OF POTATOES AND LEEK
(serves 8)

This is a particularly good way of cooking potatoes for the busy Christmas cook, as the dish looks after itself and will not spoil if you are running late.

75g/3oz butter
1.4kg/3lb potatoes
1 large leek, finely sliced
Salt and freshly milled black pepper
450ml/¾pt half chicken or goose stock and half milk
Chopped parsley to garnish

Butter a wide, shallow ovenproof dish generously, then peel the potatoes and cut them into thinnish slices. Arrange a layer over the base of the dish, then sprinkle on a little sliced leek and season with salt and pepper. Continue with another layer of potatoes and so on, until the vegetables are all in, finishing with a layer of potatoes. Season the top layer well, then pour in the mixed stock and milk. Finally, dot with the remaining butter.

Cook at the top of a pre-heated moderate oven 350°F; 180°C; Gas Mark 4 for 45–60 minutes, or until the potatoes are tender and the top layer is golden brown. Garnish with chopped parsley and serve with roast goose, duck, chicken, pork or with cold meats at the buffet table.

BRAISED RED CABBAGE WITH PEARS
(serves 8)

Dessert pears are used in this dish instead of the more usual apples. Adding grated beetroot towards the end of cooking improves the colour.

1.4kg/3lb red cabbage
50g/2oz butter
350g/12oz onion, finely sliced
675g/1½lb dessert pears
2 garlic cloves, finely chopped
2 generous pinches ground cinnamon
2 generous pinches grated nutmeg
2 generous pinches ground cloves
1.25ml/¼tsp dried thyme
5ml/1tsp grated orange rind
30ml/2tbsp sugar (optional)
Salt and freshly milled black pepper
45ml/3tbsp wine or cider vinegar
150ml/¼pt chicken or vegetable stock
1 small raw beetroot, grated (optional)

Cut the cabbage into quarters, remove the hard stalk, and shred the cabbage finely. Melt the butter in a large saucepan and cook the cabbage for about 5 minutes. In a large casserole, layer the cabbage with the onion slices and the pears, peeled, cored and thinly sliced. Sprinkle over the garlic, spices, thyme, orange rind and sugar, if using. Season well with salt and pepper and pour over the vinegar and stock. Cover with a tightly fitting lid and cook very gently on top of the stove or in a very moderate oven 325°F; 170°C; Gas Mark 3 for 1½ hours. Stir in the grated beetroot, then continue cooking for a further 1 hour or until very tender. Adjust the seasoning before serving.

☆ Red cabbage is an ideal vegetable when entertaining as it can be kept warm without spoiling.

☆ Chopped cooking apples can be used instead of pears and 175g/6oz chopped streaky bacon or chopped stoned prunes can also be added for a change. Dry fry the bacon before you cook the cabbage in butter, then continue as before.

CREAMED PARSNIPS WITH PINE NUTS
(serves 8)

The natural sweetness of parsnips goes well with the richness of goose and this purée makes a change from roast parsnips. It can be made the day before you need it or can be frozen.

900g/2lb parsnips, peeled and roughly chopped
50g/2oz butter
150ml/¼pt hot single cream
Salt and freshly milled black pepper
25g/1oz pine nuts, toasted
Freshly grated nutmeg

Cook the parsnips in boiling salted water for about 30 minutes or until very tender. Drain well, then dry off over a low heat before puréeing in a blender or food processor, adding the butter and hot cream. Reheat the purée gently and season to taste, adding more cream if you wish, then pile into a warmed vegetable tureen for serving and garnish with pine nuts and a sprinkling of grated nutmeg.

SPICED AND STUFFED BAKED APPLES FOR ROAST GOOSE
(serves 8)

These are also good served with roast duck, pork and ham. Small cooking apples may be used instead.

8 crisp eating or small cooking apples
25g/1oz butter
1 small onion, finely chopped
50g/2oz fresh cranberries
50g/2oz seeded raisins, finely chopped
25g/1oz walnuts, finely chopped
15ml/1tbsp orange liqueur
Pinch of ground cinnamon
Pinch of ground allspice
Sugar to taste

Wipe the apples and remove the cores. Using a potato peeler, pare off about 1cm/½in of the skin from the top of each apple and place in a greased baking dish. Melt the butter in a saucepan and soften the onion in it. Remove from the heat and add the cranberries, raisins, walnuts, orange liqueur and spices. Mix together thoroughly and sweeten if you wish. Pack into the cavity of each apple. Pour in just

enough water to cover the bottom of the dish, then bake with the goose for the last 25–30 minutes of roasting time. Keep warm until needed, then arrange around the goose on its serving platter.

GREEN PEAS WITH HAZELNUTS
(serves 8)

Flaked almonds or chopped walnuts can be used instead if you wish.

450g/1lb frozen petits pois
50g/2oz butter
125g/4oz hazelnuts
Juice of ½ lemon
15ml/1tbsp chopped parsley
Salt and freshly milled black pepper

Cook the petits pois in a little boiling salted water or stock for a few minutes, until just tender. Meanwhile, melt the butter in a small saucepan and cook the hazelnuts over a gentle heat until golden brown. Stir in the lemon juice and parsley. Season with salt and pepper to taste. Drain the peas well, then toss with the hazelnuts and butter. Serve at once.

BETTY'S RIB OF BEEF WITH YORKSHIRE PUDDING
(serves 10–12)

Great sides of beef have been popular for the Christmas feast since Elizabethan days and a rib of beef still makes an interesting and attractive joint for today's large family gathering. It is best cooked on the bone for extra flavour and is even better when bought from a butcher who understands about hanging beef.

Betty, the wife of a farming neighbour of ours when we lived in Buckinghamshire, cooks her Yorkshire pudding around the joint with the most delicious results. The batter needs to be stiffer than normal to absorb the meat juices. This is her recipe which will serve 10–12 hot, or 6 if you want ample for cold the next day.

3kg/7lb beef forerib
Freshly milled black pepper
50g/2oz dripping

FOR THE YORKSHIRE PUDDING
225g/8oz plain flour
Pinch of salt

Freshly milled black pepper
3 medium eggs
300ml/½pt milk

Wipe the beef with kitchen paper and place, fat uppermost, in a large roasting tin approximately 37.5×27.5cm/15×11in to allow sufficient room for the Yorkshire pudding. Season with black pepper and smear with dripping, then cook at 425°F; 220°C; Gas Mark 7 for 12 minutes per 450g/lb plus 12 minutes; 15 minutes per 450g/lb plus 15 minutes; for medium, and 20 minutes per 450g/lb plus 20 minutes for well done. Meanwhile, make the Yorkshire pudding in plenty of time to let it stand for at least 30 minutes before cooking. Sieve the flour with the salt into a bowl. Stir in plenty of black pepper, then beat in the eggs and milk to form a smooth batter of pouring consistency. Leave to stand.

One hour before the beef is cooked, baste it well, then drain off any excess fat leaving enough to well coat the roasting tin. You can make gravy with this later. Pour the Yorkshire pudding mix around the joint and return to the oven. 30 minutes later, turn the tin around to allow the pudding to cook and rise on the other side.

Lift out the beef and Yorkshire pudding onto a warm serving platter and carve at the table. Serve with gravy and Horseradish Cream. Accompany with roast potatoes, parsnips or carrots and a green vegetable.

TO CARVE THE BEEF

Stand the joint on a plate with the rib bones underneath. Cut between the bones, that are now standing upright, and the meat and remove the upright bones in one piece. Turn the joint onto its side, then cut between the rib bones and the thin end of the meat to loosen it. Stand the joint on the rib bones again, then cut thin slices down towards the ribs. Cut underneath to release and serve the slices of beef.

HORSERADISH CREAM
(serves 10–12)

Grating fresh horseradish is an awful job because it smells so strongly, so if you want to opt out it is possible to buy preserved grated horseradish which is not nearly so hot. Omit the vinegar from this recipe if using preserved horseradish.

30ml/2tbsp grated horseradish, fresh or preserved
15ml/1tbsp white wine vinegar (optional)
300ml/½pt double cream

Pinch of caster sugar
Salt and freshly milled pepper
Dash of prepared English mustard

Pour the wine vinegar onto the horseradish, if using fresh. Stir in the cream and season to taste with sugar, salt, pepper and mustard. Keep at room temperature until needed and serve with hot or cold roast beef or smoked mackerel or trout.

VEGETARIAN CHRISTMAS LUNCH

BRAZIL-NUT BAKE WITH CHESTNUT STUFFING AND CRANBERRY SAUCE
(serves 6–8)

If you want to keep Christmas lunch as traditional as possible, but wish to serve a vegetarian menu, I suggest this savoury nut roast served with roast potatoes, sprouts, cranberry sauce and bread sauce.

125g/4oz vegetarian fat
4 medium onions, finely chopped
225g/8oz brazil nuts, finely chopped
225g/8oz brazil nuts, ground
2 garlic cloves, crushed
2 large tomatoes, skinned and chopped
2 small eating apples, peeled and diced
25g/1oz rolled oats
10ml/2tsp dried sage or 20ml/4tsp fresh sage
1 egg, beaten
Stock or milk to moisten
Salt and freshly milled black pepper

FOR THE STUFFING
225g/8oz chestnuts, cooked and mashed
40g/1½oz fresh wholemeal breadcrumbs
12g/½oz butter, melted
Grated rind of ¼ lemon
5ml/1tsp chopped parsley
Salt and freshly milled black pepper
A little vegetable stock or milk

Grease and line a 900g/2lb loaf tin with non-stick silicone paper. Heat the fat in a pan and gently fry the chopped onion for about 10 minutes, until softened. Put the chopped and ground nuts in a mixing bowl and mix in the onions, garlic, tomatoes, apple, rolled oats and sage. Stir thoroughly, then add the beaten egg and enough vegetable stock or milk

to make a fairly moist mixture. Season to taste.

To make the stuffing, pound the chestnuts with the breadcrumbs, butter, lemon rind and parsley. Season to taste then bind together with a little stock or milk.

Press half the nut mixture into the prepared tin, then add a layer of chestnut stuffing pressing it down well. Cover this with the remaining nut mixture. Press down well and cover with buttered foil. Bake in a moderate oven 350°F; 180°C; Gas Mark 4 standing in a roasting tin half-filled with water, for about 1 hour or until firm to the touch. After this, remove the foil and if the top is not brown enough, put it back into the oven, uncovered, for a further 10 minutes.

Allow to cool for about 5 minutes, before turning out onto a warmed serving plate. Surround with golden roast potatoes and serve with Wine Sauce (below) or Tomato and Whisky Sauce (below) and Brussels sprouts. Accompany with a Cranberry Sauce and Bread Sauce if you wish (pages·61–3).

TOMATO AND WHISKY SAUCE
(makes about 600ml/1pt)

35ml/2tbsp olive oil
1 medium onion, finely chopped
3 garlic cloves, crushed
900g/2lb tomatoes, skinned and roughly chopped
15ml/1tbsp chopped parsley
10ml/2tsp dried basil
10ml/2tsp tomato purée
Salt and freshly milled black pepper
90ml/3fl oz malt whisky

Melt the oil in a pan and fry the onion gently for about 5 minutes until soft. Add all the other ingredients and bring the sauce gently to the boil. Cover with a lid and simmer very gently for about 20 minutes, then uncover the pan and simmer for a further 10–15 minutes for the sauce to reduce a little. It can be served as it is, sieved, or blended in the liquidiser or processor until smooth.

WINE SAUCE
(makes 600ml/1pt)

Serve with the Brazil-nut Bake instead of gravy.

25g/1oz vegetarian fat or butter
30ml/2tbsp olive oil
1 medium onion, chopped

2 large garlic cloves, crushed
4 large tomatoes, roughly chopped
900ml/1½pt vegetable stock
300ml/½pt red wine
Salt and freshly milled black pepper

Heat the vegetarian fat and oil in a saucepan and fry the onion for about 5 minutes without browning. Add the garlic and tomatoes and cook for a further 3–4 minutes. Pour in the stock and wine and simmer gently until the liquid has reduced by about half. Strain and season with salt and pepper.

CREAMY JERUSALEM ARTICHOKES
(seves 6–8)

Another vegetable dish which can be prepared well in advance and finished off in the oven later. It is excellent with turkey, chicken, beef and ham and can also be served as a light lunch or supper dish.

900g/2lb Jerusalem artichokes
450ml/¾pt milk
150ml/¼pt chicken stock
Salt and freshly milled black pepper
40g/1½oz butter
30ml/2tbsp flour
225g/8oz button mushrooms, sliced
50g/2oz Gruyère cheese, grated
25g/1oz Parmesan cheese, grated
150ml/¼pt double cream, lightly whipped
25g/1oz fresh breadcrumbs

Scrub the artichokes and scrape them if necessary. Put them in a large saucepan in one layer if possible, then pour over the milk and stock. Season lightly with salt and bring to the boil. Simmer gently for about 15 minutes, or until just tender. Drain the artichokes, reserving the cooking liquor. Measure the liquid and reserve 450ml/¾pt.

Melt 25g/1oz butter in a saucepan and stir in the flour. Cook for a minute, then gradually stir in the artichoke liquor, stirring vigorously and cook until the sauce is smooth. Bring to simmering point and cook gently for 6–8 minutes, stirring frequently.

Meanwhile, peel the artichokes and cut into thick slices. Arrange in a shallow baking dish with the sliced mushrooms.

Remove the sauce from the heat and beat in ⅔ of the cheeses, mixed together. Let the sauce cool slightly, then gently mix in the lightly whipped cream. Season to taste, with salt and pepper, then pour over the artichokes and mushrooms. Sprinkle

with the remaining cheese and the breadcrumbs. Dot with the remaining 12g/½oz butter and bake near the top of a preheated oven at 400°F; 200°C; Gas Mark 6 for 20–25 minutes, or until golden brown. Serve immediately.

CREAMY LEEK AND CHEESE CROUSTADE
(serves 6–8)

The base of this dish is a mixture of breadcrumbs, cheese and nuts and combines very well with the creamy topping. Any nuts can be used in the base, or any mixture of nuts.

250g/9oz wholemeal breadcrumbs
75g/3oz butter or vegetarian fat
175g/6oz Cheddar cheese, grated
175g/6oz hazelnuts, finely chopped
¾tsp dried thyme
2 garlic cloves, crushed
Salt and freshly milled black pepper

FOR THE TOPPING
75g/3oz butter or vegetarian fat
5 medium leeks, sliced
40g/1½oz plain flour
450ml/¾pt milk
6 medium tomatoes, skinned and chopped
Salt and freshly milled black pepper
Freshly grated nutmeg
90ml/6tbsp fresh wholemeal breadcrumbs
125g/4oz Cheddar cheese, grated

Place the breadcrumbs in a mixing bowl and rub in the butter or fat. Stir in the other ingredients, then press the mixture into a roasting tin, or oven-proof dish 30×20cm/12×8in. Bake in a preheated hot oven 425°F; 220°C; Gas Mark 7 for 15–20 minutes, or until golden brown.

To make the topping, melt the butter or fat in a large saucepan. Fry the leeks gently for about 5 minutes until soft, then stir in the flour. Cook for 1–2 minutes, then gradually stir in the milk. Cook very gently until thick, and bring to the boil. Reduce the heat and add the chopped tomatoes. Simmer for a few minutes to soften the tomatoes, then season well with salt, pepper and nutmeg. Spoon the vegetable mixture over the cooked base and sprinkle with the breadcrumbs mixed with the cheese. Cook in a moderate oven 350°F; 180°C; Gas Mark 4 for 20–30 minutes until the cheese has melted and is golden brown. Serve at once with a green salad.

ALTERNATIVES TO CHRISTMAS PUDDING

CHRISTMAS TANGERINE SOUFFLÉ
(serves 6–8)

This cold soufflé can be made in a pretty glass or china bowl, or in a soufflé dish prepared with a collar. It makes a lovely refreshing pudding after a rich meal.

6 eggs, separated
175g/6oz caster sugar
Grated rind of 5 tangerines or mandarins
300ml/10fl oz tangerine juice
90ml/3fl oz lemon juice
12g/½oz powdered gelatine
300ml/½pt double cream

Place the egg yolks in a large bowl together with the sugar, grated rind and tangerine juice. Set the bowl over a saucepan of gently simmering water and whisk until the mixture is thick and mousse-like (until the whisk leaves a heavy trail in the mixture when lifted). Meanwhile, place the lemon juice in a cup and sprinkle over the gelatine. Leave for about 10 minutes to dissolve, then heat the cup in a small saucepan of hot water until the gelatine has melted. Allow to cool a little then whisk into the egg mixture.

Whisk the egg whites until stiff, but not dry, and half-whip the cream until the whisk leaves a distinct trail. Stand the egg mixture in a sink of cold water, stirring from time to time to ensure even cooling. When the mixture is cool but not setting, quickly fold in the cream and finally the stiffly beaten egg whites until thoroughly blended. As the mixture begins to set, turn it into a serving bowl or prepared 1.5 litre/2½pt soufflé dish and chill overnight until set, preferably in a cool pantry, otherwise the bottom of the fridge will do.

Decorate the soufflé with fresh tangerine slices or gold- and silver-coated almonds and ribbon, making it look as pretty as possible.

TO PREPARE A DISH FOR A COLD SOUFFLÉ

Cut a piece of non-stick silicone paper long enough to go around your soufflé dish with a 5–7.5cm/2–3in overlap. Fold the paper into 2 thicknesses and wrap around the dish to stand 7.5–10cm/3–4in above the rim. Hold in place with sellotape at the top, middle and bottom, and tie firmly in place with string just under the rim of the dish. Stand on a plate for easy handling.

TO REMOVE THE PAPER COLLAR

Cut the string and sellotape. Hold the back of a palette knife against the paper where the mixture is revealed. Pull the paper against the knife gently, so that the edge of the soufflé is not damaged.

PINK CHAMPAGNE SORBET
(serves 8)

The pink champagne can be replaced by dry sparkling wine or cider. Don't keep this sorbet for more than 2 weeks in the freezer, because wine-based sorbets have a tendency to separate if kept for a long time.

300g/10oz sugar
240ml/8fl oz water
600ml/1pt pink champagne
45ml/3tbsp lemon juice
2 egg whites
60ml/4tbsp icing sugar, sieved
Lemon slices and lemon balm or mint to decorate

Dissolve the sugar in the water in a saucepan over gentle heat. When completely dissolved, bring slowly to the boil. Boil rapidly for about 5 minutes, or until the syrup is thick. Cool, then stir in 360ml/12fl oz of the champagne and the lemon juice. Pour into freezer trays and freeze for about 1 hour, or until mushy. Pour the mixture into a bowl and beat well for 2 minutes. Return to the freezer trays and freeze for a further 30 minutes. Beat again. Repeat the freezing and beating every 30 minutes for the next 2 hours to break down the ice crystals.

Beat the egg whites until stiff, then gradually beat in the icing sugar. Beat the frozen mixture again, then fold in the meringue. Return to the freezer and freeze until firm. Transfer the sorbet to the fridge about 30 minutes before serving to soften a little.

Serve in chilled champagne glasses, or in hollowed-out lemon shells. Pour a little of the remaining champagne over each serving of sorbet and decorate with lemon slices and sprigs of lemon balm or mint.

Christmas Bread

Bread baked on Christmas Eve or Christmas Day was said to be a good remedy for stomach disorders and generally to have magical and healing powers, particularly if moistened with Christmas dew. Sometimes it was dried and powdered to be 'sown' in spring to ensure a good harvest.

LIME AND ALMOND ICE CREAM
(serves 6–8)

Serve this refreshing ice cream after the rich traditional Christmas turkey or goose and save the plum pudding for Boxing Day.

4 eggs, separated
125–175g/4–6oz caster sugar
Grated rind and juice of 4 limes
450ml/¾pt double cream
75g/3oz flaked almonds, toasted

Beat the egg yolks with 125g/4oz caster sugar and the grated rind and juice of the limes. Whip the cream and add to the egg yolk mixture. Taste and add more sugar if necessary. Whisk the egg whites stiffly and fold into the mixture, then pour into a lidded container and freeze until slushy. Whisk the ice cream again, then stir in the toasted almonds. Return to the freezer until completely frozen. Remove from the freezer 20–30 minutes before serving and place in the fridge.

Scoop out and serve piled in stemmed glasses or in an ice bowl (see below) with Petticoat Tails (page 117).

TO MAKE AN ICE BOWL

An ice bowl makes an unusual and decorative container for ice cream and sorbets. It will last for at least 30 minutes at room temperature, more if it is a very large one.

You need 2 bowls, one of which is small enough to fit inside the other with a gap of at least 2.5cm/1in all the way round. Put a few ice cubes in the large bowl and stand the smaller bowl on top of them. Place a heavy weight in the small bowl to keep it at the right height, then put some more ice cubes down the sides in the larger bowl and pour in some iced water. To decorate the bowl, put a few sprigs of mistletoe or holly, holly berries, laurel leaves, tiny fir cones and sprigs of rosemary into the water, then add more ice cubes on top to hold them down, plus more water to reach to the top of the larger bowl.

Freeze the bowls until there is solid ice between them; this will take at least 6 hours and is best done overnight. When you are ready to use the bowl, remove the weight and pour a little lukewarm water into the smaller bowl and ease it out. Dip the larger bowl into lukewarm water and gently unmould the ice bowl.

Fill the bowl with scoops of ice cream or sorbet and place it on a serving plate covered with a thick napkin to absorb the water as it melts.

VANESSA'S BREAD PUDDING
(serves 8)

Vanessa and her husband, Ian, run The Kitchen restaurant in the tiny Cornish fishing village of Polperro. Their delightful, informal restaurant is a favourite with us. Ian does most of the cooking, but Vanessa specialises in the puddings. Her recipe for bread pudding is my idea of heaven and I would much rather eat this than traditional plum pudding – see what you think.

350g/12oz wholemeal breadcrumbs
450ml/¾pt milk
200g/7oz mixed dried fruit
75g/3oz butter, melted
140g/4½oz soft brown sugar
2 small eggs, beaten
Grated rind of ½ orange
15ml/3tsp mixed spice
50g/2oz glacé cherries, halved
Freshly grated nutmeg

Soak the breadcrumbs in the milk for about 30 minutes in a mixing bowl. Add the dried fruit, melted butter, sugar, beaten eggs, orange rind and spice and mix well. Pour half the mixture into a greased 900g/2lb loaf tin, sprinkle over the halved glacé cherries, then add the rest of the mixture. Grate fresh nutmeg over the top and bake in a moderate oven 350°F; 180°C; Gas Mark 4 for about 1¼ hours. Turn out onto a warm serving dish and decorate with holly.

Serve warm with vanilla ice cream, chilled cream or one of the sauces on pages 32–3, and cut into slices.

Dumb Cake

An old English Christmas Eve custom was the baking of 'Dumb Cake', a sort of fruit loaf, by any single girl wanting to find out whom she would marry. She made the cake alone and in silence, pricked it with her initials then went to bed, leaving the door open. At midnight, her husband-to-be was supposed to enter and prick his initials on the cake next to hers. A variation involved him coming in and just turning the cake as it cooked in the oven.

Ice Bowl (above) with Lime and Almond Ice Cream (above) and Pink Champagne Sorbet served in lemon shells (page 75)

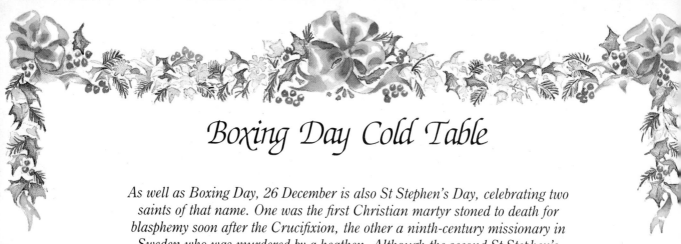

Boxing Day Cold Table

As well as Boxing Day, 26 December is also St Stephen's Day, celebrating two saints of that name. One was the first Christian martyr stoned to death for blasphemy soon after the Crucifixion, the other a ninth-century missionary in Sweden who was murdered by a heathen. Although the second St Stephen's feast day was some way away from Christmas, somehow the two celebrations have become mixed up. The latter St Stephen was made the patron saint of horses for his alleged love of these animals and over the centuries various traditions have been observed on his feast day. Sick animals, especially horses, were brought on pilgrimages to the church built over his grave and in Sweden groups of 'St Stephen's men' used to get up long before daybreak and race from village to village waking the inhabitants with a folk song and expecting to be treated to ale or spirits in return. In Munich men on horseback would ride around the inside of the church during the St Stephen's Day service, their mounts gaily decorated with ribbons, while in other countries horses were fed consecrated bread, salt or corn or blessed in church by the priest. In England, horses were ceremonially 'bled' to get rid of evil spirits, which might cause illness during the following year, and today there are many traditional Boxing Day meets, racing events and sporting fixtures in Britain, which would seem to be a direct link with the old feast of St Stephen.

CURRIED PARSNIP AND APPLE SOUP
(serves 10–12)

This is a lovely warming soup to serve before a cold meal. The apples can be omitted if you wish.

125g/4oz butter
675g/1½lb parsnips, peeled and roughly chopped
1 large onion, chopped
2 small eating apples, cored and roughly chopped
1 large garlic clove
25g/1oz flour
2.5ml/½ scant tsp medium curry powder
1.8 litres/3pt chicken or turkey stock
Salt and freshly milled pepper
300ml/½pt single cream (optional)
Fresh coriander leaves, chopped

Melt the butter in a large saucepan and add the parsnips, onion, apples and garlic. Stir well until the vegetables are moistened with butter, then cover with a lid and cook very gently for about 10 minutes. Remove from the heat and stir in the flour and curry powder. Cook for a further 2 minutes then gradually stir in the stock until well blended. Bring gently to the boil then cover with a lid again and simmer very gently for about 30 minutes until the vegetables are soft. Purée in a blender or food processor until smooth, then season to taste.

Slowly reheat in a clean saucepan and serve hot with swirls of cream and a sprinkling of chopped coriander leaves. Accompany with croûtons if you wish, but anything with a strong flavour, like garlic bread, should be avoided because the soup has rather a delicate flavour.

ALMOND AND CELERY SOUP
(serves 10–12)

1 very large or 2 small heads of celery
50g/2oz butter
1 garlic clove, crushed
2 carrots, thinly sliced
1 small parsnip, thinly sliced
1.8 litres/3pt chicken stock
125g/4oz flaked almonds, toasted
30ml/2tbsp Parmesan cheese
Salt and freshly milled black pepper
Celery salt
300ml/½pt single cream
Paprika to garnish

Take the head of celery apart and wash well. Reserve about 75g/3oz of the delicate inner stalks. Slice the rest of the celery thinly.

Melt 25g/1oz of the butter in a large saucepan and add the sliced celery, crushed garlic, carrots and parsnip. Cover the pan tightly and cook gently for about 10 minutes, or until the vegetables have softened, but not coloured. Pour in the stock and bring gently to the boil. Cover the pan, reduce the heat and simmer for 30 minutes, or until the vegetables are very soft.

Meanwhile, chop 75g/3oz of the almonds very finely in a blender or processor. Add a ladle of stock from the soup pan and process again, then rub through a sieve. Purée the rest of the soup, then rub through a sieve to remove any stringy pieces of celery. Blend the almond mixture into the smooth celery purée, then stir in the cheese. Season with salt, pepper and celery salt. Cover with a lid and leave on one side for at least 4 hours to allow the flavours to develop.

To serve, stir in the cream and the reserved celery cut into crescent-shaped slivers. Reheat the soup gently, but don't let it boil again. Check the seasoning and serve garnished with the remaining 25g/1oz of toasted almonds and a sprinkling of paprika.

SPROUT AND HAZELNUT SOUP
(serves 10–12)

Don't be tempted to use cooked left-over sprouts in this soup because both the flavour and colour will be unacceptable. Any nuts may be used.

125g/4oz butter
1 large onion, chopped
675g/1½lb fresh Brussels sprouts, roughly chopped
225g/8oz hazelnuts, chopped
225g/8oz potato, chopped
2 celery sticks, chopped
2 bay leaves
1.8 litres/3pt chicken or turkey stock
Salt and freshly milled black pepper
300ml/½pt single cream (optional)

Melt the butter in a large saucepan and add the onion. Cook until soft but not brown, then add the sprouts, hazelnuts, potato, celery and bay leaves. Cover with a lid and leave to 'sweat' over a very gentle heat for a few minutes, then stir in the stock. Slowly bring to the boil stirring frequently, then simmer until the sprouts are just tender – don't

overcook or the lovely green colour will be lost. Blend or process until smooth, then season to taste. Serve hot in warmed soup bowls with a swirl of cream and accompanied by extra toasted hazelnuts or croûtons.

☆ FREEZING SOUP

All these soups may be cooked in advance and frozen in rigid containers, but take care when re-heating not to overcook, as they all have rather delicate colours and flavours. Freeze without the cream and add just before serving.

CREAM OF CHESTNUT SOUP
(serves 10–12)

This rich soup is ideal for serving on Boxing Day before the cold buffet. It can be made 2 or 3 days before Christmas and kept in the fridge; it also freezes very well. Dried, canned or frozen chestnuts can be used as well as chestnut purée. A couple of small cooking or eating apples may be included to make Chestnut and Apple Soup.

450g/1lb chestnuts, when prepared
75g/3oz butter
1 small onion, chopped
1 medium parsnip, chopped
2 sticks of celery, chopped
3 medium carrots, chopped
1 large potato, chopped
1 bay leaf
1.8kg/3pt chicken or veal stock
300ml/½pt single cream
Salt and freshly milled black pepper
Generous pinch of ground mace
90ml/6tbsp Madeira or dry sherry
Croûtons or chapons to garnish

Roughly chop the chestnuts. Melt the butter in a large saucepan and fry the onion until soft. Add the parsnip, celery, carrots, potato and bay leaf. Stir well, cover tightly with a lid and 'sweat' the vegetables for about 10 minutes, then add the chestnuts. Pour on the stock and bring slowly to the boil. Cover and simmer gently for about 45 minutes until the vegetables and chestnuts are soft. Purée the soup in a blender or processor, then reheat gently, stirring in the cream. (Don't allow the soup to boil again.) Season with salt, pepper and mace and flavour to taste with Madeira or sherry.

Serve immediately garnished with croûtons or chapons.

TO MAKE CHAPONS

Cut slices of white bread into small cubes. Shake them in a polythene bag with crushed garlic to flavour the bread, then fry in walnut oil until golden brown and crisp.

COLD POACHED FRESH SALMON

Salmon is still a very traditional Christmas dish in the north of England and Scotland. It is an expensive dish, but a whole fish costs slightly less than fish bought by the piece and is very suitable for a large party. Allow 125–175g/4–6oz per person, but remember when calculating the amount you will need that the head accounts for about one fifth of the total weight.

1 salmon 2.8–3.6kg/6–8lb
Salt and freshly milled pepper
Olive oil
1 medium onion, sliced
1 carrot, sliced
3 sprigs parsley, including their stalks
Bouquet garni
2 bay leaves
6 whole peppercorns
2 lemon slices
300ml/½pt dry white wine
5ml/1tsp salt

Gut and clean the salmon if your fishmonger has not already done so, taking care to remove the gills as well as the insides. Run your thumb down the backbone of the fish to remove the dark membrane which lies against it. Wash the salmon under cold running water. Do not remove the head or tail but snip away the fins with scissors and trim the tail into a sharp 'V' shape. (This is known as vandyking the tail.) Leave the salmon unscaled as the scales will give extra protection during cooking and make the skin easier to remove afterwards. Dry thoroughly and season the inside of the fish. Wrap in a cloth dipped in olive oil or brush the surface of the fish with oil to protect it during cooking. Place gently on the trivet of a fish kettle or on a rack in a large roasting tin and put in all the other ingredients. Add enough water to just cover the fish and cover with a lid or a sheet of kitchen foil. Set the kettle or roasting tin on the lowest heat possible and bring to the boil as slowly as possible. Immediately boiling point is reached, remove from the heat without removing the lid and put on one side to cool in the cooking liquor.

Lift the salmon out and drain on kitchen paper while it is still slightly warm. This makes it easier to skin. Peel off the skin very carefully to preserve the contrasting brown and pink flesh and remove the eyes with the handle of a teaspoon. Place on a large oval platter or tray, then decorate all over with thinly sliced cucumber to represent the scales, or with a line of cucumber and lemon or hard-boiled egg slices running down the length of the fish. You can make more complicated patterns with shapes cut from cucumber and aubergine skin, red pimentoes, hard-boiled egg, black olives and stuffed green olives. Coat the decorated fish with aspic to fix the decorations and give a very professional finish, then finish with piped cream cheese and parsley sprigs.

Serve with a bowl of mayonnaise (see following recipes) and a cucumber salad. I also like serving warm Hollandaise sauce with cold salmon for a change (see page 39).

TO SERVE A WHOLE SALMON

Fish servers are a great help when dividing up a whole salmon, but a knife and cake slice will do. Cut the salmon along the backbone to release the flesh, then cut into portions along the side uppermost. When this side has been eaten, turn the fish over and slice the other side into portions.

MAYONNAISE
(makes approximately 450ml/¾pt)

Mayonnaise can be made in advance and kept in a cool place for up to 1 week.

3 large egg yolks
2.5ml/½tsp dry English mustard
2.5ml/½tsp sea salt
Large pinch of cayenne pepper
23–30ml/1½–2tbsp white wine vinegar or lemon juice
450ml/¾pt good-quality olive oil

Before starting to make the mayonnaise, make sure all the ingredients are at room temperature. Warm your mixing bowl and dry it carefully. Beat the egg yolks in the bowl for 1–2 minutes until thick and creamy. Add the seasoning and all but a few drops of the wine vinegar or lemon juice and beat for a further 1–2 minutes. Add the oil in drops, whisking continuously. Continue adding the oil very slowly until the mayonnaise begins to thicken. Once this has happened, the oil can be added a little faster. When the mayonnaise has thickened too much to whisk, add a few more drops of lemon juice or wine

vinegar and continue adding the oil until it has all been absorbed. Check the seasoning and adjust if necessary. Serve immediately in a chilled bowl, or store in a screw-top jar in a cool place.

☆ Make sure you add the oil drop by drop at the beginning or the mayonnaise will curdle. If this *does* happen, start again with a fresh egg yolk in a clean basin and add the curdled mixture to this drop by drop, then continue adding the oil as before.

HERBY MAYONNAISE

Make a basic mayonnaise as before, then blanch 12g/½oz each of fresh parsley, chives, tarragon and chervil and 25g/1oz young spinach and watercress leaves in boiling water for 2 minutes. Drain in a sieve and cool under cold running water. Press out all the moisture and pound to a paste. Mix this into the prepared mayonnaise just before serving with the salmon.

ORANGE MAYONNAISE

Make the basic mayonnaise as before, but beat the egg yolks with the grated rind of 1 orange. Use only 15ml/1tbsp lemon juice and make up the quantity with orange juice, omitting the wine vinegar. Serve with the salmon.

MOUSSELINE MAYONNAISE

Fold in 225ml/7½fl oz lightly whipped double cream into the basic mayonnaise and serve with the salmon.

GARLIC MAYONNAISE

Beat the egg yolks as before with the seasoning, then add 8 crushed garlic cloves, before adding the oil. Continue as before.

OLD ENGLISH PORK AND RAISIN PIE
(serves 10–12)

'Stand pies' have always been traditional fare at Christmas. In Yorkshire pork pies were usually served for breakfast on Christmas morning.

FOR THE JELLIED STOCK
Pork bones from the meat used to make the filling
2 pig's trotters or 1 veal knuckle
1 large carrot, sliced
1 medium onion stuck with 3 cloves
10 whole black peppercorns
3 litres/5pt water
Bouquet garni

FOR THE PASTRY
575g/1¼lb plain flour
2.5ml/½tsp salt
1.25ml/¼tsp icing sugar
1.25ml/¼tsp ground mace
225g/8oz lard
200ml/⅓pt water

FOR THE FILLING
1kg/2¼lb boned shoulder of pork or spareribs, with approx ¼ fat to ¾ lean meat, finely chopped
225g/8oz thinly sliced unsmoked bacon, chopped
5ml/1tsp dried sage
2.5ml/½tsp ground cinnamon
2.5ml/½tsp grated nutmeg
2.5ml/½tsp ground allspice
5ml/1tsp anchovy essence
Salt and freshly ground black pepper
125g/4oz stoned raisins
1 egg, beaten

First make the stock. Put all the ingredients in a large pan, bring to the boil and skim off any scum. Cover the pan and simmer steadily for 3–4 hours. Remove the bouquet garni and strain off the stock into a clean pan and boil down until about 450ml/¾pt stock is left. Season with salt and add more pepper if you like. Cool and skim off any fat. The stock will set to a delicious firm jelly.

To make the pastry, sieve the dry ingredients into a large mixing bowl. Bring the water and lard to the boil, then pour it quickly into the dry ingredients and mix rapidly together to a smooth dough with a wooden spoon or an electric beater. Leave the dough covered in a warm place until it cools just enough to handle it easily, but do not allow it to go cold or it will disintegrate.

Cut off about a quarter of the dough and keep covered for the lid. Put the remainder into a hinged raised pie mould or an 18cm/7in or 20cm/8in round cake tin with a removable base. Quickly and lightly mould the pastry up the sides of the tin, leaving no cracks. Set on one side.

Mix together all the ingredients for the filling except the raisins. Pack one third of this meat mixture into the pastry case and cover this with half the raisins, repeat this once more then finish with the remaining meat mixture, letting it round up over the rim of the tin a little.

Roll out the remaining dough for the lid. Brush the edges of the pastry case with a little beaten egg and press the lid on firmly. Trim the edges using the surplus pastry for decoration. Cut a hole in the centre of the lid and decorate the top with pastry

holly or ivy leaves. Make a Christmas rose from the scraps of pastry to cover the central hole. Brush over with beaten egg and bake in the centre of a pre-heated oven at 400°F; 200°C; Gas Mark 6 for 30 minutes to firm the pastry and give it a little colour, then reduce the oven temperature to 325°F; 160°C; Gas Mark 3, and cook for a further 1½–2 hours to allow the meat to cook. Cover the pie with foil or brown paper if it is browning too quickly.

Remove the pie from the oven and leave to cool a little. Take it out of the mould or cake tin and brush the sides with beaten egg. Return to the oven for about 10 minutes to colour. When the pie crust is lightly brown all over, remove from the oven, lift off the rose and pour in some of the warmed jellied stock using a small funnel or a cone of cardboard. This stock will fill the gaps left by the shrinking meat and will turn to jelly when cold. Replace the rose and leave the pie for at least 24 hours in a cool place before serving.

If you wish, decorate the pie with small gold paper leaves and surround its base with a wreath of Christmas greenery and more gold paper leaves or small baubles. Fresh, brightly coloured flowers would also look very effective or Christmas roses if you are lucky enough to have them growing in your garden. A raised pie provides a spectacular centre-piece for a cold buffet table so be as imaginative as you like.

☆ ALTERNATIVE FILLINGS

Other meat and game can be used to make raised pies using the same method. Try a combination of veal and ham and/or egg, venison and veal, phea-sant, partridge, hare, chicken and ham, turkey and ham, duck, or goose.

The Story of Rosemary

Rosemary, with its attractive scented grey-green leaves, was once one of the most popular Christmas decorations, but fell from popularity in the nineteenth century. The herb was believed to have acquired its scent when Jesus' swaddling clothes were hung over it and is a symbol of remembrance and friendship.

Boxing Day Cold Table: (left to right) Rich Old English Christmas Trifle (page 97), Cold Poached Fresh Salmon (page 80), Pear and Ginger Tart (page 97), mixed green salad, Christmas Salad (page 93), Old English Pork and Raisin Pie (page 81)

CHRISTMAS SPICED BEEF
(serves 12–15)

This is a very traditional way of cooking beef for a celebratory dish dating back to Elizabethan times and particularly popular in Scotland and the north of England. In the past, the most enormous pieces of meat weighing 18kg/40lb or more would be prepared and served over the twelve days of Christmas. Spiced beef is not a complicated dish, but it must be planned ahead as the joint needs to be cured for 10 days before cooking. It is marvellous for entertaining as it keeps for 3 weeks and makes a handsome addition to the cold buffet table.

Saltpetre can be bought from good chemists.

2.5–2.7kg/5½–6lb topside or best-quality silverside, cut and tied for salting
2.5ml/½tsp ground mace
2 whole cloves
12g/½oz allspice berries
25g/1oz whole black peppercorns
10ml/1dsp dried thyme
125g/4oz dark brown sugar
125g/4oz sea salt
6 bay leaves
25g/1oz juniper berries
10ml/2tsp saltpetre
1 bouquet garni
2 carrots, chopped
2 celery sticks, chopped
1 onion, chopped
2 wineglasses port
300ml/½pt beef stock

Grind the mace, cloves, allspice, peppercorns and thyme together. Stir this mixture into the sugar.

Untie the beef, cover with the spice and sugar mixture, then re-roll and tie up with string. Place in a very clean earthenware casserole crock or dish, cover and leave in a cold place for 24 hours.

Next day, grind the salt, bay leaves and juniper berries to a coarse powder and mix in the saltpetre. Rub this mixture into the beef and let it steep in the earthenware casserole, or crock, in a cold place for a further 9 days. Turn the meat and rub it with the gradually liquefying spice mixture every day.

When the cure is completed, rinse the meat under a cold running tap and wipe off any remaining spices with kitchen paper. Put the joint into a heavy casserole which holds it snugly. Surround it with the bouquet garni and chopped vegetables and pour over the port and stock. Cover tightly with a sheet of greaseproof paper, a sheet of foil and then the lid.

Cook in a low oven 275°F; 140°C; Gas Mark 1 for 4½–5 hours, or until very tender. Don't open the casserole as it cooks, or the moisture will escape. Let the joint cool in the unopened casserole until lukewarm, then take out the meat and drain it well. Save the cooking liquor to enrich soups and stews.

Dry the beef with kitchen paper, wrap in grease-proof paper and put between two boards with a 1.4–1.8kg/3–4lb weight on top. Leave it like this in a cold place overnight.

Next day it is ready to eat, or it can be wrapped in clean greaseproof paper and foil and stored in the fridge until needed. Bring the meat back to room temperature at least 2 hours before serving. Carve into paper-thin slices and arrange on a large platter. Garnish with finely sliced gherkins and encircle the platter with sprigs of mistletoe and evergreen.

Serve with plenty of pickles and strong English mustard. Potatoes baked in their jackets are an excellent accompaniment. The Avocado and Cream Cheese Dip on page 106 also makes a perfect partner.

COLD GLAZED TONGUE
(serves approx 16)

Some butchers only sell ox tongues that have been trimmed of bone and gristle; if this is the case, you need 2 tongues 1–1.4kg/2½–3lb in weight instead of 1.8–2.3kg/4–5lb as in this recipe which is the untrimmed weight. Try to buy tongues that have been smoked as well as salted, because the flavour is particularly good.

2 pickled ox tongues weighing 1.8–2.3kg/4–5lb each
1 large onion, sliced
2 large carrots, sliced
2 sticks celery, chopped
1 bouquet garni
1 sprig fresh rosemary
2 blades mace
5ml/1tsp black peppercorns
30ml/2tbsp Madeira
15ml/3tsp gelatine powder
23ml/1½tbsp water
450ml/¾pt cooking liquor, reduced

Rinse the tongues and soak in cold water overnight, changing the water once.

Next day, rinse well, then place in a casserole which just holds them. Cover with cold water and bring to the boil. Skim, then taste the water; if it is very salty, drain and cover with fresh water. Bring to the boil again, then add the vegetables, herbs,

mace and peppercorns. Cover with a lid and cook in a pre-heated cool oven 300°F; 150°C; Gas Mark 2 for about 4 hours or until very tender. Test with a skewer in the root ends of the tongues.

Drain the tongues when cooked, reserving the cooking liquor, and skin them while still hot. Remove all the small bones, fat and gristle if the tongues are untrimmed, then curl them round each other in a large smooth-sided round cake tin or soufflé dish while still warm. Skim off all the fat from the reserved cooking liquor and reduce to a scant 450ml/¾pt by boiling rapidly. Taste and adjust seasoning as necessary, then stir in the Madeira.

To glaze the tongues, melt the gelatine in the water then blend in the cooking liquor. Pour over the tongues to fill in any gaps, reserving any excess.

Put a plate which just fits inside the tin over the tongues and press them down with heavy weights on top of the plate. Leave overnight in a cold place until the meat and jelly are set. Chill the excess jelly separately. To serve, unmould the tongues on to a round serving dish. Garnish the dish with bay or laurel leaves and fresh cranberries, orange slices or whole kumquats. Accompany with English Mustard, Caper, Cumberland, Orange and Horseradish, or Raisin Sauce (pages 86 and 90).

TO SERVE TONGUE HOT

Tongue is also delicious served hot: Christmas Eve would be a suitable festive occasion. After cooking, carve it in thin slices while still hot and arrange on a large warm serving dish. Pour a suitable hot sauce over it, cover the dish with foil and place in the oven for about 10 minutes to heat through.

Serve extra sauce separately. Cumberland, Orange and Horseradish, English Mustard, Caper or Raisin Sauce are all delicious with hot or cold tongue.

☆ TONGUE-PRESS

Traditional tongue-presses usually measure about 12.5–15cm/5–6in in diameter and will take one tongue. A smooth-sided round cake tin or soufflé dish of similar size will do just as well.

Dipping Day

Christmas Eve is often called Dipping Day in Sweden because many families still go through the ritual of 'doppa y grytan' – dipping rye bread in the hot cooking liquid from the Christmas ham.

ENGLISH MUSTARD SAUCE
(serves 8)

This is a splendid sauce for serving with ham, tongue, spiced beef or brawn.

50g/2oz butter
50g/2oz flour
600ml/1pt milk
10ml/2tsp prepared English mustard
Salt and freshly milled pepper

Melt the butter in a saucepan and stir in the flour. Cook gently for 2 minutes, then remove from the heat and add the milk gradually, stirring all the time. Return to the heat and cook gently, stirring continuously until the sauce is thick and creamy. Simmer gently for 5–10 minutes then stir in the mustard. Season to taste with salt and pepper. Serve warm.

CAPER SAUCE
(serves 8)

Serve with tongue or spiced beef.

25g/1oz butter
25g/1oz flour
450ml/¾pt milk
15ml/1tbsp caper vinegar (from the jar of capers)
20ml/2tbsp capers, chopped or whole
Salt and freshly milled pepper
30ml/2tbsp double cream

Make a basic white sauce as for Mustard Sauce above, and when it is cooked, stir in the caper vinegar and the whole or chopped capers. Season to taste. Simmer for a further 5 minutes, then stir in the cream. Serve very hot.

SMOKED SALMON

If you are having a Christmas party or are expecting a number of guests to drop in over the Christmas period, a whole side of smoked salmon is a wonderful addition to the larder. Scotch salmon is a luxury, but don't economise by buying cheap imported fish which will be rubbery and tasteless. Offcuts from the side of salmon can be used to make mousses, creams, pâtés, quiches, fillings for vol-au-vents, pancakes and sandwiches, soups and savoury ices.

TO SLICE

Cut off any fins from the side of salmon with scissors, then cut off 6mm/¼in all the way round the salmon where the flesh and skin meet at the edge.

Slide a sharp knife under the group of fine bones which are usually found on the surface of the thicker end of each side (the head end), and remove. Slide your forefinger down the salmon just above the group of bones you have removed and you will feel a lot of little bones. Pull these out with a pair of eyebrow tweezers.

Cut the salmon into diagonal slices about 5cm/2in wide, as thinly as possible, slanting the knife away from the tail end and towards the head. Arrange the salmon slices on a flat dish in single layers separated by sheets of plastic film or greaseproof paper.

TO SERVE

Allow about 75g/3oz per person.

Arrange the slices of salmon on individual plates or on a large platter. Serve with wafer-thin slices of buttered brown bread with the crusts removed, and lemon quarters. Some people like freshly milled black or white pepper with their smoked salmon.

The Story of Mistletoe

Mistletoe played an important part in certain Druid rites linked with human and animal sacrifice. The Druids regarded the 'Golden Bough' as the healer of all things and because it grew on oak trees it was believed to hold the life of the tree through the winter. Those attending the sacrificial rites are said to have taken home sprigs of the mistletoe to put over their doors to promote fertility, protect against witchcraft and work miracles of healing. Kissing under the mistletoe is peculiar to Britain and may have something to do with the pagan belief of its powers of fertility. In the old days, the man plucked a berry from the bough each time he kissed a girl; when all the berries were gone, the kissing stopped! In Scandinavia mistletoe was the plant of peace, and enemies who met under it would lay down their arms and declare a truce.

In spite of a Christian myth that the Cross was made from mistletoe wood and the plant then shrank to its present size from shame, mistletoe remained irredeemably pagan. It was not allowed inside churches, although at one time an exception was made at York, where mistletoe was ceremonially carried into the Cathedral on Christmas Eve and laid on the high altar, after which a universal pardon was proclaimed in the city. However, even today, mistletoe is rarely used in church decorations.

SMOKED TROUT

After Scotch smoked salmon, this is the most delicious of smoked fish to me and is now an affordable price. Small, hot-smoked trout and the newer cold-smoked pink rainbow trout or salmon trout can both be eaten without cooking.

TO FILLET AND SERVE A SMALL SMOKED TROUT

Cut off the head and tail and fins and remove the skin. Cut down the spine with a sharp knife and lift out the bone. Re-form the fish into its original shape and arrange on an individual plate, or large platter. Allow 1 fish per person. Serve with thin brown bread and butter and lemon quarters. Accompany with Horseradish Cream (page 72) and freshly milled black pepper or a dash of cayenne.

TO SLICE AND SERVE LARGE SMOKED TROUT

Slice and serve as you would smoked salmon, allowing about 75g/3oz per person.

CHRISTMAS HAM BAKED IN A HUFF

This old-fashioned way of baking ham in a flour and water or 'huff' paste dates back to medieval times. The juices and flavour are completely sealed in the paste case so the ham remains moist, full of flavour and there is less shrinkage. It can be finished off with a variety of glazes or beautifully crumbed with homemade dried breadcrumbs. You can use two large sheets of foil to wrap the ham up in a parcel instead of the huff paste if you wish, but you will not get such a good result. Try to buy a smoked ham which has a particularly good flavour.

1 whole ham 4.5–6kg/10–14lb
1.4kg/3lb flour
750ml/1½pt cold water

Scrape the ham well with the back of a knife, removing any rust from the underside. Place in a very large pan, bowl or bucket and cover with cold water. Soak overnight, changing the water at least once. Next day, drain off the water, rinse well and dry with a clean tea-towel.

Put the flour in a large mixing bowl and mix to a paste with the water. Roll out on a floured board and place the ham in the middle. Wrap around the ham and seal firmly wetting the edges with water.

Transfer to a large roasting tin and bake in a preheated moderate oven 350°F; 180°C; Gas Mark 4 allowing 25 minutes per 450g/1lb. When cooked, break open the huff case with a small hammer or rolling pin. Remove the ham and strip off the skin, finishing with a glaze or with breadcrumbs.

Serve hot or cold displayed on a large serving platter or a special raised stand. Finish off with a ham frill (page 88) and decorate as you wish (page 88). Encircle the platter or ham stand with a wreath of rosemary and bay leaves. Gold-painted rosemary or bay leaves also look very attractive.

Serve with a suitable sauce (page 90) and accompany with Spiced Orange Rings, Spiced Kumquats or Prunes in Port (pages 90–1).

TO GLAZE THE CHRISTMAS HAM

After stripping off the skin, score the ham fat into diamond shapes using a sharp knife. Insert a whole clove into each diamond if wished and spread or sprinkle your chosen glaze over the whole surface of the ham. Return to a fairly hot oven 400°F; 200°C; Gas Mark 6 for about 30 minutes until sizzling and golden brown.

SUGGESTIONS FOR GLAZES

MUSTARD AND SUGAR
30ml/2tbsp prepared English mustard
60ml/4tbsp soft dark brown sugar
300ml/½pt cider

Coat the ham with the mustard and press on the sugar. Pour the cider around the ham in the roasting tin and finish off in the oven.

MUSTARD AND REDCURRANT JELLY
30ml/2tbsp Dijon mustard
40ml/2 heaped tbsp redcurrant jelly
20ml/2dsp brown sugar
Juice of 2 oranges

Mix all the ingredients to a thick paste and spread over the surface of the ham. Finish off in the oven.

SUGAR, SPICE AND WHISKY
75g/3oz butter
175g/6oz brown sugar
5ml/1tsp ground cinnamon
45ml/3tbsp whisky
300ml/½pt Guinness

Mix the butter, sugar, spice and whisky together to make a thick paste. Press onto the ham then pour the Guinness into the roasting tin. Finish in the oven.

HONEY, ORANGE AND GINGER
45ml/3tbsp clear honey
45ml/3tbsp fresh orange juice
2.5ml/½tsp ground ginger
15ml/1tbsp grated orange rind

Mix all the ingredients together and spread all over the ham. Finish off in the oven.

SUGAR AND SPICE
225g/8oz Demerara sugar
5ml/1tsp ground ginger
5ml/1tsp ground mixed spice

Mix all the ingredients together and sprinkle over the ham. Finish off in the oven.

HONEY AND VINEGAR
45ml/3tbsp clear honey
45ml/3tbsp white wine vinegar

Stir the honey and wine vinegar together and spread over the ham. Finish off in the oven.

HONEY AND MUSTARD
45ml/3tbsp clear honey or golden syrup
45ml/3tbsp dry English mustard

Mix the honey with the mustard powder and spread on the ham. Finish off in the oven.

MARMALADE
Spread 75–90ml/5–6tbsp tangy orange or ginger marmalade all over the ham. Finish off in the oven.

BREADCRUMBS AND SUGAR
75g/3oz dry breadcrumbs
60ml/4tbsp brown sugar
2.5ml/½tsp ground mace or nutmeg

Mix all the ingredients together and sprinkle over the ham. Finish off in the oven.

BREADCRUMB, PARMESAN AND REDCURRANT JELLY
50ml/3 heaped tbsp jelly
75g/3oz dry breadcrumbs
75g/3oz grated Parmesan cheese
Freshly milled black pepper

Brush the surface of the fat of the ham with redcurrant jelly. Mix the breadcrumbs and cheese together and season well with black pepper. Press the mixture onto the redcurrant jelly and finish in the oven.

SUGGESTIONS FOR DECORATING A HAM

Remove the ham from the oven after glazing and serve hot, or leave to cool completely.

Decorate the ham with apple or pineapple rings, orange slices, candied fruits, blanched almonds, fried bread shapes or sprigs of rosemary, laurel or bay leaves. Finish by attaching a ham frill to the bone.

TO MAKE A HAM FRILL

Cut a piece of paper into a rectangle about 15cm/6in × 12.5cm/5in. Fold the paper in half along the longer length, then cut a fringe on the folded side at 6mm/¼in intervals and 5cm/2in in length. Wrap around the ham bone and fasten with sellotape or pins. White paper makes a very clean professional frill, but green, blue, silver or gold metallic paper is very effective and festive, particularly if you decorate the ham with small coloured tree baubles.

The Boar's Head

The boar's head was once a regular dish at Christmas and is still served with ceremony at a few places in Britain. Among the pagans the boar was sacrificed to the sun god, for the injury that animal was fabled to have done him; Adonis was said to have died of a wound from a boar's tusk. The Saxons offered a boar to the sun at the winter solstice, while a similar observance existed in Rome. With its round face and golden bristles the boar was a solar symbol in Scandinavia, where boars' heads were also eaten at Christmas time.

Boar hunts were a popular Christmas sport in the Middle Ages so the boar's head with an apple or orange stuck in its mouth became the traditional centrepiece of the medieval English nobleman's Christmas table. It was set on a gold or silver dish and carried in procession to the accompaniment of drums, trumpets or carols and decorated with sweet rosemary and bay. The custom still survives at Queen's College, Oxford, on the Saturday before Christmas where the boar's head is borne in on a silver salver by the chef accompanied by a herald and a procession of singers.

The Christmas Ham

Traditionally villages all over Europe have fattened their pigs for Christmas, curing them as hams and using the fresh meat for brawns. The Christmas ham is the main dish on Finnish tables served with a cabbage or beetroot salad and casserole dishes of carrots, liver, swedes or candied potatoes.

Decorated Christmas Ham (page 87 and above)

CUMBERLAND SAUCE

This spicy sauce is delicious at Christmas served with hot or cold gammon, tongue, duck, goose and all kinds of roast game and raised pies. It keeps very well for several weeks, so you can prepare it well in advance and make a large quantity to last the festive season.

2 oranges
2 lemons
450g/1lb redcurrant jelly
150ml/¼pt ruby port
Pinch of salt
10ml/1 level dsp dried English mustard powder
10ml/1 level dsp ground ginger or ground mace

Using a potato peeler, remove the rind from the oranges and lemons, then cut into very fine strips, about 1cm/½in long and as thin as possible. Boil the shredded rind in enough water to cover for about 5 minutes, then drain well in a sieve. Cool the rind under cold running water, then drain again and leave on one side.

Place the redcurrant jelly in a saucepan with the port and melt over a very gentle heat for about 10 minutes, stirring to dissolve the jelly.

Mix the salt, mustard and ginger with the juice of 1 of the lemons to make a smooth paste, then add the juice of the two oranges. Finally stir in the redcurrant mixture and reserved strips of the orange and lemon rind. Pour into jars and cover. Cool, then store in the fridge. Serve chilled.

ORANGE AND HORSERADISH SAUCE
(serves 6–8)

30ml/2tbsp redcurrant or quince jelly
Grated rind and juice of 1 lemon
Grated rind and juice of 3 oranges
10ml/2tsp creamed horseradish
5ml/1tsp French mustard
5ml/1tsp wine vinegar

Place the redcurrant or quince jelly in a small saucepan and heat gently until it melts. Add the grated rind and juice of the lemon and oranges and stir well. Add the remaining ingredients and heat through.

Serve hot or cold with ham, pork, game or raised pies.

RAISIN SAUCE
(serves 6–8)

25g/1oz butter
25g/1oz flour
300ml/½pt ham stock
60ml/2fl oz dry cider
50g/2oz seedless raisins
2 sticks of celery, finely chopped (optional)
Pinch of grated nutmeg
30ml/2tbsp whipping cream

Melt the butter in a saucepan and stir in the flour. Cook for about 2 minutes then gradually add the stock, stirring continuously. When smooth, stir in the cider, followed by the raisins and celery, if using. Taste and adjust seasoning if necessary adding the nutmeg as well. Cook very gently for 10–15 minutes, then stir in the cream just before serving.

SPICED ORANGE RINGS

Oranges were once preserved in this way when citrus fruit was scarce and expensive. They make an excellent accompaniment to cold pork, ham, duck, goose, tongue, pheasant and partridge and a really attractive present. Whole kumquats can be preserved in the same way.

6 medium thin-skinned oranges
Water to cover
450ml/¾pt white wine or cider vinegar
350g/12oz sugar
5ml/1tsp whole cloves
3 blades mace
7.5cm/3in stick of cinnamon
Few extra cloves, to finish

Wash the oranges well and dry them. Cut into slices about 6mm/¼in thick and remove the pips. Place the slices in a saucepan and barely cover with water. Bring to the boil, cover and simmer for about 30 minutes, or until the orange skin is just tender. Drain the cooking liquor into a clean pan and add the vinegar and sugar. Tie up the spices in a piece of muslin and add to the pan. Heat very gently, stirring frequently, until the sugar has dissolved, then bring to the boil. Boil hard for 10 minutes, then place the well-drained orange rings, a few at a time, in the syrup. Simmer gently for 25–45 minutes until the rind is very tender and translucent, but the oranges have not disintegrated.

Remove the orange slices with a draining spoon

and pack carefully into clean warm jars. Discard the spices then boil up the syrup again for about 10 minutes, until it begins to thicken. Leave until cool but not cold, then pour over the oranges to completely cover them and fill the jars. Add a few cloves to each jar, then cover and seal. Store in a cool dark place for at least 6 weeks, before serving.

SPICED KUMQUATS

Boil the vinegar with the spices and sugar for 10 minutes as before. Place 675g/1½lb whole kumquats in the syrup and simmer very gently for about 20 minutes until the fruit is tender. Continue as before.

Serve the kumquats whole or cut across in halves as an accompaniment to tongue, ham, roast game and duck.

PRUNES IN PORT

Brandy or sherry can be used as alternatives to the port in this recipe, which is absolutely delicious with cold pork and ham and cold or hot roast goose, or the prunes can be eaten with cream as a dessert.

450g/1lb large prunes, unpitted
Fresh tea to cover
20ml/2dsp light soft brown sugar
Port, brandy or sherry

Wash the prunes well in hot water and soak in tea overnight with the sugar. Next day, put the prunes and soaking liquor into a saucepan and bring slowly to the boil. The prunes will be plump and there will be little liquid left. Pack the prunes into clean, dry jars and when cool, cover with port, brandy or sherry and any left-over liquid. Seal the jars tightly and store in a cool dark place for 3 months. Serve as an accompaniment to cold pork, ham, tongue, spiced beef and poultry.

APPLE AND JUNIPER JELLY

Make this jelly with windfalls in the autumn. Crab apples can also be used. Apple jelly is a good base to which you can add a number of different spices, herbs and flavourings. The combination of apple and juniper is particularly good with pork, ham and strongly flavoured meats like venison and hare.

1.4kg/3lb cooking apples
Water to cover
12g/½oz juniper berries

Wash and cut up the apples. Tie the juniper berries in a piece of muslin and place with the apples in a large pan. Pour over enough water to cover, then simmer very gently for about 1 hour, or until the apples are very soft and pulpy. Strain through a jelly-bag overnight.

Next day, measure the juice and place in a clean pan. Add 450g/1lb sugar for each 600ml/1pt apple juice, then heat very gently until the sugar has completely dissolved. Bring to the boil and boil rapidly until setting point is reached. Pour into clean warm jars, cover and store until needed.

MY FATHER'S SPECIAL FRUIT CHUTNEY

My father invented this mellow chutney because he couldn't find a sweet fruit recipe that he thought was really good and could be made at any time of the year. Well, here it is and all our family love it. The chutney is good with all Christmas cold meats and makes a very acceptable gift.

225g/8oz red or green tomatoes
300ml/½pt malt vinegar
900g/2lb cooking apples when prepared
225g/8oz onions, peeled and quartered
450g/1lb dried apricots
450g/1lb pitted dates
450g/1lb stoned raisins
125g/4oz preserved stem ginger
6g/¼oz garlic
3g/⅛oz dried chillies
675g/1½lb soft brown sugar
50g/2oz cooking salt
23ml/1½tbsp mixed spice

Skin the tomatoes (if they are red) and cut into small pieces. Put in a large pan with the vinegar. Cook very slowly for about 30 minutes, until soft. Peel, core and quarter the apples. Mince them with the onions, apricots, dates, raisins, ginger, garlic and chillies, then add to the pan. Stir in the sugar, salt and spice and heat gently, stirring well, to dissolve the sugar. When the sugar has dissolved completely, increase the heat and bring to the boil. Simmer for about 1 hour, or until the chutney is thick and rich in colour. Pour into clean, warm jars, cover and seal. Store in a cool dark place for several months if you want a really mature chutney, otherwise leave for 1 month at least before serving.

Making gifts for friends and family solves all the nightmare problems of Christmas shopping and the results have a special quality; a sense of time and trouble taken, which is much nearer to the true spirit of Christmas.

Pot chutney, jelly and preserves in small jars and top with Christmas wrapping paper or material. Label and attach gift tags with ribbon to the top of the jars.

ROWAN JELLY

Rowanberries are the fruit of the mountain ash, common throughout Britain. They are best picked in October and make a reddish-orange jelly with a tangy bite which is excellent with game birds, hare and venison as well as pork, ham and goose. A jar would make the perfect present for the discerning gourmet.

450g/1lb rowanberries
450g/1lb cooking apples
Water to cover
Juice of 1 lemon
Sugar

Remove any stalks from the berries and wash well. Wash, then cut up the apples, including the peel and cores. Put rowanberries and apples in a pan with enough water to just cover. Simmer very gently for about 30–40 minutes, or until soft and pulpy. Strain fruit through a jelly-bag overnight.

Next day, measure the juice, including the lemon juice, and put in a saucepan. Heat very gently, stirring in 450g/1lb sugar to each 600ml/1pt juice, until it has completely dissolved. Bring to the boil and boil rapidly for about 15 minutes until setting point is reached, a temperature of 220°F; 110°C on a sugar thermometer.

Pour into clean warm jars, cover and store.

Julklapp

On Christmas Eve it is the custom in North Germany and Scandinavia for an unseen person to fling open the door and throw in a large parcel wrapped in many layers of paper for each member of the family, which when opened reveals a very small gift. In Sweden the Julklapp is addressed to just one person and is usually a very tiny, but expensive present wrapped in layers and layers of paper.

SALADS FOR THE BUFFET TABLE

RED CABBAGE, DATE AND BLACK GRAPE SALAD
(serves 10–12)

900g/2lb red cabbage
8 juniper berries, crushed
Grated rind of 1 large orange
90ml/6tbsp orange juice
75g/3oz fresh or dried dates, finely chopped
225g/7½fl oz natural yoghurt
Salt and freshly milled black pepper
575g/1¼lb black grapes
Fine strips of orange rind to garnish

Shred the cabbage finely. Crush the juniper berries and mix with the orange rind and juice. Add the chopped dates, then gradually beat in the yoghurt. Season with a little salt and plenty of black pepper and leave to stand for about 1 hour.

Toss the cabbage in the dressing about 1 hour before serving and leave to stand. Remove the seeds and skin from the grapes, then stir most of them into the cabbage just before serving, reserving a few for decoration. Sprinkle a few strips of orange rind and the remaining grapes over the salad and serve slightly chilled.

TANGY PEAR, PINEAPPLE AND RADISH SALAD
(serves 10–12)

2 bunches of radishes
1 small pineapple
8 ripe dessert pears
Juice of 2 lemons
300ml/½pt sour cream
150ml/¼pt mayonnaise
Salt and freshly milled black pepper
5ml/1tsp ground cardamom
15ml/1tbsp chopped parsley

Trim and clean the radishes and cut into slices. Place in a bowl of cold water, cover with clingfilm and leave to chill for 2 hours in the fridge.

Remove the skin and core of the pineapple and cut into chunks. Peel and core the pears and cut into long strips. Put the pears into a bowl with the lemon juice and toss lightly. Place the pineapple in a

separate bowl. Cover both bowls with clingfilm and leave to chill for 2 hours.

Just before serving, mix the sour cream and mayonnaise together and season with salt, pepper and cardamom. Drain the pears and carefully fold into the dressing with the pineapple. Pile into a pretty serving dish or salad bowl. Drain the radishes and dry well. Arrange over the top of the salad and serve sprinkled with parsley.

QUAILS' EGG AND BACON SALAD
(serves 12)

12 quails' eggs or small hens' eggs
4 sticks of celery, diced
A selection of salad leaves, washed, dried and torn into
   even-sized pieces
1 large parsnip, grated
4 large carrots, grated
8 rashers of smoked streaky bacon
120ml/8tbsp single cream
5ml/1tsp prepared English mustard
5ml/1tsp sugar
20ml/4tsp white wine vinegar
Salt and freshly milled black pepper

Place the eggs in a saucepan of cold water, bring to the boil and simmer for 3 minutes. Drain and cover with cold water. When the eggs are cold, carefully remove the shells and cut in half.

Arrange a mixture of the vegetables on a shallow serving platter. Cut the bacon into snippets and fry gently until the fat begins to run, then increase the heat to crisp the bacon. Remove and leave on one side to cool.

To make the dressing, whisk the cream, mustard, sugar and vinegar together. Season to taste. Pour over the salad, add the bacon, reserving a little for garnishing and toss together lightly. Arrange the eggs on top of the salad and scatter with the reserved bacon. Serve at once.

CHRISTMAS SALAD
(serves 10–12)

450g/1lb fresh young spinach leaves or a mixture of lamb's
   lettuce or watercress
75g/3oz walnuts, roughly chopped
105ml/7tbsp walnut oil
3 slices wholemeal bread, cut into small cubes
30ml/2tbsp sunflower oil

10ml/2tsp tarragon vinegar (page 95)
5ml/1tsp French mustard
175g/6oz Stilton, farmhouse cheddar or chèvre, coarsely
   crumbled
1 large pomegranate to garnish
25g/1oz walnut halves, to garnish

Wash and thoroughly dry the greenstuff. Tear any large leaves into pieces. Roast the chopped walnuts in a moderate oven 350°F; 180°C; Gas Mark 4 for about 15 minutes, then leave to cool.

Heat 75ml/5tbsp walnut oil in a frying pan and add the cubed bread. Fry until evenly golden and crisp, then keep warm. Mix the remaining walnut oil with the sunflower oil, the vinegar and the mustard and place in a salad bowl. Add the greenstuff and toss gently until well coated with dressing.

Just before serving sprinkle over the cheese, the chopped walnuts and the warm croûtons and toss again lightly. Scoop out the seeds from the pomegranate, discarding the shell and yellow pith. Scatter the seeds and the walnut halves over the salad to garnish. Serve immediately.

Traditional Boxing-Day Customs

December 26 is devoted to recovering from the excesses of the previous 2 days with the accent on informality, visiting, outdoor and indoor sports, entertainments, pantomime and parlour games.

In Holland 'Second Christmas Day' often includes a play, a concert or dinner in a restaurant. In Hungary, cinema and theatre-going feature in towns and fortune-telling in villages. The circus, a direct descendant of the Roman games, is a common event of the day in many European countries and in Britain, Boxing Day saw the opening of the pantomime season which became inseparable from Christmas in the Victorian period, although its origins can be traced back to the great court masques and plays.

Parlour games, another peculiarly British institution, were also very popular with the Victorians and today indoor games are still a traditional part of the relaxed atmosphere of Boxing Day. Sports and outdoor games make a welcome and healthy change from overeating and overdrinking. In Australia there is surfing, swimming, tennis and cricket and each Boxing Day sees the start of the Sydney to Hobart yacht race. In Canada there is skating, skiing, tobogan-ning, ice hockey and curling. The Irish go in for hurling, horse racing and greyhound coursing, while in Britain there is a full programme of football fixtures and horse racing as well as traditional fox hunting and the Boxing Day shoot.

CRIMSON SALAD
(serves 10–12)

2 heads of radicchio
8 spring onions, finely chopped
8 large tomatoes, skinned, seeded and chopped
150ml/10tbsp tarragon-flavoured olive oil (page 95)
Juice of 1 orange
2 cloves of garlic, crushed
30ml/2tbsp chopped parsley
Salt and freshly milled black pepper
125g/4oz salted peanuts, roughly chopped
30ml/2tbsp fried breadcrumbs to garnish (optional)

Wash and thoroughly dry the radicchio leaves, then tear into even-sized pieces. Place in a salad bowl with the spring onions and chopped tomatoes.

To make the dressing, mix the oil with the orange juice, garlic and parsley. Season to taste and mix thoroughly again. Stir in the chopped peanuts. Spoon the dressing over the prepared salad ingredients and toss lightly together. Sprinkle with the fried crumbs if you wish and serve immediately.

WARM POTATO SALAD WITH SOUR CREAM DRESSING
(serves 10–12)

1.4kg/3lb small new potatoes
225ml/7½fl oz dry white wine
22ml/1½tbsp garlic-flavoured olive oil (page 95)
Salt and freshly milled black pepper
2 onions, red-skinned if possible
4 hard-boiled eggs, roughly chopped (optional)
450ml/¾pt sour cream
12ml/1 heaped dsp mild English mustard
Juice of ½ lemon
Chopped chives to garnish

Cook the potatoes in their skins in boiling salted water for 10–15 minutes until tender. Drain well and dry over a gentle heat, then slice if they are larger than bite-size. Mix the wine with the oil, then sprinkle over the potatoes. Season lightly and keep warm. Chop the onions finely and mix with the hard-boiled eggs if using.

To make up the dressing, mix the mustard and lemon juice with the sour cream. Pour into a large warmed serving dish. Just before serving, mix the chopped onion and egg mixture into the potatoes. Fold the potato mixture into the dressing and garnish with chives.

ENDIVE, ORANGE AND HAZELNUT SALAD
(serves 10–12)

The flavour of curly endive is rather bitter like chicory and is best used with other ingredients in a mixed salad. The combination with orange is excellent.

2 heads of curly endive
2 bunches of watercress
6 large oranges
2 small red peppers
50g/2oz hazelnuts
150ml/5fl oz natural yoghurt or sour cream
15ml/1tbsp sugar (optional)
60ml/4tbsp thyme-flavoured sunflower oil (page 95)
30ml/2tbsp lemon juice
Salt and freshly milled black pepper

Wash the endive and watercress and dry thoroughly. Tear gently into pieces and place in a salad bowl. Grate the rind of 1 orange into a small bowl, squeeze in the juice and reserve. Remove all the peel and pith from the remaining 5 oranges and divide into segments. Add these to the endive. Seed the red peppers and cut into thin strips. Add to the salad bowl. Toast the hazelnuts lightly under a hot grill, rub off the loose skins in a tea-towel and chop roughly.

To make the dressing, mix the yoghurt, or sour cream, with the sugar, if using, and reserved orange rind and juice. Beat in the oil gradually and stir in the lemon juice. Season well.

Just before serving, spoon the dressing over the salad and toss lightly. Sprinkle with the nuts and serve immediately.

ALISON'S GARLIC DRESSING
(serves 10–12)

This recipe was given to me by the daughter of a book illustrator friend of mine. Garlic-flavoured oil (page 95) can be used, but omit the whole garlic.

30ml/2tbsp white wine vinegar or lemon juice
5ml/1 scant tsp caster sugar
Salt and freshly milled black pepper
Dijon mustard
90ml/6tbsp sunflower oil
90ml/6tbsp Flora cooking oil
2 large garlic cloves, crushed

Dissolve the sugar in the vinegar or lemon juice. Season well and whisk in the oils. Adjust seasoning as necessary and add the crushed garlic.

HAZELNUT VINAIGRETTE
(serves 10–12)

Use walnut oil for a change if you wish. The sherry vinegar should be a good quality and pale. Use herb-flavoured oils for a change.

60ml/4tbsp sherry wine vinegar
5ml/1 scant teaspoon caster sugar
5ml/1 scant teaspoon salt
Freshly milled white pepper
90ml/6tbsp hazelnut oil
90ml/6tbsp groundnut oil
3 cloves of garlic, peeled

Dissolve the sugar in the vinegar, add the seasoning, then add the oils, whisking vigorously. Cut the garlic cloves in half and add to the dressing. Taste and adjust as necessary. If the vinegar is too strong, add a little more hazelnut oil.

☆ I find it best to make salad dressings in a screw-topped jar, which can then be shaken easily.

HERB VINEGARS

Herb vinegars originated as an attempt to store herbs for winter – the result was delicious vinegars in themselves. They are very simply made by steeping 50–75g/2–3oz bruised leaves from the chosen herb in 600ml/1pt red or white wine vinegar for 6–8 weeks. After steeping, strain through a jelly-bag or muslin into a clean warm bottle and add a fresh sprig of the appropriate herb. Seal tightly.

Suitable herbs are tarragon, basil, thyme, rosemary, sage, lavender, marjoram, fennel, mint, dill, salad burnet and lemon balm. Garlic and lemon peel can be added for extra flavour. Use for flavouring salads, salad dressings and sauces.

FLOWER VINEGARS

These subtle-flavoured vinegars are ideal for use in salad dressings and marinades. Rose petals, violets, primroses, cowslips, flowers from herbs, marigolds, elderflowers, broom flowers and nasturtiums all make excellent prettily coloured vinegars. In Elizabethan days, the preserved flowers themselves were used in winter salads, not just the vinegar.

Pick the flowers on a dry day and shake to remove any insects. Half-fill a large jar with the flowers, pressing them down well. Pour over enough white wine vinegar to fill the jar, seal tightly and leave to steep in a sunny place for 2 days. Top up the jar with extra vinegar and leave for at least 10 days. Strain through a jelly-bag or muslin and pour into a clean warm bottle. Seal tightly and store in a cool, dry place.

FRUIT VINEGARS

These are usually made from well-flavoured, fully ripened soft fruits such as raspberries, blackberries, blackcurrants and elderberries. Pick over 450g/1lb fruit and place in a large bowl. Bruise the fruit gently with the back of a wooden spoon and pour over 600ml/1pt white wine vinegar. Cover with a clean cloth and leave to stand for 7 days, stirring every day. Press fruit again and strain through a jelly-bag or muslin, then pour into clean sterilised bottles. Seal tightly and leave to stand in a cool place for at least 3 weeks.

Use in salad dressings and marinades.

HERB AND FLAVOURED OILS

Delicious herb-flavoured oils are useful for salad dressings, sauces, marinades and for frying, grilling and roasting. Many herbs can be used with good results and the method is the same. Select 2 or 3 fresh sprigs of your chosen herb. Crush the leaves a little to release the aromatic oils and place in a bottle. Pour over 5ml/1tsp wine vinegar and 450ml/ ¾pt good-quality oil. Seal tightly and leave to steep for 2–3 weeks in a sunny place, shaking daily. Use as you wish, topping up the bottle each time with fresh oil to cover the herbs, until the herb flavour begins to fade, but don't keep any herb oil more than 6 weeks.

Lavender, thyme, basil, tarragon, rosemary, sage and marjoram and mixtures of these are all suitable. Experiment with different combinations and try including cloves of garlic and chillies. A delicious oil for salads or cooking can be made simply by putting garlic in a jar of olive oil, or placing whole lemons and one cut in half and studded with whole cloves in a large jar of good olive oil.

☆ Flower, fruit and herb vinegars and herb and flavoured oils make unusual and interesting gifts for friends who enjoy cooking. Finish them with hand-written labels suggesting perhaps a few ways of using them, and tie ribbon around the neck of the bottle or jar to attach a gift tag.

RICH OLD ENGLISH CHRISTMAS TRIFLE
(serves 10–12)

The trifle is a very traditional Christmas dish, but this recipe is rather different from the more usual custard and jam confections. The topping is syllabub which has to be started the day before, but is extremely simple. Use exotic fresh fruit such as pineapple, kumquats, mangoes, nectarines and Kiwi fruit for a change.

FOR THE BASE
8 trifle sponges
125g/4oz ratafias
120ml/8tbsp apple or quince jelly
150ml/¼pt medium sherry, Madeira, orange liqueur or Kirsch
450g/1lb mixed fresh fruit, prepared

FOR THE CUSTARD
600ml/1pt single cream
Vanilla pod
6 egg yolks
10ml/2tsp cornflour
50g/2oz caster sugar

FOR THE TOPPING
Finely grated rind and juice of 1½ lemons
125g/4oz caster sugar
45ml/3tbsp brandy
45ml/3tbsp sweet pale sherry or white wine
450ml/15floz double cream

FOR THE DECORATION
Crystallised or fresh fruit slices
Gold, silver or coloured dragées or sugared almonds
Extra ratafias
Small sprigs of fresh rosemary

Cut the trifle sponges in half and spread with jelly, then sandwich together, and arrange in the base of a pretty glass or china bowl. Cover with the ratafias, then sprinkle with sherry or liqueur. Arrange the prepared fruit on top and put to one side.

To make the custard, heat the cream very gently with the vanilla pod until almost boiling. Beat the egg yolks with the cornflour and sugar until pale, remove

Edible gifts: (left to right) My Father's Special Fruit Chutney (page 91), Spiced Orange Rings (page 90), Rowan Jelly (page 92), Herb-flavoured Oil (page 95), Raspberry Vinegar (page 95)

the vanilla pod from the hot cream, then pour onto the egg mixture, stirring continuously. Rinse out the cream pan, leaving a film of cold water in the bottom. Return the custard to the pan and stir well over a low heat until it thickens enough to coat the back of a wooden spoon. Leave to cool before pouring over the trifle. Then leave to cool completely.

To make the syllabub topping, soak the lemon rind with the lemon juice, brandy, sherry or wine and sugar. Stir until the sugar has dissolved, then leave to stand overnight. The next day, strain the mixture into a small bowl. Whip the cream lightly until it is just beginning to hold its shape, then gradually add the liquid, whipping continuously. (Take care not to over-beat.) Spread the topping over the layer of custard and chill well.

Decorate with crystallised or fresh fruit slices, coloured dragees or almonds, ratafias and sprigs of fresh rosemary.

PEAR AND GINGER TART

225g/8oz plain flour
Pinch of salt
125g/4oz unsalted butter
200g/7oz caster sugar
1 egg yolk
30ml/2tbsp ice-cold water
2–3 drops vanilla essence
4 firm dessert pears, halved
50g/2oz preserved stem ginger, chopped
3 eggs
1 level 15ml/1tbsp cornflour
250ml/½pt single cream
15ml/1tbsp Kirsch or Framboise (optional)

Sieve the flour and salt together into a mixing bowl. Cut the butter into the flour until well coated and in small pieces. Rub in with the fingertips until the mixture resembles fine breadcrumbs. Stir in 25g/1oz caster sugar. Mix the egg yolk with the cold water and vanilla essence and stir into the flour mixture. Mix to a firm dough adding more water if necessary. Knead lightly until smooth and chill in fridge for about 30 minutes.

Roll out on a lightly floured board and line a 25cm/10in flan tin. Chill again and then bake blind in a fairly hot oven 400°F; 200°C; Gas Mark 6 for 10–15 minutes. Remove from the oven and take out foil or baking beans and return to the oven for 5 minutes.

Cool the pastry and then fill with the pears. Sprinkle with 125g/4oz caster sugar. Beat the eggs, remaining sugar and cornflour together until almost

white. Stir in the cream, ginger and liqueur, if using. Pour over the pears and bake in the centre of a moderate oven 350°F; 180°C; Gas Mark 4 for 35–40 minutes or until the custard is set.

Serve hot or warm, sprinkled with caster sugar. Accompany with whipped cream or yoghurt.

CHESTNUT AND CHOCOLATE PROFITEROLES
(serves 12)

Unfilled profiteroles can be made up to 3 months in advance and frozen. Open freeze and pack in rigid containers.

125g/4oz butter, cut into pieces
300ml/½pt water
150g/5oz plain flour
10ml/2tsp caster sugar
4 eggs, beaten

FOR THE FILLING
225g/8oz canned chestnut purée
30ml/2tbsp rum
150ml/¼pt double cream

FOR THE TOPPING
225g/8oz good-quality plain chocolate
30ml/2tbsp soft brown sugar
45ml/3tbsp water
125g/4oz butter

Melt the butter in a saucepan with the water and bring to the boil. Sieve the flour and stir in the sugar. Add all at once to the pan after removing from the heat. Stir quickly with a wooden spoon until the mixture is a smooth ball and leaves the side of the pan clean. Gradually beat in the eggs a little at a time until the mixture is smooth and glossy.

Grease 2 or 3 baking sheets and dampen under cold running water. Place teaspoons of the pastry onto the baking sheets, then cook in a hot oven 425°F; 220°C; Gas Mark 7 for about 25 minutes, or until well risen, firm and golden brown. Remove from the oven and make a slit in each bun to allow the steam to escape, then return to the oven for 3–4 minutes to dry out.

To make the filling, beat the chestnut purée and rum together until smooth. Whip the cream until stiff and fold into the chestnut mixture. Spoon into a piping bag fitted with a plain 6mm/¼in nozzle and fill the buns. Leave on a wire rack.

To make the topping, melt the chocolate together with the sugar and water in a basin fitted over a saucepan of simmering water, stirring until you have a smooth sauce. Beat in the butter a little at a time, until the sauce is hot and has a glossy appearance.

Just before serving, pile the profiteroles in a shallow dish, one on top of the other to make a pyramid. Pour the chocolate sauce over them and serve immediately.

Boxing Day Drinks Party

More casual invitations to 'drop in for a drink' are made in the latter part of December and the beginning of January than at any other time of the year. Whether the drink be a simple glass of sherry, a glass of mulled wine or a delicious glass of apple punch, you need to provide your guests with something to nibble. For a small gathering some nuts you have prepared yourself such as Buttered Almonds or Curried Cashews (see pages 102 and 104) will be a pleasant surprise, but with a little forethought and advance planning you can offer a selection of appetising tit-bits for a larger drinks party. None of these need be complicated and I think it is better not to offer a huge variety of food. Concentrate on 2 or 3 delicious savouries, both hot and cold, providing plenty of each one and maybe 2 dips with various accompaniments. Whatever you serve must be very appetising and small enough to eat with your fingers. Always serve hot savouries as hot as possible and well drained if they have been fried. Balsa wood or plastic mini forks are much easier and safer than cocktail sticks. Make sure you provide lots of paper or china plates and piles of mini paper napkins. Sachets of cologne-impregnated finger-wipes are a good idea for coping with greasy fingers. Remember to provide a really good non-alcoholic punch for guests who may be driving or may just prefer not to drink.

WHITE WINE CUP
(serves 12)

The amount given here will serve 20 guests with 1 wine glass each. Double the quantities for more.

3 bottles dry white wine, chilled
60ml/4tbsp orange liqueur
180ml/6fl oz brandy
Good dash of Angostura bitters
Approx 450ml/¾pt tonic water
Cucumber slices to garnish
Pineapple, apple and orange slices
Crushed ice

Mix all the ingredients except the cucumber, fruit and ice in a large bowl about 1 hour before serving. Transfer to large jugs containing crushed ice and add the cucumber and fruit slices just before serving. Pour into frosted wine glasses (page 108).

☆ QUANTITIES OF WINE
If you are providing just 1 wine cup or punch, either hot or cold, you need to allow 2 glasses per head. 1 × 75cl wine bottle serves 5 × 150ml/5fl oz glasses.

MULLED RED WINE PUNCH
(serves 20)

This is an economical but excellent recipe for a party. To save complicated last-minute preparations, the spicy syrup base can be made before Christmas and stored in a covered container in the fridge. It can then be heated and the wine added when required. The quantities of spices and wine may be varied to suit individual tastes and the wine does not have to be of the best quality. I have this wine on the go the whole of the Christmas holiday for unexpected callers – its spicy welcoming smell pervades the whole house.

FOR THE SYRUP BASE
6 large oranges
225g/8oz sugar
5ml/1tsp ground cinnamon
5ml/1tsp grated nutmeg
10ml/1dsp whole cloves
1.8 litres/3pt water

2 bottles dry red wine

Roughly cut up the oranges and place in a saucepan with all the other ingredients. Heat gently until the

sugar has dissolved, then bring to the boil. Simmer gently for about 30 minutes without covering. Strain through a fine sieve. Your syrup base is now ready and can be kept in the fridge until required.

When you want to serve your mulled wine, first bring the syrup to the boil in a large pan, then add the red wine. Warm up again, but don't bring to the boil. Serve in warmed wine glasses.

☆ When you are heating any punch make sure you do *not* bring it to the boil as this will ruin the flavour. The water and spices on their own *can* be boiled.

FRUIT CUP
(serves 20)

This is a good non-alcoholic punch, which you can dress up as much as you like. It can be served hot or cold.

4 lemons
225g/8oz caster sugar
1 litre/2pt boiling water
1 litre/2pt fresh orange or apple juice
1 litre/2pt ginger ale
4 oranges or apples, finely sliced
Crushed ice

Halve and squeeze the lemons, reserving the juice. Put the lemon halves in a bowl with the sugar and boiling water. Stir to dissolve the sugar and leave to get cold. Strain into a jug, add the reserved lemon juice and then the orange or apple juice. Chill well.

Just before serving, add the ginger ale, orange or apple slices and plenty of crushed ice. Serve in frosted glasses to make this drink look even more festive.

Origins of Boxing Day

Christmas is a time when people have always tried to think of others and give money generously to the poor. Boxing Day is said to derive its name from the alms boxes which were placed in churches over the festive period. The day after Christmas was the day these boxes were broken open and the contents distributed to the poor. Also on this day, apprentices and servants broke open the small earthenware boxes in which their masters had deposited small sums. The tradition of giving out Christmas Boxes to postmen, milkmen, dustmen and newspaper boys is all that remains of the custom today.

☆ TO FROST GLASSES

Run a cut lemon around the top edge of the glass, then dip into caster sugar. If you want a coloured frosting, colour the caster sugar with a little edible food colouring. To make a frosted pattern on a glass, paint any design you like with a paint brush and water, or beaten egg-white, then roll the glass in caster sugar. The sugar will stick to the pattern you have painted.

☆ FRUIT-JUICE ICE CUBES

Freeze pure fruit juice in ice-cube trays and add to cold punches and fruit cups just before serving.

☆ FLOWERS, SUMMER FRUITS AND FRESH HERBS IN ICE CUBES

A lovely idea is to preserve small flowers, fruits and sprigs of herbs, especially mint and borage, in ice cube trays ready to pop into cold punches and fruit cups at Christmas parties. Your guests will be delighted.

☆ STORING EXTRA ICE CUBES

Make ice cubes before Christmas and store in strong polythene bags in the freezer. Crushed ice can be stored in the same way; if you want to break it up before using, wrap the polythene bag of ice in a thick towel and hit it with a rolling pin.

APPLE AND ELDERFLOWER PUNCH
(serves 20)

Serve this non-alcoholic punch either hot or cold with as much fruit and herb garnish as you wish. Homemade elderflower cordial can of course be used and will be that much more delicious.

2 bottles Copella apple juice
Approx ¼ bottle Rock elderflower cordial
1 litre/2pt lemonade
Lemon and apple slices and mint to garnish

Place the apple juice in a suitable bowl and add the elderflower cordial to taste. Just before serving, add the lemonade and the fruit garnish. Serve in frosted wine glasses (above).

Fruit Cup (above), Mulled Cider (page 102), White Wine Cup (page 99), Mulled Red Wine Punch (page 99)

MULLED CIDER
(serves 20)

This quantity will make enough to serve in 300ml/½pt glasses. Brandy can be used instead of orange liqueur.

6 small eating apples
24 whole cloves
5 oranges, sliced
5 litres/10pt dry still cider
150ml/10 level tbsp soft light brown sugar
Juice of 5 oranges
Juice of 2½ lemons
15ml/3tsp ground ginger
10ml/2tsp ground nutmeg
2 × 10cm/5in cinnamon sticks
150ml/10tbsp orange liqueur or brandy

Core the apples, keeping them whole, and slit the skin round the centre of each one. Stick 4 cloves in each apple and bake in a moderate oven 350°F; 180°C; Gas Mark 4 for 20 minutes.

Place the sliced oranges, cider, sugar, orange and lemon juice, and spices into a large pan. Heat gently to dissolve the sugar, then bring slowly to serving temperature, but don't allow to boil. Stir in the orange liqueur. Put the baked apples and cloves into a punch bowl and pour over the heated cider. Serve immediately in warmed 300ml/½pt glasses.

BUTTERED ALMONDS
(serves about 20)

Hazelnuts, walnuts, pine nuts, pecans, cashews, brazils and peanuts can also be used, or a mixture.

75g/3oz butter
15ml/1tbsp corn oil
225g/8oz blanched almonds
Sea salt (optional)

Heat the butter and oil in a large frying pan until foaming. Add the almonds and toss over the heat for a few minutes until golden brown on both sides. Remove the nuts with a slotted spoon and drain on absorbent kitchen paper. Sprinkle generously with salt if you wish and leave to cool before serving.

Once the nuts are completely cold, they can be stored in an airtight jar or tin for 6–8 weeks.

☆ *Devilled nuts* are a hot, spicy version prepared as above with the addition of 2.5ml/½tsp cayenne pepper with the salt.

Spiced nuts can be made as before with the addition of 2.5ml/½tsp mixed spice with the salt.

Curried nuts can be made by frying the nuts as before, then sprinkling with a mixture of 5ml/1tsp salt, 10ml/2tsp mild curry powder and 3.75ml/¾tsp ground cumin and frying for another 2 minutes.

ANCHOVY TWISTERS
(makes about 40)

125g/4oz puff pastry
1 egg, beaten
2 × 50g/1¾oz tins of anchovies
A little milk
30ml/2tbsp Parmesan cheese, grated

Roll out the pastry to a 30cm/12in square and trim the edges. Brush with beaten egg, then cut the pastry into quarters. Cut each quarter into 1–2cm/½–¾in wide strips.

Drain the anchovies and cut in half lengthways. Soak for a few minutes in a little milk to reduce the saltiness, then drain well. Lay a piece of anchovy in the centre of each pastry strip and press lightly to make it stick. Sprinkle with the cheese. Twist each strip once or twice and lay on a greased baking tray lined with non-stick silicone paper. At this stage, you can leave the twisters loosely covered in a cool place and cook them at the last minute.

Bake in a preheated hot oven 425°F; 220°C; Gas Mark 7 for about 12 minutes, or until lightly browned. Cool on a wire rack, then store in an airtight container. Serve warm.

WALNUT AND BLUE CHEESE NIBBLES
(makes 20)

150g/5oz Danish blue cheese
25g/1oz unsalted butter
Freshly milled black pepper
40 walnut halves

Crumble the blue cheese in a small bowl and cream it with the butter. Season with pepper. Sandwich the walnut halves together in pairs with the blue cheese mixture and serve in a gold foil or paper sweet case.

☆ Instead of blue cheese try plain cream cheese or one of the many herb-flavoured cream cheeses now available.

STILTON PUFFS
(makes about 24)

These simple hot savouries can be made very quickly and easily using puff pastry trimmings.

225g/8oz puff pastry
125g/4oz Stilton cheese
7.5ml/½tbsp brandy
15ml/1tbsp double cream
25g/1oz walnuts, finely chopped
Beaten egg and salt to glaze

Roll out the pastry on a lightly floured board to 3mm/⅛in thickness. Cut into 5cm/2in squares. Crumble the Stilton into a basin, add the brandy and cream and blend together roughly with a fork, but don't make a paste. Put a little of the cheese mixture into the centre of each pastry square and sprinkle with a few of the chopped nuts. Moisten the edges of the square with a little water and fold over into a triangle. Seal the edges well and crimp them together. Place the triangles on greased baking trays and glaze with beaten egg and salt.

Bake in a pre-heated hot oven 425°F; 220°C; Gas Mark 7 for about 12 minutes, or until each pastry triangle is puffed up and golden brown. Serve hot on a napkin-covered dish.

FRIED STILTON PUFFS

Make into triangles as before, but deep fry in lightly smoking oil until puffed up and crispy. Drain on kitchen paper.

Origin of Punch

Punch is said to come from the Hindu word 'panch', meaning five, a reference to the five ingredients used in its seventeenth-century form. However, it seems to have been well known before this date; Sir Edward Kennel, the Commander-in-Chief of the English Navy, made a huge punch for his ships' crews on 25 October, 1599. He used 80 casks of brandy, 9 casks of water, 25 thousand limes, 80 pints of lemon juice, 1,300 pounds of sugar, 5 pounds nutmeg and 300 biscuits together with a large cask of Malaga. This was served by the ships' boys from a vast marble bowl to 6 thousand guests. Apparently, the fumes were so powerful that the boys had to be replaced every 15 minutes!

Nowadays, punch is usually a mixture of wine or spirits, sugar, lemon juice, cloves and spices and hot water.

CHICKEN AND ALMOND GOUJONS WITH ORANGE MAYONNAISE
(makes about 30)

Dover sole, lemon sole or plaice make excellent goujons and halved scallops can be cooked in the same way.

4 large boned chicken breasts
Seasoned flour
Beaten egg
120ml/8tbsp blanched almonds, very finely chopped
Sunflower oil to deep fry
Orange segments and watercress to garnish
150ml/¼pt orange mayonnaise (page 81)
100ml/3fl oz double cream

Cut the chicken breasts into thin strips about 6mm/¼in wide and 6–7.5cm/2½–3in long. Dust with the seasoned flour, dip into the beaten egg and roll in the chopped nuts to get an even coating. Deep fry in the oil for a few minutes, until golden and tender. Drain thoroughly on absorbent kitchen paper and serve hot in a white napkin-lined basket. Garnish with orange segments and watercress.

Just before serving, lightly whip the double cream, stir into the mayonnaise and serve with the goujons.

DEVILS ON HORSEBACK
(makes 20)

20 large prunes
Red wine, port or water
1 bay leaf
Approx 75ml/5tbsp apricot or apple chutney
10 rashers smoked streaky bacon
Chopped parsley to garnish

Place the prunes in a bowl and cover with hot red wine, port or water. Cover and soak overnight.

Next day, transfer the prunes to a saucepan with the soaking liquor and the bay leaf. Simmer very gently for about 10 minutes until tender, then drain. Allow the prunes to cool, then remove the stones. Dry well on absorbent kitchen paper. Chop up the chutney finely and fill the cavity of each prune. Remove the rind from the bacon and cut each rasher in half. Flatten on a board and stretch slightly with the back of a knife, then wrap each half rasher round a prune. Place on a baking tray and bake in a preheated hot oven 425°F; 220°C; Gas Mark 7 for 7–10 minutes, or under a moderate grill, turning once, until the bacon is crisp. Serve hot.

CURRIED CASHEWS
(serves about 20)

The nuts in this recipe are not fried so are not quite as fattening as the last recipe. Almonds, peanuts, walnuts, brazils, hazelnuts and pine nuts can be used instead of cashews.

225g/8oz unsalted cashew nuts
5ml/1tsp ground coriander
5ml/1tsp ground turmeric
2.5ml/½tsp ground cumin
5ml/1tsp garam masala
Large pinch of ground ginger
Large pinch of ground chilli
Pinch of grated nutmeg
Salt and freshly milled black pepper
2 egg whites

Mix all the spices together on a plate. Break up the egg whites lightly with a fork and dip in the cashews, a few at a time, then roll them in the spices. When they are evenly covered, place on a baking tray and bake in the top of a very low oven 225°F; 110°C; Gas Mark ¼ for about 1 hour, or until the spicy coating on the nuts is quite dry. Leave to cool before serving.

The nuts can be stored in an airtight jar or tin for several weeks.

GARLIC CHEESE AND HERB DIP
(serves about 20)

225g/8oz cream cheese
150ml/¼pt sour cream
1 medium onion, finely chopped
2 cloves of garlic, finely chopped
15ml/1tbsp fresh chives, chopped
15ml/1tbsp fresh parsley, chopped
Salt and freshly milled black pepper
Chopped chives to garnish

Mix the cream cheese with the sour cream and stir in the remaining ingredients. Season to taste and garnish with chives. Chill well before serving.

☆ Soured cream can be made by adding 5ml/1tsp lemon juice to 150ml/¼pt single cream. Leave to stand in a cool place for ½–1 hour.

DEVILLED CRAB DIP
(serves about 20)

350g/12oz cream cheese
60–90ml/4–6tbsp thick mayonnaise
10ml/2tsp chilli sauce
10ml/2tsp Worcestershire sauce
255g/8oz crabmeat, brown and white mixed
Salt and freshly milled black pepper
Pinch of cayenne pepper

Beat the cream cheese until soft, then gradually add the mayonnaise until a soft, creamy consistency is achieved. Stir in the sauces, then fold in the crabmeat. Season to taste with salt and black pepper. Spoon into a shallow serving bowl, sprinkle with cayenne pepper and chill in the fridge before serving.

☆ ACCOMPANIMENTS FOR DIPS

Avoid crisps and fragile biscuits where possible as they break and crumble making the dip look unappetising.

Homemade savoury biscuits, crackers, rye breads or melba toast are excellent, but also provide a selection of crisp raw vegetables (crudités). A large shallow bowl is best for these, where each vegetable can be attractively grouped and ice cubes or crushed ice piled in and among them. Decorate with flowers and herbs. Melon shells also make attractive containers. As well as sticks of carrot and celery the following vegetables are ideal for dips: cauliflower or broccoli broken into florets, tiny Brussels sprouts, strips of fennel, baby button mushrooms, mini sweetcorn, chicory leaves, sticks of cucumber, blanched whole young beans, or mange-tout and strips of red, yellow and green pepper. Hot baby new potatoes are also very popular as are small pieces of fried chicken or turkey breast, scampi, scallops, prawns, cocktail sausages, tiny meatballs, potato cakes, fish cakes and tiny rissoles.

Garlic Cheese and Herb Dip (above) and Devilled Crab Dip (above)

SALMON SAVOURY PUFFS
(makes about 24)

These savoury profiteroles can be filled with many different mixtures of cheese, anchovies, prawns, crab, pâté, chicken, turkey, ham, avocado and leek purée, etc – try experimenting with any left-overs that you might have, using cream cheese, white sauce, mayonnaise or cream to bind together. Season with curry powder, herbs and spices. Brushing with beaten egg mixed with a little Bovril or Marmite before baking makes a good savoury topping. The tops can also be sprinkled with chopped nuts.

FOR THE CHOUX PASTRY
60g/2½oz plain flour
150ml/¼pt water
50g/2oz butter
Pinch of salt
Pinch of cayenne pepper
Pinch of freshly milled black pepper
2 eggs
30ml/2tbsp Parmesan cheese, grated
Beaten egg and salt to glaze

FOR THE FILLING
225g/8oz fresh or tinned salmon
2 hard-boiled eggs, chopped
30ml/2tbsp mayonnaise
5ml/1tsp grated lemon rind
Salt
Pinch of paprika

Sieve the flour on to a piece of greaseproof paper, so that it is easy to tip into the pan. Put the water and butter into a fairly large heavy saucepan and gradually bring to the boil, letting the butter melt before the water boils. When bubbling, draw the pan aside immediately and tip in all the flour at once; if the flour is added gradually, it cooks into lumps. Stir vigorously with a wooden spatula until the mixture is smooth and pulls away from the pan to form a ball. Add salt, cayenne and black pepper to taste and beat again. Cool for a few minutes.

Beat in the eggs one at a time and continue beating for about 3 minutes until the dough looks glossy, then add the cheese. Using a piping bag fitted with a plain 1cm/½in nozzle, pipe small balls of the choux dough on to dampened baking sheets. Allow room for spreading as the choux paste rises quite a lot during baking. Brush the top of each ball with the beaten egg and salt glaze. Bake in a preheated fairly hot oven 400°F; 200°C; Gas Mark 6 for about 15 minutes, or until brown and very crisp

to the touch. Transfer to a wire rack immediately and split the puffs to allow the steam to escape or the pastry will become soggy.

To make the filling, flake the salmon removing any skin and bones. Mix with the eggs, mayonnaise, lemon rind and season to taste. Fill the profiteroles with the salmon mixture and dust with paprika. Serve while still warm.

AVOCADO AND CREAM CHEESE DIP
(serves 20)

Make this a short time before serving to avoid discoloration.

2 large ripe avocados
30ml/2tbsp lemon juice
10ml/2tsp grated onion
1 clove garlic, crushed
125g/4oz cream cheese
60ml/4tbsp thick natural yoghurt
30–60ml/2–4tbsp mayonnaise
A dash Tabasco sauce
5ml/1tsp paprika
Salt and freshly milled white pepper

Peel and halve the avocados. Remove the stones and blend the flesh in an electric blender or processor with the lemon juice. Add the onion and garlic, then gradually blend in the cream cheese, yoghurt and mayonnaise to a smooth cream. Season to taste with Tabasco, paprika, salt and pepper. Place in a shallow serving bowl and cover tightly with clingfilm. Store in the fridge until needed.

YOGHURT AND STILTON DIP
(serves about 20)

175g/6oz Stilton cheese
150ml/¼pt double cream
300ml/½pt natural yoghurt
15ml/1tbsp brandy (optional)
15ml/1tbsp fresh parsley, chopped
Salt and freshly milled black pepper
A dash of Tabasco
5ml/1tsp paprika

Mash the Stilton until soft. Lightly whip the cream and mix with the cheese. Stir in the yoghurt, brandy if using and parsley and season to taste with salt, pepper, Tabasco and paprika. Turn into a shallow serving bowl and chill well before serving.

New Year's Eve Dinner Party

Before the New Year can be welcomed in, the Old Year's evil and bad luck must be banished so that everyone can start with a clean slate. The commonest way was to burn the evil ceremonially. In some districts of Holland, Christmas trees are collected for huge bonfires; some countries burn effigies of the Old Year and others ritually buried the dead twelve months of the year. Sober folk may choose to contemplate the coming year in church at Watch Night services, but throughout the world people generally welcome in the New Year in a fashion similar to Scotland's, with balloons and funny hats, streamers and 'Auld Lang Syne', drinking, dancing and much merry-making. Many of these customs and practices, which seem just part of the fun today, have pagan implications. The buffoonery, funny hats and streamers recall the Roman festivals of Saturnalia and Kalends as well as the medieval Lord of Misrule. The practice of holding hands in a circle to sing 'Auld Lang Syne' goes back to the pagan meetings round a stone circle. The very sentiment of the song – not written originally for the New Year – is in tune with the ancient belief that at the New Year ancestors return to the family hearth. As midnight strikes across the world, glasses are filled and raised in a toast to the New Year and to the health and happiness of family and friends. It is a comforting thought that our ancestors were passing round steaming bowls of wassail to signify friendship and goodwill all those centuries ago.
Parties for New Year's Eve can take several forms, but perhaps the most pleasant is a fairly formal dinner for a few special friends, followed by a bowl of punch, Wassail Cup (page 118), or Het Pint (page 115) to celebrate the New Year, served with a few traditional dishes for the 'first-footers'.

POTTED SMOKED TROUT
(serves 8)

Smoked salmon or mackerel may also be used in this very simple recipe, which can be made well in advance and stored in the fridge.

350g/12oz smoked trout, skinned and boned
75g/3oz butter, softened
175g/6oz cream cheese
45ml/3tbsp sour cream or natural yoghurt
Juice of ½ large lemon
Few dashes of Tabasco sauce
3.75ml/¾tsp ground mace
Salt and freshly milled black pepper
75g/3oz clarified butter
Fennel fronds to decorate

Purée the trout in a blender or processor. Gradually add the remaining ingredients, except the clarified butter and fennel, to form a smooth purée. Spoon into a pretty pot or dish and pour over a film of clarified butter. Leave to set in the fridge.

Take out of the fridge at least 1 hour before serving. Serve decorated with fennel fronds and accompanied by hot, dry brown toast.

TO MAKE CLARIFIED BUTTER

From 225g/8oz butter you will get 175g/6oz clarified butter because the moisture and salt are removed. Clarified butter is excellent for frying and grilling because it is less likely to burn when heated.

To clarify butter, cut it up and place in a heavy-based saucepan. Melt over a gentle heat and once melted, continue to cook until it is foaming well. Skim well, then strain through muslin into a basin and leave to settle. Pour into another basin, leaving the sediment behind. Use the butter at once, or melt it down to pour into pots, which should be covered before storing in the fridge for future use.

GRAPEFRUIT AND ORANGE SALAD
(serves 8)

3 large grapefruit
5 large oranges
45ml/3tbsp gin
3–4 pieces of stem ginger (optional)

Cut the grapefruit and oranges in half across and remove the half-segments. Squeeze out any remaining juice. Add the gin and mix together gently. Chill before serving in wide champagne or grapefruit glasses standing on small plates covered with gold or Christmas paper doileys and decorated with stem ginger, if wished. Decorate the plates with sprigs of holly and berries.

WINTER SOUP
(serves 8)

Make this soup from the carcass of the Christmas turkey or goose and any vegetables which you might have left over from the festive season. Remove the peel from an orange and dry out in the oven to make dried orange peel for the recipe.

FOR THE STOCK
1 turkey or goose carcass
Water to just cover
1 large onion, quartered, including the skin
1 bay leaf
Bunch of parsley stalks, tied
Dried peel of 1 orange
12 bacon rinds

FOR THE SOUP
1.5 litres/2½pt strong turkey or goose stock
2 leeks, thinly sliced
2 celery sticks, thinly sliced
3 large carrots, sliced
1 large onion, chopped
2 large potatoes, chopped
Salt and freshly milled black pepper
Celery salt
150ml/¼pt single cream
Chopped parsley to garnish

To make the stock, break up the carcass into pieces and place in a large saucepan. Pour over enough water to just cover, then add all the other ingredients. Bring gently to the boil, then simmer gently for 2 hours. Strain and leave to cool, then remove all the fat.

To make the soup, place the stock in a large pan and add all the vegetables. Season with salt, pepper and celery salt, cover and simmer very gently for 30–40 minutes. Purée in a blender or food processor and reheat gently. Adjust seasoning to taste and stir in the cream. Sprinkle with parsley and serve.

If serving this soup for lunch or before a light main course, accompany with grated cheese and croûtons or chapons (page 80).

HONEY AND MUSTARD ROAST PORK
(serves 12–15)

A splendid leg of home-produced pork is as traditional at Christmas time as roast turkey or goose. It can also be a good buy and ideal for a large family gathering.

This is an old recipe where the joint is prepared and left overnight in its coat of honey, mustard and spices. Any meat left over is really excellent cold.

2.7–3.6kg/6–8lb leg of pork
1 large garlic clove
75ml/5 level tbsp Dijon mustard
75ml/5 level tbsp thick honey
30ml/2tbsp vegetable oil
Pinch of dried thyme
Pinch of dried marjoram
Pinch of dried sage
Pinch of ground ginger
Freshly milled black pepper
75g/3oz butter
Coarse salt

The day before, remove the rind from the pork with a small sharp knife and reserve in the fridge. Weigh the joint and place in a large roasting tin lined with a piece of foil large enough to loosely wrap the joint the next day. Rub the flesh of the meat all over with the cut clove of garlic.

Mix the mustard, honey, oil, herbs and ginger together in a small bowl and season with plenty of pepper. Smear this mixture all over the joint and leave overnight in a cool place.

On New Year's Eve, when you are ready to cook the pork, wrap the foil over the joint and roast at 375°F; 190°C; Gas Mark 5 for 35 minutes per 450g/1lb plus an extra 25 minutes. Open up the foil for the last 35 minutes of cooking time, baste the joint and leave to brown.

Grapefruit and Orange Salad (above)

Meanwhile, dry the reserved pork rind with kitchen paper and cut into strips with kitchen scissors. Place in a roasting tin, then rub with the butter and sprinkle with coarse salt. Cook in the oven with the joint for about 1½ hours, or until crisp.

Serve the leg of pork on a large warm meat platter, together with the crackling. Arrange baked apples and Apricot Stuffing Balls around the pork and garnish with watercress. Accompany with gravy, roast potatoes and vegetables. The pork is delicious cold, served with a fruit sauce (pages 66–70) or fruit pickles (pages 90–2).

TO CARVE A LEG OF PORK

Make a cut in the centre of the joint down towards the bone, then make a second cut close to the first. Angle the knife slightly to free the slice and remove. Continue carving, working either side of the first slice. Slice the meat from the side of the joint parallel to the bone.

APRICOT STUFFING BALLS
(makes 12 balls)

Sage and Onion Stuffing Balls can also be served with the pork (see page 65).

125g/4oz dried apricots, soaked overnight
125g/4oz celery, finely chopped
175g/6oz fresh white or wholemeal breadcrumbs
2.5ml/½ level tsp dried sage
Large pinch mixed spice
25g/1oz melted butter
Salt and freshly milled black pepper
1 small egg
15ml/1tbsp Dijon mustard

Drain the apricots well and chop finely. Put them in a mixing bowl and add the celery, breadcrumbs, sage, spice and butter. Season well and mix together thoroughly. Beat the egg with the mustard and use to bind the stuffing mixture together; if necessary, moisten with a little stock or milk. Shape into 12 balls and roll in a little flour.

An hour before the pork is cooked, arrange the stuffing balls around the joint and continue cooking as before, removing the foil as before.

The stuffing balls can be prepared the day before and kept in the fridge overnight or they can be frozen. They can also be cooked in a separate tin, or fried if this is easier for you.

CHÂTEAU POTATOES
(serves 8)

The name comes from Châteaubriand as this type of potato is often served with Châteaubriand steak. They are also very good with roast meat, poultry and game. New potatoes can also be used, but leave them whole and don't blanch first.

900g/2lb old potatoes, peeled
60ml/4tbsp olive oil or clarified butter
Salt

Cut the potatoes into pieces a little smaller than the normal size for roast potatoes. Trim off the sharp edges to make ovals. Blanch for 7 minutes in boiling salted water, then drain well.

Heat the oil or butter in a shallow casserole or sauté pan and add the potatoes. Cook over a moderate heat until golden brown, shaking the casserole occasionally to stop them from sticking. Season lightly with salt, cover with a lid and finish in a fairly hot oven 400°F; 200°C; Gas Mark 6 for 10–12 minutes. The potatoes should be crisp on the outside and tender in the centre.

SAVOY CABBAGE WITH FENNEL
(serves 8)

Any cabbage can be used instead of savoy, but the latter is so lovely and crisp.

1.3kg/2½lb savoy cabbage, finely shredded
30ml/2tbsp olive oil
1 medium onion, finely chopped
2 garlic cloves, crushed
Salt and freshly milled black pepper
100ml/3½fl oz sour cream (optional)
5ml/1tsp fennel or caraway seeds

Gently heat the oil in a large heavy-based saucepan and soften the onion for 5 minutes. Add the garlic and fry for another couple of minutes, then stir in the shredded cabbage. Season with salt and pepper, cover with a lid and cook for 10 minutes, stirring once or twice so that it cooks evenly.

Stir in the cream if you wish and toss the mixture with two forks, sprinkling in the fennel or caraway seeds and adjusting the seasoning if necessary. Serve immediately.

Hogmanay

Ever since the Reformation, the Scots have always celebrated New Year's Eve rather than Christmas. When the Protestant reformers first attacked the traditions of Christmas, the Scots took it to heart more than the English. They cut back heavily on Christmas celebrations, transferring them instead to the New Year. The English went on happily celebrating both Christmas and the New Year!

Traditionally Hogmanay is a communal celebration and people used to gather in the streets in Scottish towns. Bonfires were lit, torches were waved and tar barrels burnt to celebrate the Old Year being burnt out before the New could begin. During these ceremonies the Scots enjoyed the traditional drink of Hogmanay, het pint, to toast the New Year.

Inside the house, Hogmanay was the time for putting everything in order before the New Year arrived. The whole house had to be swept and polished, clothes mended, clocks wound up, sheets changed, pictures straightened, borrowed things returned and debts paid. Special Hogmanay food was prepared; oatcakes, cheeses, shortbread, black bun, treacle bannocks and gingerbread loaves, with plenty of whisky and wine to drink. The fire was piled up high; the bigger the flames, the greater the luck to come.

On the stroke of midnight the head of the house used to open the front door or windows until the last stroke of the church clock's bell had died away, to let out the Old Year and let in the New. As the midnight bells rang out, trays were banged, household bells rung, and pots clanged to drive out any evil spirits lurking in the dark corners of the rooms. Family and friends would cross arms and join hands in a circle to sing Robert Burns' 'Auld Lang Syne', drink more het pint and wait for the first-footer, before staggering off to bed.

CARROTS WITH RAISINS
(serves 8)

Carrots like this go particularly well with roast pork, turkey and chicken. The dish reheats well, so can be made well in advance.

75g/3oz large, seeded raisins
50g/2oz butter
30ml/2tbsp olive oil
1 garlic clove, crushed
900g/2lb carrots, finely sliced
Salt and freshly milled black pepper
Generous pinch of nutmeg or ground mace
Juice of 1 large orange
30ml/2tbsp chopped parsley

Soak the raisins in lukewarm water for 15–20 minutes. Melt the butter in a heavy-based saucepan, add the oil and fry the garlic for a few minutes. Add the carrots, stir well, then season with salt, pepper and nutmeg or mace. Pour over the orange juice and add the drained raisins, then cover the pan tightly and cook over a very low heat for about 30 minutes until the carrots are tender, just shaking the pan and turning the ingredients occasionally. Take care not to let the carrots brown or to let the pan burn dry; add a splash of stock or water if necessary. The vegetables should absorb most of the oil, butter and orange juice during cooking. If there is more than a spoonful of the liquid left in the pan at the end of the cooking time, remove the lid and cook for a few minutes more until it evaporates.

When ready to serve, season the carrots again to taste if necessary and sprinkle with parsley.

BRAZIL-NUT MERINGUE CAKE
(serves 8)

Hazelnuts, walnuts and almonds can be used instead of brazil nuts for a change. Toast the nuts in a moderate oven and grind in a coffee or nut mill, a blender or a processor.

5 large egg whites
300g/10oz caster sugar
5–6 drops of vanilla essence
5ml/1tsp vinegar
175g/6oz toasted ground brazil nuts

FOR THE FILLING
5 large egg yolks
2.5ml/½tsp cornflour
25g/1oz caster sugar
23ml/1½tsp brandy
180ml/6fl oz milk
60g/2½oz plain chocolate, coarsely grated
Sieved icing sugar to finish

Grease 2 × 20cm/8in sandwich tins and line the bases of the tins with greased silicone or grease-proof paper.

Whisk the egg whites until stiff, then add the sugar, 15ml/1tbsp at a time. Continue beating until the mixture is very stiff and stands in peaks. Whisk in the vanilla essence and vinegar, then, using a metal spoon, lightly fold in the ground brazil nuts. Divide the mixture evenly between the two prepared tins and smooth the top with a palette knife. Bake in the centre of a moderate oven 375°F;

190°C; Gas Mark 5 for 35–40 minutes, until firm to the touch. The top of the meringue will be crisp and the inside soft like a marshmallow. Leave to cool a little then turn out onto a wire cooling rack and remove the base papers.

While the meringue cakes are cooking you can prepare the filling. Put the egg yolks in the top of a double boiler, or in a bowl over a pan of hot water, with the cornflour, sugar and brandy and mix together. Stir in the milk and cook until thick, stirring all the time with a wooden spoon. Stir in the chocolate until melted and the mixture is smooth. Remove from the heat and transfer the mixture to a bowl to cool.

To assemble the cake, invert one meringue base onto a serving plate. Spread the chocolate mixture evenly over the base and top with the second meringue. Chill in the fridge before serving.

Dredge liberally with sieved icing sugar.

CHRISTMAS PANCAKES
(serves 8)

The pancakes can be made ahead, wrapped and refrigerated, then reheated the next day, or can be frozen. They are piled on top of each other in this recipe and should be served by cutting in wedges like a cake.

FOR THE PANCAKES
125g/4oz plain flour
Pinch of salt
12g/½oz caster sugar
Grated rind of 1 medium orange
1 large egg
150ml/¼pt milk ⎱
150ml/¼pt water ⎰ mixed together
30ml/2tbsp melted butter
Little extra butter for cooking

FOR THE FILLING
225g/8oz cream cheese
1 egg, beaten
25g/1oz caster sugar
Finely grated rind of 1 orange
Finely grated rind of 1 lemon
70ml/7dsp homemade mincemeat (page 52)

FOR THE TOPPING
4 egg yolks
125g/4oz caster sugar
45ml/3tbsp brandy or rum

To make the pancakes, sieve the flour and salt together into a basin, then stir in the sugar and orange rind. Make a well in the centre of the flour and add the eggs. Gradually beat in the eggs and the milk and water mixture until a smooth batter is formed. If possible leave the batter to stand for a couple of hours.

Just before cooking the pancakes, stir the melted butter into the batter. Cook the pancakes in a heavy-based medium-sized frying pan, using a little melted butter to prevent them from sticking to the pan. Pour in a little batter, tilting the pan until it covers the base. When the surface is set turn the pancake over and cook the other side for a few seconds. Slide each cooked pancake out of the pan onto a warmed plate with sheets of greaseproof paper between them to prevent them from sticking together. Cover with foil and keep warm over a saucepan of simmering water. The mixture will make about 8 pancakes.

To make the filling, cream the cheese with the beaten egg, sugar and orange and lemon rind until smooth. Spread 7 pancakes with a little of this filling followed by 10ml/1dsp of mincemeat and pile them into a stack. Top with the remaining pancake.

To make the topping, whisk the egg yolks with the sugar and brandy or rum in a basin over a saucepan of hot water until thick and frothy. Spoon this over the pancakes and place under a hot grill until golden brown and bubbling.

Serve immediately with ice cream or clotted cream.

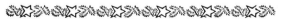

First-footing

This was once familiar to everyone in Scotland, a large part of the north of England and some parts of the south. The first person to set foot in a house in the New Year will decide its luck for the year. It is generally agreed that to bring good luck this person should be a male who is not cross-eyed, flat-footed, blind or lame. Each area has its own ideas about the 'lucky' colour of the first-footer's hair, but all agree that it should never be a woman. However, it is possible to cancel the bad luck by sprinkling salt on the fire!

A first-footer should enter the house by the front door carrying coal, bread and salt, symbolising warmth, life and hospitality, and a sprig of evergreen and mistletoe. He should leave by the back door, thus taking good luck right through the house. He is generally expected to kiss all the women under the mistletoe, share a drink with the party and wish the family a happy New Year.

TO FREEZE AND REHEAT PANCAKES

Freeze the cooled pancakes separated by grease-proof paper and wrapped in polythene. Defrost by stacking them onto a warm plate with the grease-proof paper between. Cover the stack with foil and place the plate over a pan of simmering water. Alternatively they can be defrosted on a foil-covered plate in a warm oven.

FRUDITÉS WITH A CREAM AND YOGHURT DIP
(serves 8)

Frudités are a sweet version of crudités – instead of serving vegetables with mayonnaise, you serve fruit with a sweet creamy dip. The dish can be a very light and refreshing pudding or an extra treat at the end of the meal.

225ml/7½fl oz double cream
225ml/7½fl oz sour cream or yoghurt
Icing sugar, sieved, to taste
Few drops of vanilla essence
Fresh fruit, prepared

To prepare the dip, whip the two creams together with sugar to taste until standing in soft peaks. Flavour with vanilla essence. Spoon into 8 individual dishes and chill. Prepare a selection of fruit and cut into slices, divide into segments or keep whole depending on the fruit. Arrange the fruit on individual serving plates with the dishes of cream dip in the centre. Sprinkle the fruit immediately with the lemon juice, or gin if you are feeling extravagant.

Serve immediately garnished with small flowers and mint or lemon balm leaves. Accompany with Petticoat Tails (page 117). Use your fingers or small forks to dunk the fruit into the cream dip.

SLOE GIN
(makes about 600ml/1pt)

Sloe gin is a delicious winter warmer and what better time than New Year's Eve to open a new bottle with great ceremony? This traditional country drink makes an ideal gift for a very special person and is even better stored for a year before drinking.

Approx 225g/8oz ripe sloes
15ml/1tbsp sugar
Approx 600ml/1pt gin

Wash the sloes and pick them over removing any rotten ones and any stalks. Prick the fruit well with a silver fork (a darning needle will do) and place in a clean empty bottle. Sprinkle the sugar over them and pour on the gin to fill the bottle. Cork or screw down tightly and leave in a dark place for 3 weeks, shaking the bottle twice daily.

Store for 3 months before straining through muslin, or a paper coffee filter and rebottling.

ORANGE BRANDY
(makes about 600ml/1pt)

Drink this as a liqueur or use as a flavouring for custards, puddings, cakes and sauces. You can use whisky instead of brandy if you prefer.

2 large oranges
125g/4oz caster sugar
600ml/1pt brandy

Thinly pare the rind from the oranges using a potato peeler. Cut into very fine shreds and place in a jar. Squeeze the juice from the oranges and add to the jar with the sugar and brandy. Seal the jar and shake well to dissolve the sugar. Store in a cool, dark place for 1–2 months, shaking the jar occasionally. Strain through muslin, or a paper coffee filter, and bottle. It is then ready to drink.

☆ Left-over brandy-, gin- or vodka-steeped fruit can be added to fruit pies, spooned over ice cream, or made into a sauce for a steamed or baked pudding.

The Punch Bowl

The punch bowl began to take the place of the wassail bowl in the seventeenth century. The wassail bowl, a large communal drinking bowl, was filled with lambswool or spiced ale and carried round the streets and countryside on festive occasions, such as Christmas, New Year and Twelfth Night.

Punch bowls were designed with the glasses hanging from the sides and their ladles often had a coin inserted; a symbol of the coins offered with the wassail in earlier times. Most modern punch recipes are based on wine rather than spiced ale.

New Year's Day Traditions

The Old Year's gone away
To nothingness and night;
We cannot find him all the day
Nor hear him in the night.

In many countries New Year's Day is a time for visiting and for giving presents, as it was in England until the reign of James I. In Russia, Grandfather Frost, the post-Revolution gift-bringer, visits the children on New Year's Day.

While people now make resolutions about their future behaviour, New Year's Day used to be marked by even more rituals to ensure good luck for the household in the coming year. The first sight on New Year's Day was held to be an omen; in northern England to see a man with his arms loaded was lucky; elsewhere beggars and grave diggers brought misfortune. Bavarians thought it bad luck to encounter a cat, but the Scots were delighted to look out of the window and see an animal facing their way; facing the other way meant bad luck.

Games to discover one's fate were popular. In Germany molten lead was dropped into cold water and the resulting shape analysed – a strip might mean a journey, a heart a marriage. In England the shapes indicated the occupation of a girl's future husband. Several countries believed that the shape of the ashes of the previous night's fire could be 'read' first thing on New Year's Day, and in Scotland a brightly burning fire portended prosperity in the coming year, a dull one indicated trouble.

Other customs involved water; the first bucket from the village well was called the cream or flower, and whichever spinster drew this would be married to the most handsome bachelor in the district before the year was out. It was also thought to have special healing properties. Another custom allowed young men and children to dash about with a jug of newly drawn water, which they sprinkled on anyone they met.

In Gloucestershire, farmers still light dawn fires in their fields on New Year's Day; there are thirteen – one for Our Lord and twelve smaller fires for the Apostles. The fire for Judas is stamped out immediately. Wassailing the apple trees is the oldest New Year custom and in Bavaria coins are tied around trees with ribbon to make them more fruitful.

New Year's Day is now a public holiday in 125 countries and most people are happy to spend it recovering from the excesses of the previous night. Few people now believe in the old superstitions and beliefs, but most still intend to turn over a new leaf at the start of a New Year.

CRÈME DE CASSIS

The blackcurrants for this recipe should be plump and juicy. If they come from the garden pick a handful of fresh young leaves at the same time and steep them with the fruit. They add a surprising amount of flavour.

A splash of cassis is added to a glass of chilled dry white wine to make the refreshing French drink 'Kir', but it is a delicious liqueur on its own.

675g/1½lb ripe blackcurrants
450g/1lb sugar
5cm/2in piece of cinnamon stick
3 whole cloves
6 blackcurrant leaves if available
1 bottle brandy

Pick over the blackcurrants and wash them. Shake them dry in a colander and place in a bowl. Add the sugar and crush with a fork until the juices run. Pack the fruit in a wide-mouthed jar, adding the spices and the bruised blackcurrant leaves. Top up with brandy, then seal tightly.

Leave to steep in a sunny place for at least 1 month, shaking the jar from time to time. After a month, strain through muslin and pour the liqueur into clean bottles. Seal tightly and drink when you wish.

APRICOT BRANDY
(makes about 750ml/1¼pt)

Nectarines and peaches may be made into a liqueur in the same way as above – you will need 3–4 ripe fruits. Sweet ripe plums can also be used.

450g/1lb fresh ripe apricots
450g/1lb sugar
750ml/1¼pt brandy

Wash the fruit and halve it. Remove the stones, reserving them, then pack in a wide-mouthed sterilised jar, layering the fruit with sugar to cover over each layer. The fruit should be tightly packed. Screw the top of the jar on loosely and leave for 4 days. Remove the kernels from the apricot stones and chop them. Add to the apricots in the jar and pour over sufficient brandy to cover the fruit. Seal the jar tightly and leave to steep for at least 6 months at room temperature.

The liqueur may be drunk immediately, but is better stored for a further 6 months, if you can bear it!

WHISKY PUNCH
(serves 8)

Serve with Black Bun and Petticoat Tails (page 117) at the stroke of midnight to welcome the 'first-footer'.

Thinly pared rind and strained juice of 2 large lemons
225g/8oz lump sugar
1.8 litres/3pt boiling water
1 bottle whisky

Put the rind and juice of the lemons with the sugar into a punch bowl. Pour on the boiling water and stir until the sugar has dissolved completely. Add the whisky. Stir well and serve with a ladle.

RASPBERRY RATAFIA
(makes about 1 litre/1¾pt)

Raspberries make a rich, fruity, deep pink and deliciously warming liqueur. It also tastes superb in a Christmas trifle, or added to chilled white wine.

450g/1lb raspberries
900ml/1½pt vodka or gin
5–6 blanched almonds, crushed
Few drops of almond essence
450g/1lb sugar
600ml/1pt water

Pick over the berries, then pack into a wide-mouthed jar. Bruise the berries gently with the back of a wooden spoon and pour over the vodka or gin. Add the crushed almonds and the essence, then seal the jar tightly and leave to stand in a cool place for 1 month, shaking occasionally.

At the end of this time, make a syrup by dissolving the sugar in the water and boiling for 15 minutes. Leave to cool. Open the jar containing the fruit and alcohol and strain through muslin, pressing the fruit to extract as much juice as possible. Stir the sugar syrup into the fruit liqueur, then pour into clean sterilised bottles. Store in a cool place for 6 months before drinking.

HET PINT
(serves 8)

This spiced ale mixed with eggs and whisky used to be carried through the streets of Scotland in great copper kettles to welcome in the New Year. It was also drunk before a wedding and when a baby was about to be born. Het Pint is a deliciously warming drink to offer the 'first-footer' and to make New Year's Eve go with a swing.

2.4 litres/4pt pale ale
5ml/1 heaped tsp nutmeg, freshly grated
Sugar to taste
3 large eggs
300ml/½pt whisky or brandy

Pour the ale into a large saucepan and add the freshly grated nutmeg. Heat gently to just below boiling point, then stir in sugar to taste. Whisk the eggs thoroughly in a bowl and *gradually* add the hot ale, to make sure the mixture doesn't curdle. Lastly, add the whisky or brandy and reheat in the saucepan before quickly pouring back and forth into tankards or mugs until it froths. Serve immediately with Black Bun and Petticoat Tails (page 115).

SAUTERNES SUPPER CUP
(serves 8)

Serve this refreshing drink to celebrate the arrival of the New Year with Black Bun and Petticoat Tails (page 115).

2 bottles Sauternes
240ml/8fl oz vodka
Rind of 2 large oranges
2 bottles cheap dry champagne, or dry sparkling wine or dry sparkling cider
Canned apricot halves, in apple juice

Cut the orange rind into very fine shreds with a sharp knife. Soak in the vodka for 2 hours, then strain into a glass or punch bowl. Set this bowl in another larger one packed with ice. Pour over the chilled Sauternes and just before serving, pour in the champagne, sparkling wine or cider.

Place 2 or 3 ice cubes into each serving glass, followed by an apricot cap. Ladle the wine cup over the ice and serve.

BLACK BUN
(serves 10–12)

A bun is an old Scottish word for a plum cake and Black Bun is a very dark rich fruit cake made traditionally for Hogmanay or New Year's Day, although originally eaten on Twelfth Night. The cake is encased in a pastry shell to prevent the juices and flavour from escaping during baking. This original bread paste was discarded when the cake was eaten, but later the pastry was enriched with fat and became part of the cake.

At Hogmanay gatherings, great slices of Black Bun are washed down with many mugs of Het Pint (page 115). Make the cake at least 2 weeks before serving.

FOR THE PASTRY CASE
450g/1lb plain flour
Pinch of salt
2.5ml/½tsp baking powder
225g/8oz butter
Iced water to mix
Beaten egg to glaze

FOR THE FILLING
350g/12oz self-raising flour
5ml/1tsp ground cinnamon
1.25ml/¼tsp freshly milled black pepper
Pinch of salt
5ml/1tsp allspice
1.25ml/¼tsp grated nutmeg
450g/1lb seedless raisins
450g/1lb currants
125g/4oz blanched almonds, chopped
50g/2oz candied peel, grated
50g/2oz glacé cherries, chopped
30ml/2tbsp whisky
Approx 45ml/3tbsp milk

To make the pastry, sieve the flour, salt and baking powder together into a mixing bowl. Rub in the butter, then add sufficient iced water to mix to a smooth dough which will leave the sides of the bowl clean. Leave in the fridge for 30 minutes, then bring back to room temperature. Roll out the pastry thinly and use ⅔ to line a greased 450g/2lb loaf tin, or a 20cm/8in loose-bottomed cake tin, making sure there are no holes.

To make the filling, sieve the dry ingredients together into a mixing bowl, then add the fruit and

Whisky Punch (page 115), Black Bun (above), Petticoat Tails (above)

nuts. Stir together and add the whisky and enough milk to bring the mixture to a stiff consistency.

Fill the pastry-lined tin and smooth the top. Roll out the remaining pastry to make a lid and place it on loosely to allow room for the inside to rise a little. Prick the cake with a skewer in several places right to the bottom, then lightly prick the pastry lid all over with a fork. Brush well with beaten egg.

Bake in a preheated moderate oven 350°F; 180°C; Gas Mark 4 for about 2½ hours (test with a fine skewer which should come out clean). Cool the cake in the tin for 30 minutes, before turning out. Store in an airtight tin for at least 2 weeks before cutting. Sprinkle with caster sugar before serving with a glass of whisky at midnight on New Year's Eve, or with the after-dinner coffee and liqueurs.

PETTICOAT TAILS
(makes 8)

No Scottish Hogmanay is complete without these traditional shortbread biscuits, which are always offered to 'first-footers'. In fact, in Scotland, shortbread is eaten during the whole of the festive season.

The biscuits' fascinating name is thought to have come about because they were the same shape as the pieces of fabric used to make a full-gored petticoat in Elizabethan times. The original biscuits were patterned and in those days the word for a pattern was a 'tally', and so the original biscuits were known as 'petticote tallis'.

Serve at midnight with a glass of whisky or with the after-dinner coffee or liqueurs for a traditional touch.

125g/4oz butter
50g/2oz caster sugar
150g/5oz plain flour
50g/2oz ground rice
Extra caster sugar for dredging

Cream the butter and sugar together until pale and fluffy. Gradually stir in the flour and ground rice to make a smooth dough. Press into an 18cm/7in sandwich tin and pinch the edges with a finger and thumb. Prick all over with a fork to make a pattern.

Bake in a cool oven 325°F; 170°C; Gas Mark 3 for about 40 minutes, until pale golden in colour. Mark into 8 triangles with a sharp knife and leave in the tin for 5 minutes. Cut into 8 triangles and dredge with caster sugar. Remove from the tin when cold and store in an airtight container. Serve with a narrow tartan ribbon tied around the shortbread circle.

Twelfth Night Supper Party

*Nowadays in Britain, we no longer celebrate Twelfth Night or Feast of
Epiphany, the evening being marked mainly by the taking down of the
Christmas cards and dismantling of the decorations and Christmas tree; to
leave them in position any longer than midnight is said to invite bad luck,
although greenery can be left up in churches until Candlemas on 2 February.
Traditionally the greenery is buried, burned or saved until the next year.*

*In the past, Twelfth Night was notable for its good luck rituals and
processions, mostly pagan in origin, and its spirit of revelry and good humour.
Shakespeare's Twelfth Night was actually written for the frolics when duty and
convention were ignored and mirth became the order of the day. Farmers drank
and cheered round bonfires and wassailed their orchards and animals to drive
evil spirits from their fields and farms. In the streets, the fools and hobby-horses
of the Morris men joined the apprentices in playing practical jokes which were
also popular at court.*

*In many European countries Twelfth Night is still kept as a feast day with
family parties and presents for the children, and it does seem a really
marvellous opportunity to give a good supper party, maybe in fancy dress, as a
final celebration of Christmas. Try a hot buffet for a change and decorate the
edge of the table with a deep gold paper frill cut to look like a crown. Add
streamers and balloons and plenty of candles and make the food and drink as
festive as possible.*

*It was usual to leave the distribution of sweets and fruit from the Christmas
tree until Twelfth Night so it would be a lovely idea to give each of your guests
a little gift from the tree at the end of the meal or at midnight. Perhaps they
will even help you dismantle the decorations!*

ROBIN'S TWELFTH NIGHT WINE CUP
(serves 12)

*Offer this white wine cup instead of Wassail Cup, or
as an alternative, to your guests when they arrive.
Serve with small pieces of Twelfth Night Cake.*

*Robin and his wife, Christina, also serve this
excellent wine cup at summer parties in the garden
with a cucumber, borage flower and mint garnish.*

1.5 litres/2½pt hock
750ml/1¼pt gin
1.5 litres/2½pt fizzy lemonade
Orange, lemon, apple and cucumber slices to garnish

Chill the hock and the gin well and mix together in
a decorated punch bowl. Add the fruit garnish and,
just before serving, pour in the lemonade so that
the wine cup is still bubbly when you serve it.

WASSAIL CUP
(serves 12)

*Wassail, a mixture of spiced mulled ale and eggs,
used to be carried from house to house in a wassail
bowl, a large earthenware bowl decorated with
ribbons, bells and sprigs of evergreen. People would
pay a few pence to drink from the bowl to bring them
good fortune.*

*Greet your guests with a glass of Wassail Cup,
served from a decorated Wassail Bowl, and a small
piece of Twelfth Night Cake to be really traditional
and to ensure your party will be great fun – 'Wes hal',
or 'Be of good health'!*

3.6 litres/6pt good brown ale
450ml/¾pt dry sherry
3.75ml/¾tsp ground cinnamon
3.75ml/¾tsp ground ginger

3.75ml/¾tsp grated nutmeg
3 strips lemon peel
6 small red eating apples
Soft dark brown sugar to taste
3 slices crustless white bread, cut into star shapes and
    toasted

Pour 3.3 litres/5½pt ale into a very large pan and
add the sherry, spices and lemon peel. Heat very
gently to simmering point. Simmer for 5 minutes.

Meanwhile, bake the apples in a moderate oven
for about 30 minutes with a little sugar and the
remaining 300ml/½pt ale, basting them with the ale
as they cook. Add these to the spiced ale, taste and
add more sugar if necessary. Pour piping hot into a
large warmed bowl tied with a brightly coloured
ribbon around its rim. Attach sprigs of evergreen,
tiny fir cones and bells to the ribbon. Float the star
toasts with the apples on the surface of the ale just
before serving.

Ladle into warmed mugs, glasses or tankards.

SMOKED SALMON AND CREAM CHEESE PANCAKES
(serves 12)

*These small pancakes can be prepared well in advance
and finished in the oven later. Smoked trout or
mackerel can be used instead of salmon.*

24 small pancakes
350g/12oz cream cheese
Finely grated rind of 1½ lemons
30ml/2tbsp chopped chives
350g/12oz smoked salmon trimmings, finely chopped
Salt and freshly milled black pepper
Melted butter
Lemon wedges to garnish
Chopped parsley to garnish

Mix the cream cheese with the lemon rind, chives
and smoked salmon. Season to taste.

Lay the pancakes flat and divide the cream cheese
mixture evenly between them. Fold each small
pancake in half, then in half again, to form triangles.
Put the prepared pancakes into a buttered shallow
ovenproof dish and brush them with melted butter.
Cover the dish with foil and bake in a moderate oven
350°F; 180°C; Gas Mark 4 for 10–15 minutes.

Serve hot garnished with wedges of lemon and
sprinkled with chopped parsley.

Wassailing the apple trees

*In many apple-growing parts of Britain the ceremony of
wassailing the apple trees was observed, and in some areas
still is, on Twelfth Night or old Twelfth Night, 17 January.
This was done to trees that had not been wassailed on
Christmas Day or New Year's Day.*

*The custom, sometimes known as apple-howling, was
intended to drive away bad spirits from the orchard and to
encourage kindly spirits to provide a plentiful harvest the
following year. At dusk, the villagers and the farmers went
to the orchard and formed a ring round the largest apple
tree. Guns were fired between the branches and pots and
pans were banged to drive away evil spirits. The trunk was
splashed with a little wassail or cider which was then poured
around the roots and a piece of toast dipped in the wassail
was wedged in the branches. Everyone solemnly bowed and
sang the wassail song, asking the trees to bear heavy crops
of large apples. Many of these songs still exist, particularly
in the Westcountry.*

Wassailing the animals

*An old Herefordshire custom was to take a wassail bowl
into the byre and drink to the health of all the animals. A
crown cake with a hole in the centre was hung on the horn
of an ox and if tossed off meant good luck for the owners.*

POACHED SPICED PEARS WITH PARMA HAM
(serves 12)

*This is a very festive recipe and looks most attractive
on a buffet table. If the pears are on the small side,
served from a decorated wassail bowl, and a small*

900ml/1½pt red wine
8 whole cloves
Cinnamon stick
Juice of 1½ lemons
45ml/3tbsp caster sugar
900ml/1½pt cold water
Few drops of red food colouring (optional)
6 large firm pears
24 strips Parma ham
Sprigs of watercress to garnish

Put the red wine into a saucepan, just large enough
to hold the pears, with the cloves, cinnamon stick,
lemon juice and caster sugar. Stir over a very gentle
heat until the sugar has completely dissolved. Add

the water and a few drops of food colouring to give a really deep red colour.

Peel, halve and core the pears. Place the pears in the red wine liquid, cover and poach very gently for about 15 minutes, basting them with the liquid from time to time, until they are just tender. Transfer the pears and their cooking liquor into a shallow dish and leave to cool. Chill well.

To serve, remove the poached pears from their liquor and arrange on a flat serving platter, draping the slices of Parma ham partly over the pears. Garnish with small sprigs of watercress.

The Traditions of Twelfth Night

The Twelve Days of Christmas end with Twelfth Night, or the Feast of the Epiphany, one of the oldest and most important festivals in the Christian church. It marks the arrival in Bethlehem of the Three Kings from the East; Caspar, Melchior and Balthasar, bearing their gifts to honour and celebrate the birth of Christ. 6 January also marks Christ's baptism by John the Baptist and the first miracle, the transformation of water into wine at the wedding feast at Cana.

The Three Kings, bearing gold, frankincense and myrrh, were natural candidates for the role of gift-bringers. Spanish children leave out empty shoes on Twelfth Night and straw for the camels and hope that the Kings passing by on their annual visit to Bethlehem will take the straw and fill the shoes with sweets and presents. The day is a public holiday featuring parades heralding the arrival of the Kings and firework displays.

Befana and Babouschka

In Italy on Twelfth Night presents are brought not by the Three Kings, but by Befana, whose name is a corruption of Epiphany. According to legend, this old woman was busy cleaning her house when the Wise Men passed by. When she learned where they were going she asked them to wait until she had finished her work so that she could go with them, but they would not wait. Later she set out to follow them, lost their tracks and has been searching ever since for Jesus. Riding a broomstick, Befana goes down chimneys and leaves gifts in stockings for all children in the hope that one might be the Holy Child. Naughty children are supposed to receive a lump of coal, but these days it is usually made of marzipan.

Russian children used to be visited at Epiphany by a similar character called Babouschka, or grandmother. Legend has it that she misdirected the Three Kings and in atonement must wander the earth in a hopeless search for Jesus. Recently she has been replaced by Grandfather Frost.

CASSEROLED BEEF WITH PRUNES AND WALNUTS
(serves 12)

A rich casserole is ideal for a supper buffet party because it can be made well in advance and frozen if you wish, or cooked the day before and left in the oven until completely cold, before reheating the next day. The flavour is definitely improved by doing this.

1.4kg/3lb lean chuck steak
900ml/1½pt Guinness
4 medium onions, finely sliced
75g/3oz root ginger, peeled and chopped
90ml/6tbsp oil
2 bay leaves
2.5ml/½tsp dried thyme
7.5ml/1½tsp juniper berries
9 whole cloves
7.5ml/1½tsp allspice berries
½ whole nutmeg, grated
3 garlic cloves, finely chopped
450g/1lb carrots, sliced
450g/1lb parsnips, chopped
23ml/1½tbsp flour
3 thin strips of orange peel
175g/6oz walnut halves
Salt and freshly milled black pepper
24 large prunes, soaked in water

TO FINISH
25g/1oz butter
450g/1lb pickling onions or shallots, peeled
10ml/1dsp caster sugar
Chopped parsley
6 slices of crustless white bread cut into star shapes and fried

Cut the beef into large cubes and place in a china or earthenware bowl. Pour over the Guinness and add the sliced onions, ginger, 23ml/1½tbsp of the oil, the bay leaves and thyme. Mix well, then cover and leave to marinate in a cool place for 1–2 hours. Soak the prunes in water while you prepare and cook the casserole.

When ready to cook the casserole, remove the meat from the marinade and pat dry with kitchen paper. Heat the remaining oil in a heavy flameproof casserole, add the beef in batches and brown all over. Remove with a draining spoon and set aside. Grind the juniper berries, cloves, allspice berries and grated nutmeg together in a pestle and mortar and fry in the casserole with the garlic. Strain the marinade, reserving the liquid and the vegetables.

Add the onions and ginger to the casserole and cook over a very low heat, stirring frequently until soft and transparent. Add the carrots and parsnips and continue cooking until they are nicely browned. Stir in the flour, followed by the liquid from the marinade. Add the orange peel and walnuts and season to taste. Cook in a preheated slow oven 325°F; 160°C; Gas Mark 3 for about 3 hours, or until the meat is tender.

About 30 minutes before the end of the cooking time, stir the drained prunes into the casserole and return to the oven to finish cooking. (Add a little of the prune juice if the casserole is too thick.) At the end of the cooking time check and adjust the seasoning if necessary.

To finish, melt the butter in a pan and cook the pickling onions or shallots until softened. Add the sugar and cook until slightly caramelised. Just before serving, stir the onions into the casserole and transfer into a warmed shallow serving dish. Sprinkle with plenty of chopped parsley and garnish with fried bread star shapes around the edge of the serving dish.

Serve with Braised Red Cabbage with Pears or Apples (see page 71), Creamed Potatoes with Celeriac (see next recipe), or Casserole of Potatoes and Leek (page 70) or Gratin Dauphinois (below and a green vegetable or salad.

CREAMED POTATOES WITH CELERIAC
(serves 12)

Creamed potatoes go beautifully with any casserole and by adding celeriac, beetroot, swede, turnip, chopped onion, flaked almonds and chopped pine nuts (just a few examples) the dish can be made more exciting.

900g/2lb potatoes, peeled
900g/2lb celeriac
Salt
Lemon juice
Butter
150ml/¼pt double cream, hot
Freshly milled black pepper
Freshly grated nutmeg

Steam or boil the potatoes in lightly salted water or chicken stock. Meanwhile, scrub, trim and peel the celeriac and cut into even-sized pieces. Drop into acidulated water. Drain, then cook in lightly salted simmering water or chicken stock for 25–30 min-

utes, or until tender. Drain and dry both vegetables over a very gentle heat, then mash them and mix together well. Beat in a large knob of butter and plenty of hot cream. Season to taste with salt, pepper and nutmeg.

TO PREPARE CELERIAC
Celeriac is a marvellous vegetable for adding a fresh flavour to winter dishes and is very adaptable. It may be grated and served raw in salads, or cooked like celery which it resembles in flavour.

Celeriac at its best should be the size of a large cooking apple, firm and unblemished. To prepare celeriac for cooking, trim and slice or dice it, then peel it, dropping it immediately into water acidulated with lemon juice to prevent any discoloration. If the celeriac is to be cooked whole, trim and scrub it and then cook it, peeling it later. Boil sliced or diced celeriac in salted water for 25–30 minutes. Whole celeriac will take from 40 minutes to 1 hour to cook.

GRATIN DAUPHINOIS
(serves 12)

The correct version of this famous potato dish is said to be without eggs or cheese, but sprinkle grated cheese on the top if you prefer. The dish is very good-tempered and can be cooked in a cool oven for a long time, or a fairly hot oven for a shorter time.

1.4kg/3lb potatoes, peeled
124g/4oz butter
4 garlic cloves, crushed
Salt and freshly milled pepper
450ml/¾pt double cream
7.5ml/1½tsp plain flour
450ml/¾pt milk
Freshly grated nutmeg

Slice the potatoes very, very thinly into a bowl of cold water. Blanch for 2 minutes in boiling, salted water, drain well and dry off over a gentle heat.

Butter a large shallow gratin or ovenproof dish generously and sprinkle with a little of the crushed garlic. Arrange layers of potato slices sprinkled with garlic, salt and pepper into the dish. Stir the flour into the cream then mix the cream and milk together. Pour over the potatoes, then sprinkle with a little nutmeg. Melt the remaining butter and dribble evenly over the top of the potatoes.

Bake at the top of a cool oven 300°F; 150°C; Gas Mark 2 for about 1½ hours until the top is brown and crusty and the potatoes are soft.

BUTTERED CALABRESE AND ALMONDS
(serves 12)

900g/2lb calabrese
Salt
75g/3oz butter
175g/6oz flaked almonds
Juice of 1 lemon
Freshly milled black pepper

Trim and wash the calabrese. If the stems are very thick, slit them lengthways so that the heads do not get overcooked. Cook in boiling lightly salted water for about 5 minutes, until just tender, or steam.

Meanwhile, melt the butter in a small pan and cook the almonds over a gentle heat until golden brown. Stir in the lemon juice and season with pepper to taste.

Drain and dry the calabrese over a gentle heat, then toss with the buttered almond mixture. Serve at once.

BEDFORDSHIRE FLORENTINE PIE
(serves 12)

For centuries, great apple pies have been made for special feasts, such as Twelfth Night, and this recipe is particularly festive with its addition of mulled ale just before serving.

450g/1lb puff pastry
900g/2lb cooking apples
450g/1lb Cox's apples
5ml/1tsp ground cinnamon
2.5ml/½tsp grated nutmeg
6 whole cloves
50g/2oz soft brown sugar
Juice of 1 orange
175g/6oz raisins
Grated rind of 2 oranges
Milk to glaze

FOR THE MULLED ALE
300–450ml/½–¾pt light ale
10ml/1dsp clear honey
Generous pinch of nutmeg

(clockwise from left) Poached Spiced Pears with Parma Ham (page 119), Floating Cranberry Islands (page 125), Raspberry Ratafia (page 115), Smoked Salmon and Cream Cheese Pancakes (page 119), Wassail Cup (page 118)

Peel, core and quarter the apples. Place them in water acidulated with lemon juice. Put the peelings and cores in a saucepan with the cinnamon, nutmeg and cloves, then cover with water and bring to the boil. Simmer for 30 minutes to make a syrup. Strain and discard the peelings, cores and cloves, reserving the syrup. Return this to the saucepan and boil rapidly until 45–60ml/3–4tbsp of syrup are left. Dissolve the sugar in this syrup and leave to cool. Stir in the orange juice.

Put the drained quartered apples into a 1.8 litre/3pt pie dish, layering them with the raisins and orange rind. (You may need to cut the apples in half again if they are large, but don't slice them thinly or their juice will boil out and the fruit will toughen.) Pour the cold fruit syrup over the apples.

Roll out the pastry to make a lid for the pie in the usual way. Scallop the edges and make a hole in the centre of the pie to allow the steam to escape. Decorate with pastry trimmings cut into stars, crowns and roses. Brush the top with milk to glaze, then place on a baking sheet near the top of a preheated hot oven 450°F; 230°C; Gas Mark 8 for 10 minutes, then reduce the temperature to 375°F; 190°C; Gas Mark 5 and bake for a further 30–40 minutes, or until the fruit is tender. Protect the pastry with foil if it is browning too much.

Remove from the oven and leave on one side while you make the mulled ale. Heat the ale with the honey and nutmeg until hot, but not boiling. Using a small funnel inserted into the hole in the centre of the pie, pour the mulled ale over the apples. Serve immediately, decorated with extra stars and crowns cut from gold or silver paper.

Accompany with clotted cream, a sauce on pages 32–3, Ginger Ice Cream (page 41), or Foaming Lemon Sauce.

FOAMING LEMON SAUCE
(serves 10–12)

600ml/1pt milk
300ml/½pt single cream
9 egg yolks
Grated rind of 4 lemons
45ml/3 level tbsp caster sugar
15ml/3 level tsp cornflour
4 egg whites
125g/4oz caster sugar

Heat the milk and cream in a saucepan; bring slowly to the boil, then remove from the heat. Allow to cool a little. Beat the egg yolks with the lemon rind, sugar and cornflour in a basin until thick and creamy. Pour the hot milk and cream slowly onto the egg

mixture, stirring all the time. Rinse out the saucepan leaving a film of cold water in the bottom. Return the custard to the pan and stir with a wooden spoon or ballon whisk over a low heat until thick and smooth. Make sure the mixture does not boil just in case it curdles, although the cornflour should stabilise it. Allow to cool. Whisk the egg whites with the 125g/4oz caster sugar until they stand in peaks. Gradually whisk in the custard and serve immediately.

FLOATING CRANBERRY ISLANDS
(serves 12)

This elegant pudding is a modern version of a very popular Georgian dish.

450g/1lb fresh or frozen cranberries
900g/2lb frozen raspberries
250g/9oz caster sugar
Cold water
15ml/3 heaped tsp potato flour
10ml/2tsp triple-strength rose water

FOR THE MERINGUE ISLANDS
Milk and water mixture
Vanilla pod
6 egg whites
175g/6oz caster sugar

FOR THE CARAMEL TOPPING
175g/6oz sugar
60ml/4tbsp water

Wash the cranberries, then simmer very gently with the sugar and a little water for about 10 minutes, or until tender. Add the raspberries and bring gradually to the boil. Simmer until the fruit has collapsed and is soft. Strain, reserving the fruit, and measure the juice. Make this syrup up to 600ml/1pt with water and pour back into the saucepan. Bring back to the boil. Mix the potato flour with a cup of cold water. Stir into the syrup a little at a time, allowing the potato flour to thicken the syrup between each addition. As soon as the syrup is thick enough, stop adding the potato flour. Stir in the strained fruit and the rose water. Pour into a pretty shallow serving dish. Dredge the surface with caster sugar to stop a skin forming, then cool and chill.

To make the meringue islands, fill a shallow pan (a sauté- or frying-pan) with a mixture of milk and water. Add a vanilla pod for flavour and bring very slowly to simmering point. Whisk the egg whites until stiff, then gradually whisk in the sugar until the meringue mixture is smooth and shiny. Remove the

vanilla pod from the pan. Using a tablespoon, rinsed in cold water between each addition, spoon 4 'islands' into the pan of barely simmering water, spacing them well apart. Poach very gently for 2–3 minutes on each side until firm. Remove with a draining spoon and drain well on a clean tea towel. Repeat until the meringue mixture is used up, then leave to cool. About 1 hour before serving, arrange the meringue islands on top of the fruit.

To make the topping, dissolve the sugar in the water and boil rapidly until a rich golden brown. Remove from the heat and trickle over the meringues. Serve as soon as possible.

Twelfth Night Cake

Now, now the mirth comes
With the cake full of plums,
Where Beane's the king of the sport here.
Twelfe Night (Robert Herrick)

In England the tradition of the Twelfth Night cake baked in honour of the Three Kings goes back as far as the medieval court of Edward II and until the late nineteenth century was as well known as the Christmas cake is today. It was very large and extremely elaborate, more like a modern wedding cake, and contained a bean, a sacred vegetable in ancient times. According to custom, the cake was cut and divided between the serfs of the manor. The feudal lord would relinquish his authority for one day to whoever got the bean, namely the Bean King. In later centuries a pea as well as a bean was added, so that a Queen could also be chosen. Later still, other charms were sometimes added to the cake – bells or a ring for a wedding, a button symbolising a bachelor, and a thimble signifying an old maid or a seamstress.

In the nineteenth century cakemakers sold special cards with their Twelfth Night cakes and with these you could elect a whole court of characters to go with the Bean King and Queen. The cards were put in a hat and passed around for everybody to pick out a famous character to play.

It would be great fun to offer your guests a small piece of Twelfth Night Cake when they first arrive and elect a King and Queen for the evening. Either save the Christmas cake, or part of it, until Twelfth Night and plant the bean and pea in two guests' slices, or bake a special individual rich fruit cake containing a bean and pea and charms if you wish. Coat with royal icing as usual and finish with a gold cake frill cut like a crown. Decorate the top of the cake with gold paper stars and more crowns. Divide the whole cake between your guests and provide gold paper crowns for your Bean King and Queen. Serve the cake with a glass of champagne, white wine or Wassail Cup (page 118) or Mulled Red Wine Punch (page 99).

TO MAKE YOUR OWN CHRISTMAS CRACKERS

Crackers made from material and decorated with old ribbons and lace, or from crêpe wrapping or tissue paper decorated with transfers, etc, look lovely on any Christmas table or tree, and each person can be given a special individual gift.

Snaps for homemade crackers are not always easy to find, but some craft shops do have them, or you can ask regular cracker manufacturers who will sometimes supply materials or suggest firms or novelty shops who could help you with snaps, mottoes and small gifts.

MATERIALS NEEDED FOR EACH CRACKER

Tissue paper
3 toilet-roll tubes
Glue
Crêpe or fancy wrapping paper
Motto, snap, paper hat and gift
Button thread
Ribbon or gift-wrapping thread
Trimmings to decorate

Place the toilet-roll tubes end to end leaving 2.5cm (1in) between them and trim the outer rolls if you wish the two cracker ends to be shorter than the middle section. Roll the tubes up in double-thickness tissue paper cut 1cm/½in longer than the combined length of the tubes and 1cm/½in wider than their circumference. When rolled fix in place with glue.

Now roll the tubes up in crêpe or fancy wrapping paper, or any attractive paper you can find which is not too thick. This outer paper can be the same width as the tissue, or shorter if you want contrasting tissue to show. Fold in the edges of the paper, then stick with glue.

Place the motto, snap, paper hat and gift in the cracker, then wind strong button thread several times round the cracker where the tubes meet. Pull the thread tightly and finish with several knots until the cracker holds its shape; then remove the thread and replace it with loosely tied ribbon or gift-wrapping thread.

Decorate the ends of the cracker with pinking shears or cut a fringe, then decorate the body of the cracker as you wish, using sprigs of evergreen, tiny fir cones, berries, tiny posies of dried flowers, shapes made from straw and tied with ribbon, to give you an unusual natural look; or lace ribbon, feathers, fabric flowers, sequins, paper doileys, to give a more elaborate cracker. Attach the decorations with glue or double-sided sellotape.

These instructions will make a fairly simple cracker. You can, of course, be much more adventurous and wrap the cracker in several layers of different papers and make lace cuffs, etc.

TO MAKE YOUR OWN CHRISTMAS SERVIETTE RINGS

Homemade serviette rings can be made to match your crackers and look extremely attractive on the festive table; decorate them in the same way.

MATERIALS NEEDED FOR TWO SERVIETTE RINGS

Tissue paper
1 toilet-roll tube
Glue
Crêpe or fancy wrapping paper
Trimmings to decorate

Cut the toilet-roll tube in half and roll each one in double-thickness tissue paper 1cm/½in longer than its length, and 1cm/½in wider than its circumference. When rolled fix in place with glue. Now roll each tube-half in the same crêpe or fancy wrapping paper as your crackers and fold in the edges. Stick with glue to make them neat and decorate as you wish to match your crackers. Roll up a paper or material serviette and push through the serviette ring.

The History of the Christmas Cracker

Crackers are a fairly recent addition to Christmas traditions and were invented by Tom Smith, a London pastry cook, in 1840. He spent a holiday in Paris where he noticed sweets and sugared almonds wrapped in twists of brightly coloured paper. When he returned home he copied the idea and because people started to give them to each other as presents, he began to include love mottoes and riddles. The 'bang' was said to have been added after listening to the crackle of logs in his hearth.

These early crackers were called 'cosaques' and Tom Smith made them elegant as well as amusing. He commissioned quite well-known artists and authors to produce the designs and to write the mottoes. His crackers would have contained gifts such as fans, jewellery and head-dresses, in fact, all the things that crackers contain today, but on a much grander scale. The most popular Victorian cracker was for spinsters and contained a wedding ring, night cap and a bottle of hair dye!

Tom Smith opened his first cracker factory in Norwich and the business still exists today making 52 million crackers a year.

Index

Illustrations are indicated by italic numbers